J. M. KEYNES IN RETROSPECT

Everything great, a word, a deed once completed then turns itself instantly against him who did it. By the very fact he did it he is henceforth weak – he can prolong his deed no longer, he faces it no more. To have something BEHIND one that one could have never willed, something in which the knot of human destiny is tied – and to have it henceforward heavy on one's shoulders . . . is very nearly crushing. The LACUNE of greatness!

Nietzsche

J. M. Keynes in Retrospect

The Legacy of the Keynesian Revolution

Edited by
John Hillard
University of Leeds

EDWARD ELGAR

Published by
Edward Elgar Publishing Ltd
Gower House
Croft Road
Aldershot
Hants GU11 3HR
England

and distributed by
Gower Publishing Company
Old Post Road
Brookfield
Vermont 05036
USA

Printed and bound in Great Britain by
Billing & Sons Ltd, Worcester.

British Library Cataloguing in Publication Data

J. M. Keynes in retrospect : the legacy of
   the Keynesian revolution
   1. Keynes, John Maynard 2. Keynesian
   economics
   I. Hillard, John
330.15'6   HB99.7

ISBN 1 85278 012 6

Contents

Introduction

The genesis of this book lay in a desire by members of the School of Economic Studies both to commemorate the fortieth anniversary of the death of John Maynard Keynes and to mark the fiftieth year since the publication of *The General Theory of Employment, Interest and Money*. An Anniversary Series of lectures, seminars and workshops was held in Leeds during 1986 and what follows is the outcome of these deliberations. The primary objective of this volume is to contribute towards a reassessment of the Keynesian legacy from the perspective of the postwar generation.

Given the present state of fashion in economic theory and practice, a collection of essays designed to reconsider the contribution of Keynes towards economic understanding seems, at first sight, to be completely at odds with the dominant trend towards orthodox retrenchment. Indeed, such spectres as 'the Keynesian incubus' (Hayek, 1975, p. 43) have been raised to explain current economic ills and to rationalize the retreat by a significant number of academics into scholasticism and dogma. But this is more an indication of the parlous state of economic orthodoxy than a measured attempt to address the contemporary relevance of Keynes. Whereas 'the promise of a new and better economic world', as Arthur Brown (below, p. 44) describes the outcome of the debate of the 1930s, has dissolved into a renewed era of mass unemployment, the widespread reversion to the soporific doctrines of the pre-Keynesian era has introduced an element of urgency into the task of re-evaluating the Keynesian legacy. It is a truism to state that orthodoxy is powerful not because it is right but right because it is powerful, and the inclination of the economics profession towards fundamentalism is the most disturbing aspect for those who are not prepared to rest content in a world of platitudinous theoretical certainty. In the face of the orthodox counter-revolution, the present generation is confronted with the difficult struggle, as were Keynes and his contemporaries, of having 'laboriously to re-discover and force through the obscuring envelopes of our misguided education what should never have ceased to be obvious' (Keynes, CW, Vol. X, p. 101).

On the other hand, what follows is not an exercise intended to rake over the ashes of a defunct economist in the hope of stirring the embers of a lost cause. As is apparent from the subject-matter chosen by the contributors, there is no presumption that Keynes possessed all the answers. In addition, the economic setting is now substantially different from that which confronted Keynes, not least because of the changes in economic structure occasioned during the passage of the so-called Keynesian era. Rather, the continued importance of Keynes as a source of inspiration derives from the questions he posed, which according to Austin Robinson, 'are still questions [and] it is his questions we are still struggling to answer' (1973, p. 541). It remains the case that, despite a huge amount of intellectual energy spent in trying to come to terms with Keynes, it has thus far proved impossible to 'package' him. The intrinsic difficulty of classifying Keynes, particularly in relation to the economic orthodoxy which it was his stated intention to revolutionize, goes far to explain the sustained interest in his life and work. Allied to the complexity of the debate surrounding Keynes himself is the further burden imposed upon interpretation by the designation 'Keynesian' to postwar currents in economic theory and practice. Of necessity, both concerns comprise an underlying theme throughout this volume.

I wish to thank Sue Logan for invaluable clerical assistance in the compilation of the book.

1   J. M. Keynes: The last of the Cambridge economists[*]

John Hillard

The republic of my imagination lies on the extreme
left of celestial space.
(J. M. Keynes, CW, Vol. IX, p. 309)

A book that arises from a vision, like a mountain
appearing fitfully amongst its clouds, must inevitably
present an uncertain outline ... The *General Theory*
presents a wild and craggy scene compared with the
clear placid surface of the 'classical' lake ... the
subject was the human affair in all its ambitious
thoughts and passions, the heart of a man unsearch-
able even in its business manifestations. Keynes did
not seek to reduce the picture of the tumultuous
market place to a cool play of well instructed reason.
In terms of painting, Keynes was a Turner not a
Canaletto.
(Shackle, 1983, pp. 242, 248)

Illuminated missals – spires –
Wide screens and decorated quires
All these I loved, and on my knees
I thanked myself for knowing these
And watching the morning sunlight pass
Through richly stained Victorian glass
And in the colour shafted air,
I, kneeling, thought the Lord was there.
Now, lying in the gathering mist,
I know that Lord did not exist.
(John Betjeman)

I

This essay sets out to explore the enigma of Keynes' heretical stance
against the orthodox equilibrium theory of economics. In treading
this well-worn path of Keynesian scholarship, it is apparent that the
dust raised deliberately by Keynes in his declared intention 'to

[*] I wish to thank Arthur Brown, Rodney Crossley, Bill Gerrard, Hugo Radice and
Michael Surrey for critical comments and friendly debate.

revolutionise the way the world thinks about economic problems' (CW, Vol. XIII, p. 492) still pervades the intellectual atmosphere a half-century after the *General Theory* exploded on the scene. The unresolved dilemma of his motivation and purpose in choosing to run 'counter to the overwhelming weight of contemporary opinion and sentiment' (CW, Vol. IX, p. xvii) stands at the centre of the confused controversy surrounding his legacy. The modest aim of what follows is to reaffirm Keynes' antithetical achievement of his demolishing the intellectual basis of orthodox dogma, whilst reserving a degree of scepticism concerning his 'optimistic hypothesis' that the economic problem was amenable 'to reforms in the technique of capitalism' (ibid., pp. xviii, 294).

My question, therefore, is this: did Keynes embark on his 'long struggle of escape' (CW, Vol. VII, p. xxiii) from orthodox habits of mind merely to end his pilgrimage in furnishing a gloss to cover the (Neo-) Classical economic model? If this were the case, then he most clearly failed in his mission to revolutionize 'habitual modes of thought and expression' (ibid.). For as the 'Keynesian' gloss has worn thin, the self-same dogma which Keynes sought to exorcise has re-emerged in the degenerate form of New Classical economics. From this refuge of methodological individualism, the Keynesian Revolution is viewed as nothing more than an abortive palace *coup*. In terms of hard, rational logic New Classical economics represents 'the supreme intellectual achievement . . . of adopting a hypothetical world remote from experience as though it were the world of experience and then living it consistently' (CW, Vol. VII, p. 192). Consider the following critique of Keynes' theoretical outlook which encapsulates neatly the abstract rigidity of the orthodox mindset:

> Keynes founded that subdiscipline, called 'macroeconomics' because he thought explaining the characteristics of business cycles was impossible within the discipline imposed by classical theory, a discipline imposed by its adherence to the two postulates (a) that markets clear and (b) that agents act in their own self-interest . . .
> One essential feature of all equilibrium models is that all markets clear . . . If, therefore, one takes as a basic 'fact' that labour markets do not clear, one arrives immediately at a contradiction between theory and fact. The facts we actually have, however, are simply the available time-series on employment and wage-rates plus the responses to our unemployment surveys. Cleared markets is simply a principle, not verifiable by direct observation, which may or may not be useful in constructing successful hypotheses about the behaviour of these series. (Lucas and Sargent (eds), 1981, pp. 304, 311)

According to New Classicism, therefore, Keynes committed a cardinal error in his attempt to construct a macroeconomic schema at odds with the essential postulates of individual economic rationality and instantaneous market clearance. It followed that the entire Keynesian project aimed at synthesizing Keynes' novel elements with the pre-existing framework was flawed from the outset. The advent of rational expectations equilibrium with misperceptions marked a swing in the pendulum of fashion back to the totally automatic model of the economic universe. In this reborn state of perfect order, with nothing to interfere with one's peace of mind, the *General Theory* after fifty years could be consigned without conscience to the history of economic thought as the work of a minor post-Malthusian.

To be fair to the New Classicals, it *is* difficult to disagree with the contention that 'the established Keynesian doctrine is theoretically sterile and politically inoperable' (Lilley, in Skidelsky (ed.), 1977, p. 26). The pharisee reaction has been directed not so much at Keynes but rather against those proselytes who accepted 'the "classicization" of the Keynesian revolution' (Balogh, 1982, p. 43). For example, whereas a 'new Keynesian' like Stiglitz takes it as gospel that the 'central element in the Keynesian legacy [is] the importance of the assumption of wage rigidity' (Butkiewicz, Koford and Miller (eds), 1986, pp. 192–3), this ignores Keynes' insistence that such a presumption was an *orthodox* rationale for economic maladjustment and 'the essential argument' of the *General Theory* was 'precisely the same whether or not money-wages are liable to change' (CW, Vol. VII, p. 27). More disturbingly, whatever designation is applied to the various 'Keynesian' rationales for explaining a disjuncture between the law of markets and observational reality in terms of 'imperfections', they all share an *ultimate* faith in the analytical coherence of the general Walrasian model (see Eatwell and Milgate (eds), 1983, ch. 15).

In terms of a shared constellation of beliefs, those economists whom Bill Gerrard below categorizes as mainstream Keynesians and their orthodox counterparts are separated only by a fine line in their vision of how the economy operates. It is but a small step from here to a theoretical consensus which emphasizes the imperative of promoting long-run free-market adjustment whenever and wherever possible, since 'if the powerful mechanism of market adjustment via supply and demand *is* present in the economy, then it seems almost perverse not to attempt to harness these [ultimately] beneficial forces' (Eatwell and Milgate (eds), 1983, p. 261). Given the pervasiveness of the counter-revolution, the danger lies in burying Keynes alongside a doctrine purporting to take inspiration from him.

II

Anyone who has taken the trouble to read Keynes in the original cannot fail to be impressed by a distinctiveness of *style* which, even in works of 'pure' theory, indicates that he employed a profoundly different scheme of thought in approaching the economic problem. As Harrod in his *Life of John Maynard Keynes* predicted: 'those who come after will be interested in Keynes, not only on account of his teaching and influence but also for what he was in himself' (1972, p. ix). This is not the place, however, to speculate at length about the sources of Keynes' habit of mind. Recent biographical analyses, such as Skidelsky (1983) and Hession (1984), have thoroughly plumbed the depths of the 'man behind the model'. For the present purposes, I wish to focus upon Keynes' highly developed sense of intuition as an important key to understanding his revolt against the formalism of economic orthodoxy.

Writing to G. L. Strachey in 1906, Keynes presented the rather startling idea that 'the whole thing depends on intuiting the Universe in a particular way ... it is not a question of argument, all depends on a particular twist in the mind' (quoted in Harrod, 1972, p. 131). What appears at first sight to be a most uncharacteristic utterance from the supreme rationalist in fact provides a striking indication of Keynes' tacit dimension. Under the influence of G. E. Moore's intuitive ethics, Keynes engaged in taking 'fairly complete licence to judge all things anew ... in a ... quest for new values' (ibid., pp. 90, 101). The prime duty of the self-appointed Apostles of Truth was the implementation of the doctrine of intuition, that is, 'to penetrate below the surface of things and acquire depth of insight' (pp. 121–2). Notwithstanding, he remained equivocal about the potentialities of absolute intuition as 'hardly a state of mind which a grown-up person in his senses could sustain literally' (CW, Vol. X, p. 442). At least, unlike Wittgenstein, he was not burdened by the absurdity of trying to articulate 'whereof one cannot speak'.

This having been said, Keynes did retain a faith in the value 'of direct inspection, of direct unanalysable intuition about which it was useless and impossible to argue' (ibid., p. 437). Throughout his life it served as 'his religion under the surface' (ibid., p. 442). Where, then, did he stand below the surface of things? His exploration of the self beyond the semantic prison of artificial abstraction was guided by 'the principle of organic unity, on the state of affairs as a whole which [cannot] be usefully analysed into parts' (p. 436). Whereas western thought delineates sharply between analytical knowledge and intuitive understanding, the process of what Alan Watts described as *correlative vision* reveals this distinction as a corresponding pair of interdependent opposites within an organic whole. In the context of eastern symbolism, left hemisphere thought is associated with the feminine as opposed to the masculine-dominated right hand. The impact of the 'feminine' upon Keynes' identity has been stressed by a number of commentators. In noting the importance of his relationship with Bloomsbury, Harrod described it as 'in a very real sense his home, providing the feminine and human interest which were the background to his daily work' (1972, p. 208).

It is well known that his private behaviour displayed a temperament far removed from his heavy-handed, pedagogic and dogmatic colleagues in the academic establishment. But the source of his difference was not a simple reflection of his sexual leanings (cf. Skidelsky, 1983, Introduction; Hession, 1984, passim). The alleged correspondence between his sexuality and economic outlook is an oversimplification. It confuses an entity (the individual) with a category (masculine/feminine; right/left) so that an analysis of Keynes' feminine attributes which concentrates on their physical expression overstates the point. In any case, homosexuality was the rule rather than the exception in English establishment circles, which implies that Keynes' uniqueness can hardly be explained by this factor alone.

The critical feature of the principle of organic unity, especially Keynes' advocacy of 'organic unity through time' (CW, Vol. X, p. 436) was the way in which it represented a different method of thought than the predominant analytical mode of knowing. Its direct impact upon his economic perception can be traced to his concern with 'the behaviour of the economic system as a whole' (CW, Vol. VII, p. xxxii). For orthodoxy, the ascertainment of total output and employment is conveniently solved by the simple summation of 'conclusions which have been arrived at in respect of a part of it taken in isolation' (ibid.). Employing the principle of organic unity, Keynes contended that 'the whole is not equal to the sum of the parts, comparisons of quantity fail us, small changes produce large effects, the assumptions of a uniform and homogeneous continuum are not satisfied' (CW, Vol. X, p. 262). Herein lies the essence of Keynes' alternative vision – his holistic approach permits the analysis of *generalized* market failure, which, according to the imperatives of orthodox logic is defined out of court. Furthermore, Keynes' insight that the system as a whole could amount to something more or less than the sum of the parts and that the parts could be affected by the whole, has devastating consequences for the orthodox concept of the atomistic individual – 'the omniscient, maximising decision-maker possessed with full knowledge and correct expectations' (Hutchison, in Wiles and Routh (eds), 1984, ch. 1).

At issue here is the very idea of the Invisible Hand. In *The End of Laissez-Faire*, he attacked the metaphysical foundations of economic orthodoxy:

> It is *not* true that individuals possess a prescriptive 'natural liberty' in their economic activities. There is *no* 'compact' conferring perpetual rights on those who Have or on those who Acquire. The world is *not* so governed from above that private and social interest always coincide. It is *not* so managed here below that in practice they coincide. It is *not* a correct deduction from the principles of economics that enlightened self-interest always operates in the public interest. Nor is it true that self-interest generally *is* enlightened; more often individuals acting separately to promote their own ends are too ignorant or too weak to attain even these. Experience does *not* show that individuals, when they make up a social unit, are always less clear-sighted than when they act separately. (CW, Vol. IX, pp. 287–8)

On the evidence of *My Early Beliefs*, a memoir written in 1938 but published posthumously in 1949, Keynes went even further in questioning the rationality of self-interest – the conceptual cog which drives the equilibrating structure of orthodox economics. Although he had been able personally to dispense with 'the Benthamite calculus', he remained dissatisfied about his application of the philosophy of 'undisturbed individualism which was the extraordinary achievement of the early Edwardian days' (CW, Vol. X, p. 444) to the changed circumstances of the interwar period. The notion of 'unsurpassable individualism' furnishes the speculative foundation for the orthodox economic fabrication. Its embodiment takes the form of 'the mechanics of utility and self-interest' with the result that the subject of economic theory is reduced to the optimal satisfaction of selfish ends. Keynes was always dubious about orthodox economists like Robbins who claimed that 'the substantial accuracy and importance' of such a generalization was 'open to question only by the ignorant or perverse' (1935, p. 1).

In *My Early Beliefs*, Keynes dismissed the speculative philosophy of natural law and utilitarianism, which underlies orthodox dogma:

> the rationality which we attributed to [human nature] led to a superficiality not only of judgement, but also of feeling [so that such] an attribution, instead of enriching [human nature] now seems to me to have impoverished it. (CW, Vol. X, p. 448)

By carrying the 'individualism of [his] individuals too far' (p. 449) and portraying the individual as one-sidedly rational, he admitted that 'we have completely failed, indeed, to provide a substitute for these economic bogus-faiths capable of protecting or satisfying our successors' (p. 446). Dismissed by Hayek as 'a peculiar brand of rationalism' (1978, p. 288), *My Early Beliefs* none the less deserves serious attention because it comprises a frank autobiographical account of Keynes' tacit philosophy. His personal transcendence of the Benthamite tradition, which he saw in 1938 as 'the worm which has been gnawing away at the insides of modern civilisation and is responsible for its moral decay' (CW, Vol. X, p. 445), reveals a persona that intuitively recognized the individual as something more than a reflex mechanism engaged in trading off material pleasure against physical pain. His regard for 'the Benthamite calculus, based on an overvaluation of the economic criterion', as 'the enemy which was destroying the quality of the popular Ideal' (p. 445) provides a glimpse of a deep-seated revulsion he felt towards 'the pseudo-rational view of human nature' (p. 448) which underlay the ethics of self-interest.

His perception that economic orthodoxy lacked a solid diagnosis of human nature must be counted as part of his long struggle of escape from natural law fictions. For instance, his discussion of instability arising from the characteristics of human nature in Chapter 12 of the *General Theory* demonstrates the importance he attached to 'non-economic' motives in determining economic outcomes. Of course, his exploration of the 'psychological' had to be conducted 'on a different level of abstraction' (CW, Vol. VII, p. 149) but, as he emphasized in 'The General Theory of Employment' (1937), his 'general, philosophical disquisition on the behaviour of mankind' was a necessary antidote to the submission of orthodox theory to 'market-place idols' (CW, Vol. XIV, p. 115) in its assumption 'that we have a knowledge of the future of a kind quite different from that which we actually possess' (ibid., p. 122).

In all, Keynes' exploration of the self outside the confines of the intellectual drawing machine and his reluctance to inhabit an absolutist world of deductive certainty, explain his determination to introduce an element of 'plain common sense' into an orthodoxy which was 'based upon venerable, academic inventions and on assumptions which are contrary to the facts' (CW, Vol. IX, pp. 90–1). The culmination of his journey free from the shackles of naive rationalism was expressed in his preference to follow his intuitions

> to see the truth obscurely and imperfectly rather than to maintain error, reached indeed with clearness and consistency and by easy logic but on hypotheses inappropriate to the facts. (CW, Vol. VII, p. 371)

His intuitive critique of the closed-system paradigm of orthodox equilibrium economics, 'though a valuable abstraction in itself and perfectly valid as an intellectual conception' (CW, Vol. XIII, p.

411), constitutes the core of the Keynesian legacy. In his rebellion against physical determinism, where the elements contain no more information than the axioms and the course of play never affects the rules of the game, Keynes was a harbinger of the 'new view' of science and this in itself encapsulates his timeless contribution towards understanding.

In this context, it is worth commenting upon Keynes' attitude towards the subject-matter of economics. In opposition to the dominant trend within the profession, he contended that 'economics is essentially a moral science and not a natural science. That is to say, it employs introspection and judgements of value' (CW, Vol. XIV, p. 297). Such a 'normative' inclination has been taken by detractors as a quirk of indiscipline arising from his lack of professional academic training. There may exist a case for such an assertion from those who profess a blind faith in the law of markets but, as a point of principle, Keynes consciously rejected the spurious objectivity incorporated into what later came to be known as 'positive' economics. Perhaps the most refreshing aspect of Keynes' economic outlook was his overt treatment of theorizing as the means to a practical end rather than pretending it was an object in itself. As he put it: 'economics is the science of thinking in terms of models joined to the art of choosing models, which are relevant to the contemporary world' (ibid.). Or again, 'economics is the application of a frame of formal thinking to the complex confusion of daily events' comprising a blend of 'theory and fact, intuitive imagination and practical judgement' (CW, Vol. X, pp. 107, 335). This is a far cry from the abstract precision of the axiomatic method but it was Keynes' 'candid examination of [his] own inner feelings in relation to the outside facts' that impelled him to the realization that 'the current intellectual bias, the mental make-up, the orthodoxy of the day' (CW, Vol. IX, pp. 287, 294) was totally inappropriate as a means of comprehending economic reality.

Finally, it is instructive to draw a parallel between Keynes' mode of thought and that of his ancestral mentor Malthus, whom he regarded as 'the first of the Cambridge economists' (CW, Vol. X, p. 107). Keynes' invocation of 'an age-long tradition of common sense' (CW, Vol. XIII, p. 552) was largely derived from the example of Malthus, 'the inductive and intuitive investigator who hated to stray too far from what he could test by reference to the facts and his own intuitions' (CW, Vol. X, p. 95). In a remarkable passage describing the logic of Malthus' development, Keynes presents a perfect summary of his own intellectual journey where he employed the method of dialectical idealism:

(i) *Thesis*
'He approached the central problems of economic theory by the best of all routes . . . as a philosopher and moral scientist, applying the methods of the *a priori* method of the political philosopher.'

(ii) *Antithesis*
'He immersed himself in the facts of economic history and of the contemporary world, applying the methods of historical induction and filling his mind with a mass of the material of experience.'

(iii) *Synthesis*
'He returned to *a priori* thought, to the pure theory of the economist and sought to impose the methods of formal thought on the material presented by events, so as to penetrate these events with understanding by a mixture of intuitive selection and formal principle and thus to interpret the problem and propose the remedy.'
(CW, Vol. X, p. 107)

Whereas economic orthodoxy remained trapped as a static thesis based on 'the proposition that an unregulated capitalism maximized both the freedom of individual choice as well as the utilization of existing resources' (Pilling, 1986, p. 19), the facts of twentieth-century experience rendered it incapable as a means of serving as a theoretical rationale to reconcile the problems of the real world. Here, the reality of sustained depression and mass unemployment was set against the logical impossibility of anything other than an automatic tendency towards the full utilization of resources, including labour. Keynes' antithesis challenged the purveyance of 'copybook maxim' by an orthodox school who had failed to comprehend that 'theory follows not from actual facts but from an incomplete hypothesis introduced for the sake of simplicity' (CW, Vol. IX, pp. 280, 284). The *General Theory* sought to synthesize the negative outcome of the breakdown of Say's Law with the positive potential of Keynes' Law embodied in the principle of effective demand.

III

On the basis of the previous argument, I wish to propose that the importance of Keynes derives from 'the simple, fundamental ideas which underlie [his] theory' (CW, Vol. XIV, p. 111) rather than the conceptual apparatus he erected in his endeavour to revolutionize órthodoxy. The bulk of academic literature aimed at interpreting Keynes has focused upon the forms within which he embodied his vision. It is a debate, moreover, where the rules of discourse are shaped by the still dominant equilibrium method which dictates 'the basic features of the economic state of society, about what and what is not important to understand its life at a particular time' (Schumpeter, 1952, p. 268). It has to be emphasized that the orthodox outlook

> is a traditional view with a history as old as economics itself: the individual is assumed to be a maximising consumer or producer within free supply-demand markets that establish an equilibrium price for any kind of goods or service. This is an economics blessed with an intellectual consistency and one having implications that extend far beyond the realm of conventional economic theory. It is, in short, also a political philosophy, often becoming something approaching a religion. (Thurow, 1983, p. xv)

As a pure theory, the presuppositions, atmosphere and method of this market-theoretic frame of reference imbue an underlying vision of the economy as a perfectly self-correcting automaton. In his typical proto-Keynesian manner, Balogh described the working of the orthodox economic machine as follows:

> Atomistically organised producers, striving independently to maximise their own profits without regard for the actions of others, were assumed to supply identical, standard products consisting of alert consumers in possession of all the facts and with conscious, unalterable and independent tastes. This process carried with it the implicit assumption of mutual independence as between demand and supply, and a postulation not only of perfect foresight, but the unchanging repetition of an identical process, in which accidental disturbances and their effects are smoothly eliminated and the original balance restored. (1973, p. 6; past tense in original!)

Any failure of the theory to bridge the practical breach between descriptive invention and economic actuality arises from the existence of 'obstacles' which prevent the compensating motions of the adjustment mechanism from taking their 'natural' course. It is the subversion of the principle of free exchange which causes economic maladjustment and, as a corollary, the removal of the impediments which rigidify the operation of market forces constitutes the necessary condition for the restoration of economic health and stability. The reduction of economic theory to such an analytical procedure means that, in effect, it refers only 'to situations where there is no practical need for theoretical guidance, since the automatism of the system ensures that all goes well' (Lowe, 1965, p. 98). In other words, orthodox equilibrium analysis can explain 'the behaviour of imperfections only in their absence. And, in their presence, it prescribes their elimination' (Piore, 1983, p. 252).

It was precisely because such an approach destroyed the practical relevance of economic theory that led Keynes to feel to be 'breaking away from this orthodoxy, to be escaping from something, to be gaining an emancipation' (CW, Vol. VII, p. xxxi). In his endeavour to explain 'the paradox of poverty in the midst of plenty' (ibid., p.

30) he became convinced that the orthodox *laissez-faire* doctrine was 'wholly inapplicable to such problems as those of unemployment and the trade cycle, or indeed, to any of the day-to-day problems of ordinary life' (CW, Vol. XIV, p. 107). Keynes' intellectual journey culminating in the publication of the *General Theory*, involved the translation of the *intuition* that orthodox theory merely describes how the economy should function into a systematic logic of its actual behaviour.

It is a tribute to Keynes' genius that he rejected the path of seeking solace in belief and determined to discover 'the fatal flaw in that part of orthodox reasoning' which led 'to the conclusions that for various reasons (seemed to him) to be inacceptable' (p. 489). Above all, his determination to become emancipated from an intellectual standpoint which 'sees the simplified hypothesis as health and future complications as disease' (CW, Vol. X, p. 285) constitutes the most enduring facet of his legacy. His struggle to bridge the obvious gap between the logical derivations of orthodoxy and 'the facts of experience' (CW, Vol. VII, p. 3) epitomizes the *spirit* of Keynes, which, as Schumpeter predicted has 'outlived both Keynesianism and the reaction to it' (1952, p. 291). On the other hand, as Keynes discovered in his study of Isaac Newton, the very nature of genius is fraught with irreconcilable contradiction. As he reflected on Newton: 'geniuses *are* very peculiar' (CW, Vol. X, p. 363). For Keynes, nowhere was conflict more apparent than in his relationship with economic orthodoxy in his chosen role as high priest turned heretic.

In the 'fever of activity' in the build-up to the publication of the *General Theory*, Keynes outlined in a radio talk what he considered as his task in hand. He addressed the question of whether 'the existing economic system is, in the long run, a self-adjusting system', on the grounds that it constituted 'the overshadowing problem' (CW, Vol. XIII, pp. 487–8). He noted that the 'self-adjusting school' was supported by 'almost the whole body of organized economic thinking and doctrine of the last hundred years' (p. 489). Keynes allied himself with the heretics on the grounds that 'the system is not self-adjusting and, without purposive direction, it is incapable of translating our actual poverty into potential plenty' (p. 491). He noted, however, that whereas 'a very moderate amount of observation of the facts, unclouded by pre-conceptions, is sufficient to show that they do not bear it out' (p. 490), the heretics had been singularly unsuccessful in making an impression on the orthodox citadel. In his view, their failure derived from a reliance upon 'instinct, flair, practical good sense and experience of the world' (p. 489) at the expense of the *logic* which provided the basis of the citadel's power and might. He concluded that the only way to 'demolish the forces of nineteenth-century orthodoxy' was to mount an attack *within* the citadel because 'if the basic system of [ortho-dox] thought is, in its essentials, unassailable, then there is no escape from their broad conclusions' (pp. 488, 491).

The irremediable contradiction in Keynes' endeavour to talk 'a new language' (CW, Vol. XXIX, p. 68) arose from his trying to achieve the impossible of equating the liberal ideal of individualism with the necessity of some form of central control. The unresolvable tension between the orthodox and the heretic within Keynes is revealed in the *General Theory* by his rejection of certain orthodox premises as and when the need arose while stopping short of a *systematic* denial of the entire corpus of orthodox theory. (The implications of this failure are explored in the essays below by John Brothwell, John Weeks and Michael Surrey.) He defended his compromise with orthodoxy on the second-best grounds that he viewed his synthesis as 'the only practicable means of avoiding the destruction of economic forms in their entirety and as the condition of the successful functioning of individual initiative' (CW, Vol. VII, p. 380). In this light, his critique of *laissez-faire* dogma appears more pragmatic than revolutionary – 'I bring in the State; I abandon *laissez-faire* – not enthusiastically, but because, whether we like it or not, the conditions for its success have disappeared' (quoted in Harrod, 1972, pp. 405–6). He wanted to have his cake and eat it too. In the end, as he admitted, he was a Catholic turned Protestant within the economic Church (CW, Vol. VII, p. xxv); and in the preface to the French edition of the *General Theory* he surmised that 'subsequent historians of thought will regard this book in essen-tially the same tradition' (CW, Vol. VII, p. xxxi).

It will be remembered that Keynes made his peace with ortho-doxy in a giveaway remark in Chapter 24 of the *General Theory*:

> if our central controls succeed in establishing an aggregate volume of output corresponding to full employment as nearly as possible, *the classical theory comes into its own right from this point onwards*. (CW, Vol. VII, p. 378; emphasis added)

By squaring the circle in this manner, Keynes left the door open to the interpretation that the under-full employment conundrum could be resolved *within* the logical framework of equilibrium mechanics. The choice-theoretic premises of atomistic competition still held sway 'apart from the necessity of central controls to bring about an adjustment between the propensity to consume and the in-ducement to invest'. The state remained autonomous from the economy except to act as an exogenous, yet benign, *deus ex machina*, thereby guaranteeing 'the advantages of decentralisation and the play of self interest' (ibid., p. 380). On these grounds, a lightly administered reflationary balm appeared sufficient to overcome the arthritic spasms of the Invisible Hand. Accordingly, if the self-regulating mechanics of the market, *mutatis mutandis*, functioned along conventional lines it required the slightest ingenuity to recon-vert the *General Theory* into a special case of the orthodox schema. For example, from a general equilibrium perspective, the problem of under-full employment could be viewed as arising from the ab-sence of an efficient market-clearing vector so that

> all that Keynes did was to remove the auctioneer which is assumed to furnish without charge, all the information needed to obtain the perfect co-ordination of the activities of all traders in the present and through to the future. (Leijonhufvud, 1967, p. 410)

More seriously, Keynes' idealist endeavour to combine the '"Manchester System" ... with the central controls necessary to ensure full employment' (CW, Vol. VII, p. 379) never resolved convincingly how 'the traditional advantages of individualism' (p. 380) could be maintained. According to orthodoxy, the notion of *any* state interference into a field of activity which is delineated by axiomatic necessity as an independent sub-set of the societal set, contradicts the very condition that supposedly ensures the optimal allocation of scarce resources. Faced with 'the mortal disease of individualism, of sitting quietly by whilst a standard of value, governed by chance causes and deliberately removed from central control, pro-duces expectations which paralyse or intoxicate the governance of production' (CW, Vol. IX, p. 74), Keynes' proposed cure of 'allow-ing the regulation of the standard of value to be the subject of *deliberate decision*' (ibid., p. 75) necessitated the subversion of individual freedom to achieve the desired end of its preservation. From an orthodox standpoint, the danger of collective control was a paramount evil to be avoided at any cost. Whether Keynes liked it or not, if the problem of under-full employment could be resolved only through the medium of control, then the state became an *endogenous* influence on the market mechanism – a point that has been ruthlessly exploited by New Classical economists in their effort to tailor the Emperor's new clothes for an enlightenment ghost.

IV

Does this mean, after all, that Keynes was really an old-fashioned economic liberal who was seeking to rationalize the introduction of 'emergency' measures aimed at restoring capitalist stability during a period of prolonged depression? (see Corry, in Thirlwall (ed.), 1978, pp. 23–6). Was Keynes a 'Cambridge Neo-Classical' whose differences with Pigou and Robertson were concerned with what is short run and what is long run? Certainly, if one concentrates on the cures which Keynes derived from his diagnosis, the Keynesian legacy can be interpreted in these ways. (The viability of Keynes' economic policy is surveyed in the essays below by Michael Collins and Hugo Radice.) It has been stressed throughout this essay that the coexistence of orthodox and heretical elements renders the Keynesian corpus a contradictory totality which, at a general level, expressed the historical conflict within the Cambridge school between 'Lockean libertarianism [and] a curious and often unacknowledged idealism, whose emphasis upon the *social* genesis of individual rights formed the tacit background of the concern for intermediate *groups* rather than individuals' (Ogilvy, 1977, p. 307). Keynes' rejection of the Benthamite pleasure/pain calculus was tempered by a faith in

> a continuing moral progress by virtue of which the human race already consists of reliable, rational decent people, influenced by truth and objective standards who can be left to their own sensible devices, pure motives and reliable intuitions of the good. (CW, Vol. X, p. 447)

As one of 'the last of the Utopians' (ibid.) he believed in 'the improvability of man through social and political cultivation according to the higher lights of enlightenment rationality' (Ogilvy, 1977, p. 18). In the end, he failed to rid himself completely of 'the old ideas which ramify, for those brought up as most of us have been, into every corner of our minds' (CW, Vol. VII, p. xxiii) thereby negating his aim to remedy 'the lack of clearness and generality in the premises of classical theory' (ibid., p. xxi). His optimistic conclusion to the *General Theory* that, 'soon or late, it is ideas, not vested interests, which are dangerous for good or evil' looks distinctly over-tired in relation to the Keynesian Era and its aftermath.

What is clear, however, is that Keynes *did* break away from the orthodox dogma which tacitly assumes that an unregulated capitalist economy possesses 'an inherent tendency towards self-adjustment' (CW, Vol. XIII, p. 487). So doing, he committed the ultimate heresy of disavowing the existence of a determinate hidden hand without which orthodox equilibrium theory would lose meaning and purpose. In other words, Keynes' heretical posture amounted to a great deal more than an assault upon certain logical deficiencies in the premises of orthodoxy. His common-sense approach and practical idealism drove him, however unconsciously, to question the metaphysical foundations of economic orthodoxy. Starting with the 'fact of experience' that the economy possesses no 'natural' tendency 'to bring the volume of the community's ouput, and hence its real income, back to its optimal level whenever temporary forces have led it to depart from this level' (CW, Vol. XIII, p. 406), Keynes' articulation of a *monetary* theory of production exposed the fallacy of orthodoxy's hypothetical presumption that, for output as a whole, supply creates its own demand (see Chapter 9, below). His denial of 'the notion that the rate of interest and the volume of investment are self adjusting at the optimum level' (CW, Vol. VII, p. 339) is tantamount to an outright abjuration of an immutable article of orthodox faith in the efficacy of the market mechanism.

Moreover, given that Keynes' renunciation of self-regulation was not reliant upon 'outside interference to hinder the processes of self-adjustment' (CW, Vol. XIII, p. 487), it cannot be construed as being based upon assumptions of structural and/or informational imperfection. The implication is unambiguous: the market mechanism 'if left to itself is not inherently stable [and] there is no automatic tendency to re-establish full employment in conditions of unemployment' (Robinson, 1986, p. 43). Keynes' critique of the mechanical failures implicit in a generalized monetary economy is still unanswered. As Lekachman has remarked: 'enough has been said elsewhere to convince all but the blind' (in Wattel (ed.), 1986, p. 43). Yet, if there exists no balancing mechanism which ensures automatically that the economic system is always operating up to its full capacity, then the entire basis of the New Classical dogmatic reaction is undermined. But, then, on questions of faith, it is the choice of tacit vision which is paramount. Keynes expressed the problem in a letter to R. B. Bryce in 1935 by noting

> the appalling state of scholasticism into which the minds of economists have got which allow them to take leave of their intuitions altogether. Yet in writing economics one is not writing either a mathematical proof or legal document. One is trying to arouse and appeal to the reader's intuitions; and if he has worked himself into a state where he has none, one is helpless! (CW, vol. XXIX, pp. 150–1)

This essay has concentrated upon the antithetical dimension of Keynes' contribution towards economic understanding on the grounds that 'it is better to know a negative truth than to demand the unattainable' (Reichenbach, 1951, p. 324). Economic orthodoxy remains wedded to an unsustainable belief in the self-regulating processes of the market mechanism. The absorption of Keynes' economics into the mechanical equilibrium system of orthodoxy resulted in 'the only difference between the liberal Keynesian and the pre-Keynesian orthodoxy [being] some disagreement about the governmental help the market might need in order to be self-stabilising' (Balogh, 1982, p. 43). In the long run, the uneasy alliance within orthodoxy has proved untenable. During the post-war inflationary boom, lip-service was paid to the social and political implications of the top-down perspective of 'national income analysis', while everyone was able to maintain the faith in the bottom-up approach based on individual economic rationality. The holotype form of welfare capitalism created economic problems dominated by collective behaviour but Keynesian economists were caught inside a conceptual system which was ultimately biased towards the individual. (The labour-market implications are explored by Rodney Crossley in Chapter 5, below.) In the face of such paradigm displacement, even Harrod was forced to admit defeat: 'when you have overfull employment in peacetime, it is not clear by Keynesian thinking what you ought to do' (in Moggridge (ed.), 1974, p. 6).

Lacking guidance from the Master who, in any case, had not explored the theoretical and practical implications of a mixed form of economy and polity, Keynesians were forced to rely upon the advocacy of moral restraint to overcome the 'harmful' side-effects of a high and stable level of employment. Not surprisingly, the intellectual and moral impotence of bastard Keynesianism gave a false credence to the purveyors of a born-again physiocracy, which, as Eatwell says is 'not so much a re-instatement of belief in the market mechanism as the triumphant resurgence of a belief that never went away' (in Wattel (ed.), 1986, p. 65). In retrospect, Sweezy's obituary verdict on Keynes has turned out to be wildly optimistic:

> Historians fifty years from now may regard Keynes's achievement as the liberation of Anglo-American economists from a tyrannical dogma and they may even conclude that this was a work of negation unmatched by comparable positive achievements. (1946, p. 400)

For the present generation, the first step towards liberation is a reconfirmation of Keynes' 'negative' achievement without which any positive prospect will remain forever unattainable.

Economists ... have discarded the older ideas without becoming aware of the consequences.

(J. M. Keynes, CW, vol. XIV, p. 123)

The individual, when trying to order his world in accordance with his premise and seeing his attempt fail, will typically not examine the premise for any absurd or unrealistic elements of its own, but will blame outside factors (eg society) or his ineptitude. The idea that the fault might lie with the premises is unbearable, for the premises are the truth, are reality.

(Watzlawick, Weabland and Fisch, 1974, p. 54)

There's a palace in the gravy
That's holding on and on
Even after all the blue haired ladies and
                    the wheelchairs are gone
I guess the reason I'm so scared of it
I stayed there once and I almost fit
I left before I got out of it.

Neil Young

2 A worm's eye view of the Keynesian Revolution

Arthur Brown*

I

In my pocket diary for 1936, among the jottings of essay subjects, recommended readings and tea-party engagements, I find under the date 4 February, the note: 'Keynes's book to be published' – an event of which I had been forewarned by the financial columns of *The Manchester Guardian*. Immediately after breakfast on that day, I walked out to Blackwell's, purchased *The General Theory of Employment, Interest and Money* for five shillings, and settled down to struggle with it.

It is the only time I have knowingly gone out to buy a book on the day of publication. Why did I do it? I was then just over four months from the beginning of my final examination and only half a term from the point at which, by custom and practice, the search for new knowledge stopped and revision reigned supreme. Reason might have suggested that my contemporaries and I, whatever else we might have to fear from the examiners, could be considered fairly safe from the impact on our Finals of a revolution in the subject instituted only on that day. *Après nous le déluge*. But somehow it didn't feel like that. What was it about the time and place that made it so?

The time was somewhat beyond the middle of what George Shackle subsequently characterized as *The Years of High Theory* (1967). Speaking of the background of that time, he says: 'The forty years from 1870 saw the creation of the Great Theory or Grand System of Economics, in one sense complete and self-sufficient, able, on its own terms, to answer all the questions that those terms allowed ... This Great Theory was ... the theory of general, perfectly competitive, full employment, stationary (or better, timeless) equilibrium.' But by the time when I first opened a textbook of economics (in July or August 1933), the world had been through

* Emeritus Professor of Economics, University of Leeds.

nearly twenty years of war, dislocation, precarious recovery and depression, in which the economic questions with which people were preoccupied had come to be mainly those which the Grand System, in itself, excluded – above all, general unemployment, then in nearly every country near to a peak much higher than had ever been recorded before, and in this country in its thirteenth successive year at over a million. Theorizing about mass unemployment was not, of course, unknown, but it was excluded from providing in terms of the Grand System, the sort of explanation, as part of an equilibrium situation, which that System claimed to provide for the general state of the economy. It could be explained only as due to frictions in the working of markets, or to oscillations of conditions in the economy about the Grand System's equilibrium situation – and oscillations of this kind had not yet been analysed with the rigour that might have given hope of their meeting (or perhaps being incorporated into) the System on intellectually equal terms. Trade-cycle theory (or depression theory) was, moreover, visibly in disarray; there was a disagreement between economists regarded as being of the first rank as to whether going out and buying an overcoat (to quote the example used by Richard Kahn on a famous occasion) would tend to diminish unemployment or to increase it. The man in the street either resorted to crude underconsumptionist theories, such as that of Major Douglas, through which both Lionel Robbins and James Meade had first developed interests in economics, or put it all down (as does his successor in the 1980s) to labour-saving inventions. If this was the state of things when I started my course in economics, it was not much better half way through my third year.

So much for the time; what about the place? If I had been in Cambridge, I might perhaps have had some inkling (depending on who my supervisor was) of the debate within the group of young economists called the 'Circus' and between its members and Keynes, which began in the autumn of 1930 and went on until the *General Theory* was published. Indeed, it is not impossible that some hint might have reached me in Oxford, especially if Meade or Harrod had been my tutor, but in fact it did not. The background of economics in Oxford was very different from that in Cambridge. There could hardly have been said to be a long-standing tradition of Oxford economics, comparable with the Cambridge Marshallian tradition. The Drummond Chair, it is true, was an old one, and its occupants (Thorold Rogers, Bonamy Price, Edgeworth) had not been undistinguished; but they were very different from each other, and in the absence (until very recently) of any body of serious students for them to teach, and of any considerable number of teaching colleagues, they had not founded a school. The degree course in Philosophy, Politics and Economics (PPE) began only in 1920.

Nevertheless, by the time I went to Oxford, a body of economists had assembled there who were to make a considerable impact on the subject in the pre-war years. In view of the overwhelming importance of the Cambridge school in British early twentieth-century economics, it is natural to ask how far this new group in Oxford was simply a Cambridge colony on the banks of the Isis. The influence of Cambridge on it was, indeed, great, but also limited in important ways. The Drummond Professor of my time, Edgeworth's successor, was D. H. Macgregor, Cambridge graduate, contemporary of Pigou, previously professor in Leeds and in Manchester, and co-editor with Keynes of the *Economic Journal* from 1925 to 1934. He was a Marshallian to the extent that his first response to almost any economic question was to recall what Marshall had said about it, but he was also a cat that walked by himself. At the time in question, his detachment from contemporary intellectual fashion had been increased by his having been blown up by a shell in 1918, as well, probably, as by personal tragedies which he had suffered in his early Oxford years; but his independence of mind had the marks of an innate rather than an acquired characteristic. He was extraordinarily learned in earlier economic literature. His association with Keynes does not seem to have extended to participation in discussions on the genesis of either the *Treatise* or *The General Theory*, though (along with Pigou, Stamp, Layton and Salter) he had been co-signatory with him of a letter to *The Times* in October 1932, advocating an increase in both private and public spending – which drew a Hayekian counterblast from the London School of Economics. His main interest up to that time had been in the economics of industry.

The University Reader in Economics (since 1925) had been G. D. H. Cole, an Oxford graduate of a time well before the advent of PPE, whose interests were as much historical and political as economic, and whose basic economic analysis, to judge from a lively and wide-ranging course of lectures on the current economic scene which I heard him give (as well as from his numerous and famous published works) owed more to Marx than to Marshall.

Apart from these two senior economists, and excluding the economic historians and agricultural economists, the members of the economics sub-faculty in my first undergraduate year numbered about fourteen. None of them (or none whom I came to know well) was, I think, a Cambridge graduate, though two notable recruits from that university, Hubert Henderson and Richard Sayers, soon appeared. My own economics tutor, Lindley Fraser of Queen's, was a Balliol philosopher who had apparently made himself an economist (though one still very much at the philosophical end of the spectrum) during two postgraduate years in the United States, the second at the Brookings School. Redvers Opie of Magdalen was a Durham BCom who had subsequently taken a doctorate at Harvard, presumably absorbing there the Taussig brand of neo-classicism, as well as marrying Taussig's daughter. Robert Hall of Trinity (where he had succeeded Frederick Ogilvie) had read PPE at Magdalen after coming from Australia as a Rhodes Scholar with a first degree in engineering. Eric Hargreaves of Oriel had read Litterae Humaniores at Corpus Christi before taking a London doctorate, in the course of which he had become expert in public finance. Maurice Allen of Balliol was an LSE graduate; Dowdell, the remarkable blind economist of St John's was an early PPE graduate (contemporary with John Hicks). Henry Phelps Brown, who had succeeded Lionel Robbins at New College, was another Oxford product, as was Russell Bretherton of Wadham.

So too, in the first instance, were the two Oxford economists who were most active in the Keynesian Revolution, Roy Harrod and James Meade. Harrod, one of the senior post-PPE recruits (appointed in 1923 after reading Greats and Modern History) had, however, spent a term on his own initiative in Cambridge, where he was supervised by Keynes and formed a life-long friendship with him. Seven years later, Meade, appointed to a Fellowship at Hertford after reading Classical Moderations and PPE at Oriel, was sent for a year to Cambridge, where, besides being supervised by Dennis Robertson, was active in the 'Circus' and made a notable contribution to Kahn's famous article on the multiplier. The sub-faculty in my first year was thus predominantly home-grown but otherwise eclectic in its academic origins, with some resort to Cambridge for *ad hoc* extra training. The arrivals during my undergraduate years who are important for this story increased the Cambridge contribution, but also helped to maintain an eclectic character – besides Henderson and Sayers (already mentioned) from Cambridge, they were Charles Hitch, a Rhodes Scholar, who succeeded Fraser in 1935, coming from Arizona via Harvard and Worcester College (his economics tutor was Dowdell at St John's), and Jacob Marschak from Heidelberg.

What sort of economics was taught by this sub-faculty on the eve of the Keynesian Revolution? It is not easy to give an answer that would be generally valid for such a decentralized system, and I must speak mainly for myself. The First Public Examination, Pass Moderations, in preparation for which I, as a natural science scholar who had been allowed to opt for PPE, was advised to spend two terms, included in my case a political economy paper, for which the prescribed reading consisted of Henderson's *Supply and Demand* (1932), Lehfeldt's *Money* (1926) and Dalton's *Public Finance* (1923), the last a somewhat more formally analytical work than the first two. Teaching for Pass Mods was by classes within colleges; in Queen's, Lindley Fraser supplemented this reading with a textbook by Henry Clay. The economics to which I was first exposed was thus, on the whole, very Marshallian.

The same could not be said, however, of the more advanced teaching that I received in tutorials (again with Fraser, and later from Hitch) from the Trinity term of 1934 onwards. The economics teaching in that term was devoted to organization topics, but the chief piece of vacation reading in economic theory onto which I was set for the summer vacation of 1934 was Cassel's *Theory of Social Economy* (1931),[1] from which I got, among other things, an idea of general equilibrium theory, a firm statement of Say's Law, and Cassel's extraordinary near-foreshadowing of later equilibrium growth theory, together with his idiosyncratic theory of wages. In my terms of theory with Lindley Fraser, I was referred to Cassel (and to Cannan and Wicksteed) markedly more often than to Marshall. Advice to read the *Principles* (1920) from Book IV onwards, came only at the end of my second year, along with a similar commendation of the two volumes of Wicksell's *Lectures* (1934), which had appeared in translation a year earlier. More recent writing, of course, was also recommended in connection with particular essays – Robbins' *Nature and Significance* (1935) (to which Fraser had written a spirited reply in *Economica*) was very much on the menu; so were Hicks' *Theory of Wages* (1932) and the Hicks and Allen article (1934) on value theory. Among the books I worked through some time before my last year were also Pigou's *Economics of Welfare* (1920), Taussig's *International Trade* (1925), and Joan Robinson's *Economics of Imperfect Competition* (1933). So far as what is now called microeconomics was concerned, Marshall had been to a substantial extent superseded not only by the newer (largely Cambridge) work on imperfect competition and welfare economics, but in Oxford, at least, by a growing awareness of various Continental and American writers.[2]

When, in the summer of 1935, I began to prepare for the special subject, Currency and Credit, I moved more definitely into Keynesian Revolution territory, but Keynes' *Treatise* was not one of the recommendations for my long vacation reading. These recommendations included, besides the Marshall and Wicksell I have just mentioned, Pigou's *Industrial Fluctuations* (1927), MacFie's *Theories of the Trade Cycle* (1934) and the indispensable Macmillan Report. The *Treatise* did, however, come into reading for specific topics – foreign exchanges, central bank control and criteria of monetary policy. My other special subject – Public Finance – was the one on which I was being tutored in the term in which the *General Theory* came out. For the most part, my recommended vacation reading for it had been un-Keynesian – M. E. Robinson's *Public Finance* (1922), a Cambridge Economic Handbook, Pigou's meaty *Study in Public Finance* (1928) and Stamp's *Wealth and Taxable Capacity* (1922). The only essay I wrote on the subject which had an overt Keynesian content was about budgetary measures against unemployment, and Kahn's 1931 multiplier article is prominent among the references for it; but that was a month after the publication of the *General Theory* (which was also, naturally, a reference) and I am clear that I had read Kahn some time before the *General Theory*, though I have no note of the occasion for it. At about this time too, I worked through Fisher's *Theory of Interest* (1930), and Charles Hitch recommended Bohm-Bawerk's *Positive Theory of Capital* (1930), but I don't think I read it until after the Finals.

Perhaps at this point I should try to recapture what, of relevance to my present story, was uppermost in the minds of my undergraduate generation, and apparently our teachers, in or about February 1936. What I have said about recommended reading may suggest that the trade-cycle theory had a high place. Indeed it had, since it was the heading under which one looked for explanations of the depression through which the world had been passing. We were relatively modest in our attribution of British unemployment to this cause; I doubt whether there would have been really drastic dissent from an analysis in *The Economist* which appeared a week before my Finals, in which 'normal' (frictional) unemployment was estimated at 5 per cent of the insured population, from the experience of the best region in the best years, while no less than 7.5 per cent, both in 1935 and at the depth of the depression in 1932 (as compared with some 3.5 per cent in 1929) was put down to 'special' i.e. structural causes, and the remaining 'cyclical' element, zero by definition in 1929, was reckoned as having reached a peak of 6.5 per cent in 1932 and fallen to less than 1.5 per cent by 1935. My final revision notes on the British unemployment problem are full of the particular circumstances of different industries. The sensitivity of unemployment to pressure of demand is largely a post-war revelation. But still, at that time – perhaps through taking into account the fact that a similar calculation for the United States or Germany would have attributed much more unemployment to cyclical causes

– we looked to cycle theory as the potential explainer of most recent economic woes.

One might suppose that, up to the appearance of the *General Theory*, the struggle for our minds in this connection could be represented as one between Keynes' *Treatise* and Hayek's *Prices and Production*, published in 1930 and 1931, respectively. That proposition requires heavy qualification. Before coming to it, however, it is perhaps necessary, at this time of day, to recall the outlines of Hayek's contentions, to which some of his colleagues at LSE were also committed. Hayek started from the doctrine that an unfettered market economy operating on Walrasian lines, without money, would produce full employment and optimal allocation of resources. Money was the root of, at any rate, some evil; the objective was therefore to define the kind of monetary regime that would be truly 'neutral', introducing no distortion into the pure, Walrasian, market economy. This search for 'neutral' money was, indeed, by no means a Hayek monopoly; it was widespread in the literature of pure monetary theory at the time in question.

Hayek contended that the only neutral monetary regime was one in which total money expenditure (MV) was kept constant, because any increase, whether through credit creation or through dishoarding, would enable the authors of the increase to grab real resources at the expense of others, who would be subjected to 'forced saving'. This contention appears to hold only in conditions of full employment, which it was natural for a Walrasian to take as the starting-point; it has, however, a more general significance when the extra expenditure is for capital formation, because that commits the economy to a longer period of production (in the Austrian sense) which can be maintained only if the expansion of money expenditure is kept up (which will be inflationary eventually, if not at once), or if the ratio of gross savings to income is increased to provide for the higher level of capital maintenance and replacement. Hayek, and Robbins at the time, maintained that the depression of the early 1930s was an inevitable result of the credit expansion and boom of the later 1920s, not, as might have been quite cogently argued, because investment opportunities had been used up, and the marginal product of investment had fallen, but because, in the absence of continued credit expansion and its consequent forced saving, voluntary savings were not sufficient to maintain and replace the enlarged capital equipment which we had inherited.

This seemed to me at the time to be nonsense, and I remember thinking that the error lay in supposing that the cost of maintaining and replacing the increased capital stock would not be automatically incorporated in maintenance and depreciation allowances before wage-earners (in a perfectly competitive market, remember) and shareholders got their hands on the residue available for consumption. No doubt there is more to it than that. Hayek's old contemporary in the University of Vienna, Gottfried Haberler (who was very far from being a Keynesian) subsequently seemed to me to treat the argument with perfect fairness, and to demolish it, in *Prosperity and Depression* (1937). Keynes' famous verdict that *Prices and Production* showed 'how a remorseless logician, starting with a mistake, can end up in Bedlam' is well deserved; but Keynes did not seem to me to identify the mistake clearly. (Nor, on later reading does Sraffa seem to me to do so satisfactorily in his review in the *Economic Journal* (1932) – he is destructive without quite making the heart of the matter clear.) Meanwhile, the very dottiness of the overconsumptionist argument commanded attention; people were inclined to think that something derived from a sophisticated theory of capital with which most British readers were not familiar, and so repugnant to common sense, must have a logical basis which they had not comprehended, and must just possibly be the key to the equally dotty, and tragic, situation of poverty in the midst of plenty.

Was Keynes' *Treatise* an effective counter-argument to the overconsumptionists and their allies? For my part, I cannot quite say that it was, though here one has to distinguish between that book and other, less theoretically ambitious Keynesian statements. I had first become fully aware of public questions about the time of the 1929 election and, being by strong environmental influence a Liberal supporter, had absorbed most of the arguments of *Can Lloyd George Do It?*. Like, no doubt, others at the time, I could not read the *Treatise* without being aware that its author took the view that the depression was a phenomenon of deficient effective demand. Nor did the book conflict with that view, but, from the fact that the Fundamental Equations are concerned with the explanation of the price-level, not the level of activity, they do not shed much more light in that direction. If one looks for such light to what Keynes has to say about the credit cycle, even in the sections which work its course out in some detail, the result is not very inspiring. The main systematic destabilizing elements referred to are the time-lag between the decision to produce more consumers' goods and their appearance in the market (a 'cobweb' mechanism) and the swings between bullish and bearish sentiment which help to produce the investment cycle – also, in the last analysis, because of time-lags and a consequent 'cobweb' effect. I gather, however, that some readers (Robert Hall and George Shackle among them) found more theoretical enlightenment in the *Treatise* than I did. So far as I can recall how I felt about it at the tme, perhaps it is fair to say that I thought this treatment of the cycle better than Hawtrey's (with its over-insistence on the leverage exerted by short-term interest rates in a world of unstable price expectations), but a good deal less enlightening than the cautious, comprehensive, eclectic treatment of Pigou's *Industrial Fluctuations* (1927). I dismissed overconsumptionism, looked to a Keynesian policy of influencing expenditure in order to *control* fluctuations, but was inclined to be eclectic, or agnostic (or a bit of both) about the *mechanisms* of disturbance in the level of activity.

Apart from the broad shapes of theories of the cycle, there was one related matter which caused much worry at this time – how to define savings and investment in ways that helped the discussion. It was natural to say, as Hayek does for instance, that for total expenditure to be kept constant, saving and investment must be equal. But having said this, one comes up against the realization that, on the usual social accounting definitions, they are equal identically. Our attention was drawn to the fact that Dennis Robertson (also Haberler and Bode) had got over the difficulty by defining today's saving as *yesterday's* income minus today's consumption expenditure, and that Keynes in the *Treatise* had escaped it by including windfall profits in investment (increment in the value of capital), but not in saving. Word came that Myrdal had a different device. I have various notes on this, some taken apparently, directly from the relevant paper in *Beitrage zur Geldtheorie* (which had not been translated), some possibly from a seminar paper given by Edward Jackson. But the version of the pure doctrine which I tried to concoct in my final revision notes evidently got into a muddle; a page has been torn out and the passage leading to it crossed out. To handle both saving and investment in *ex ante* and *ex post* versions seemed tricky; the essence of the solution can, fortunately, be grasped by keeping *ex ante* and *ex post* saving always equal and letting the two investment concepts differ simply by the value of stock accumulation or depletion. I see that Ohlin's two-part article on the Stockholm Theory in the *Economic Journal* (1937) is heavily annotated in my copy; but that was too late for Finals. And here, the *General Theory* did not help.

II

This brings me back to the moment when I returned with my copy of the *General Theory* to my room at the top of the Bell staircase in

Queen's and read with some apprehension the opening words of the Preface: 'This book is chiefly addressed to my fellow economists. I hope that it will be intelligible to others.' After fifty years during which, I imagine, the majority of readers of the book have been told in advance something of what they are expected to find in it, the impact on the first generation of readers who lacked this (true or false) guidance is not easy to recapture. The *General Theory* is the work of an author who has a number of new things to say, several of them of major importance to his theme, one or two much less so, and who has not had time to stand back and sort out his priorities for optimal exposition. It tends to start with the difficulties. By the time I had got to the Appendix on User Cost (an admitted digression, pp. 66–73) I was in need of comfort and reassurance, which my mentors were not yet wholly able to supply.

I cannot remember how far I got – certainly not to the end of the book – before word came to us, I think in a revision seminar which Charles Hitch was running, that Harrod had spoken. What he was reported to have said was an augmented version of the now famous passage in his correspondence with Keynes in the previous summer, by which he had established his claim to have understood what Keynes was really trying to say: 'Volume of investment determined by marginal efficiency of capital schedule and rate of interest; rate of interest determined by liquidity preference schedule and quantity of money; volume of employment determined by volume of investment and multiplier; multiplier determined by propensity to save' (Keynes, CW, Vol. XIII, p. 553). The augmentation consisted of a similar account of the 'classical' system, of which Keynes might not have approved, but which appeared later in Harrod's 'Keynes and Traditional Theory' (1937): 'Marginal product of capital a function of amount invested per unit of time; amount invested per unit of time a function of the rate of interest; rate of interest = marginal product of capital.'

This was the key to the scriptures. It made clear what Pigou, thirteen years later, admitted he had not understood in reviewing the *General Theory*; the respect in which it claimed to be general. Like the Hicksian interpretation in *Mr Keynes and the Classics* (1937) which I was to encounter a few months later, it may have made me and others oversimplify the book's manifold messages. It enabled us to understand the theory in terms of what we knew (or nearly knew) already. I thought I understood the marginal efficiency of capital (until John Brothwell, years afterwards, insisted that what Keynes really meant was the marginal efficiency of investment) because I had studied Fisher's *Theory of Interest*. I understood the marginal propensity to consume and the multiplier from

Kahn. I found little difficulty about the schedule of liquidity preference, basically, I think, for the rather odd reason that someone –
possibly Macgregor – had drawn my attention to Wicksteed's
concept of the 'total demand curve' – the occasion for his ringing
statement about the supply curve: 'I say it boldly and baldly: There
is no such thing' (1910, p. 785). The liquidity preference schedule is
the total demand curve for money. At least, I think some of the
credit for my understanding, such as it was, should go to a Leeds
loiner.

On the other hand, the Keynesian aggregate supply curve and
aggregate demand curve passed over my head without visible effect
until I came back to them many years afterwards and decided,
helped by the writings of Sidney Weintraub and his disciples, that
they are marvellous tools of analysis. How much even the slightest
sense of familiarity helps! In our mystification, and the source of our
enlightenment, we were not alone. Paul Samuelson states firmly
that 'no-one in Cambridge, Mass. really knew what the *General
Theory* was about for some 12 or 18 months after its publication',
and that it was the mathematical models of Meade, Lange, Hicks
and Harrod that made it plain – even, he suggests, to Keynes
himself. And even with our proximity to some of these sources of
light, we still had difficulties. Discussion of the *General Theory* in a
seminar run by Opie and Hall in the Trinity term was not very
successful – for some of us, the approach of Finals probably contri-
buted to this result.

Did what knowledge I had of the *General Theory* help me in my
Finals? I've not the least idea. I probably managed to bring some of
it in somewhere – indeed, it would not be very easy to keep it out
altogether, even if the examiners did not set any questions specifically referring to it (I don't recall that they did). It certainly helped
my morale. But Harrod was the Chairman of Examiners, and the
only question he asked me in my formal *viva voce* examination was
about the demand curve of the firm!

The tailpiece to my undergraduate studies – or the introduction to
my postgraduate work – which is relevant in this connection was
the European meeting of the Econometric Society, held in Oxford
in September 1936. There, in successive sessions, we heard: (1)
Harrod's 'Keynes and Traditional Theory', with the bones of which
I had already some acquaintance, as I have mentioned, but the sting
was in the tail – a throwaway remark that he would like to dynamize
the system by making investment depend on rate of change of
income as well as on interest; (2) James Meade's 'A Simplified
Model of Mr Keynes's System', an eight-equation model for which
he deduces stability conditions and the effects of changing interest,

money-supply, wages and thriftiness; (3) Hicks on 'Mr Keynes and the "Classics"', the first revelation of the IS–LM system. These three papers, published over the following twelve months, were, of course, those to which Samuelson referred as bringing light to Harvard. We also heard Tinbergen on one of his short-lag dynamic explorations of the American trade-cycle, and Frisch on something too far above my head for me to make coherent notes on it. It was a stunning revelation of the new world of economics, into which I was entering.

What was the impact of the *General Theory* on Oxford – on what people taught, what they talked about, what they wrote? It is hard to generalize about the impact on teaching, because of the decentralized nature of that activity in a collegiate university. One clue is to be found in the content of reading lists. No official university lists were issued in connection with the subjects to which the book in question was directly relevant; the subject-matter of economic theory was not defined, beyond its title, while the Regulation for the Currency and Credit paper said only: 'To be studied in modern textbooks and the Reports of recent public inquiries. Candidates will be expected to show a knowledge of the chief foreign systems of banking and of international aspects of currency policy.' There was however, an unofficial Select Bibliography, of which the first edition I have was 'Printed for the Oxford Association for Politics, Philosophy and Economics', and later editions were published by Blackwell's over the signatures of three compilers. In the 1935 edition, the economics compiler was Eric Hargreaves; in the 1937 edition, James Meade.

One might hope to find, in the difference between these two last-mentioned editions, some sign of the *General Theory*'s impact, more especially as James Meade was himself so much in the forefront of the Keynesian Revolution. If so, one would perhaps be disappointed. Apart from some reshuffling between headings, the only changes relating to 'Theory' and to 'Currency and Credit' are the additions of six new publications (including the *General Theory*) to the 69 existing ones. Nothing is thrown out.

In the regulations for the Political Economy paper in Pass Moderations, however, reading matter was officially specified. I have mentioned that, in 1933–34, this consisted of three books: Henderson, Lehfeldt and Dalton. At some time before I started teaching in 1938, the prescription was changed to Taussig's *Principles of Economics* (1921). This massive two-volume work, unaltered since the 1921 edition, and somewhat daunting for the non-American student, even if one omitted the large sections of it relating to specifically United States institutions and history, as was commonly done. Not surprisingly, the only reference to Keynes concerned *Indian Currency and Finance*, described as 'an able book, touching on wider questions than its title indicates'. In 1940, the Sub-Faculty recommended a further change to Benham's *Economics* (1938). Excellent and deservedly popular though that book was, it was no Keynesian work. 'Considerable concessions', says the author in his Preface, 'have been made to the views of Mr Keynes, but I can hardly be regarded as one of his followers.' The only concession I can find is the use of the concept of liquidity preference, but this is not in relation to the determination of interest, which is discussed without any mention of variation of income as one of the means of equating 'the amount of free capital offered by lenders with the amount demanded by borrowers'. There is no mention of the possibility of underemployment equilibrium (even attributing such a belief to 'some economists', as Benham is apt to do with controversial ideas). Nor is the multiplier mentioned under that name, though there is a brief descriptive account of the 'snowball effect' of the housing boom of the 1930s.

At this distance of time, one is apt to ask why we (for I was, I think, of the company on that occasion) did not specify something more up-to-date in this respect. The question would have been, what? The only obvious candidate would have been Meade's *Introduction to Economic Analysis and Policy* (1936). I have no recollection of the question being raised. Probably most of us thought it a good thing for students to start with some knowledge of traditional theory before coming – as they certainly would come, under the Oxford system – to the latest developments.

Of course, the emphasis placed in practice on different books did change; a friend who graduated in 1938, two years after me, tells me that his generation did not read Pigou's *Industrial Fluctuations*, for instance. I cannot say anything about changed emphasis in lectures, since I did not attend any undergraduate lectures within the Keynesian sphere of influence after I graduated, and the lectures I gave early in the war, were either introductory (and thus constrained by prudence to keep within the Taussig/Benham orbit) or, as it happened, in microeconomics or elementary statistics. On that, in fact, limited part of the syllabus which by custom and practice was open to revolutionary macroeconomic influences, the revolution no doubt occurred, but it was *de facto* rather than *de jure*.

Although individual views were known to differ, I do not remember that there was any division of the Sub-Faculty into pro- and anti-Keynesian factions. The members who were most prominent in publication – Harrod and Meade – were obviously active revolutionaries, and within the modal age-range of Oxford economists,

Harrod was relatively senior (about as old as the century). Macgregor, nearly a generation older, took up no extreme public attitude. When he wrote later on effective demand and employment in his *Economic Thought and Policy* (1949), he was concerned mainly to trace the roots of Keynesian macroeconomics rather than to evaluate it, but this tone was far from hostile, and the main note of criticism – a typically moderate one – is that implied in the judgement that 'the modern analysis gains rather than loses authority by recognising, instead of depreciating, the growth of its ideas in the work of earlier writers.' It is a judgement with which some others, including Harrod, agreed. Of those whom I came to know well, Redvers Opie was sceptical about the *General Theory* in a way natural to one steeped in neo-classical doctrine, but did not take a confident stand against its specific hypotheses. The same may have been true of some others. The one prominent figure known to be hostile to the *General Theory* and whom I knew well, was Hubert Henderson. His hostility, however, was in the main a part of his dislike of grand theory in general – he once told Harrod that he did not believe in the neo-classical general theory of value, either.

No prominent member of the Oxford Sub-Faculty felt himself under personal attack in the *General Theory*, as Pigou did, or thought Keynes had strayed from a path they had been exploring together, as did Robertson. Nor was there any hard core of commitment in Oxford to a rival theory claiming to explain the troubles of the time, as there was in LSE. And the absence of an established local doctrinal school perhaps helped to foster an enquiring and receptive attitude towards new ideas promising light on the manifest problems of the day.

III

The middle and later 1930s were a stimulating time in Oxford, in which the young Sub-Faculty was just coming to the size to support a variety of interests, and in which such interests received powerful stimuli in the shape of the Oxford Economists Research Group and the Institute of Statistics. Both of these enterprises were just pre-revolutionary – starting in 1935. The Research Group, of which some account has been given by F. S. Lee in *Oxford Economic Papers* (1981), became best known for its interviewing of businessmen about their policies, and the economic influences which they thought most important, and its best known conclusions, published in the first two numbers of *OEP* (October 1938 and May 1939) were that interest rates were not regarded as important outside a relatively narrow range of long-term capital formation activities, and that manufactures were priced, not by the use of marginal cost and marginal revenue estimates to maximize profits, but by a simple form of cost-plus. The latter of these two discoveries was then reconciled with the still new conventional theory of imperfect competition by the hypothesis of the 'kinked' demand curve, due to Charles Hitch and Robert Hall.

There was nothing especially Keynesian about the motivation, or the conduct, of this group of enquiries. The influence of interest rate, however, had been important in the *Treatise*, as in Wicksell, and is still important in the *General Theory*. It may be argued that to cast doubt on the effectiveness of the variable which in 'classical theory' is solely responsible for equating saving with planned investment, must tend to strengthen the *General Theory*'s central point, that the onus of adjustment falls to a substantial extent on the level of income. I do not remember this argument being used at the time. In the later part of my article 'Interest, prices and the demand schedule for idle money' (1939), I tried to defend the honour of interest rate – rather mistakenly, as Richard Sayers pointed out in the next issue of the *Papers* (1939). The 'Pigou Effect' of interest on saving, which works in favour of automatic full employment, had not then been enunciated.

The Research Group had, however, another major activity which has received less attention, and which started late enough to be regarded as 'post-revolutionary', though its inspiration is Kahn, 1931, rather than Keynes, 1936. It was the Bretherton, Burchardt and Rutherford study entitled *Public Investment and the Trade Cycle in Great Britain* started in 1937 and (because of wartime delays) not published until 1941; a valuable contribution to the history of the 1930s which should be studied again in the 1980s – it reads remarkably well after nearly fifty years, and disposes of a number of myths which have come into circulation in the meantime.

The second main Oxford development of the time which I have mentioned was that of the Institute of Statistics. Part of this development – certainly the financing of the Readership which went with it – was due to decisions in All Souls, which had for most of its history been a poor College, but which struck oil (or the equivalent) in the later 1920s when one of its agricultural estates was overwhelmed by the sprawl of the north-west London suburbs. After much discussion, of which stories were still told in my time, the College agreed to extend its traditional arts-based range of interests in the direction of quantitative social science. This fitting in with university aspirations, the Institute was established in 1935, and domiciled in an old house in Broad Street (with a medieval Dance of

Death painted ominously on the wall of its back-door passage) – the first of many homes that it was to occupy in the first thirty years of its existence. The Readership in Statistics and Directorship of the Institute went to Jacob Marschak, who had been a refugee first from Russia (his father was a supporter of Kerensky) to Germany where he eventually taught at Heidelberg; then from the Nazis. He was the author of a work (in German) on the elasticity of demand, and of the theoretical part of the pioneering study (with Lederer), *Kapitalbildung*. In Oxford, his main interest started to turn towards decision under uncertainty, which was to be a main component of his long and distinguished life work (from 1940 in the United States). In my time, however (I was doing graduate work in the Institute from 1936 to 1938), his Institute housed a remarkably wide range of empirical studies.

Not very many of these bore any specifically *General Theory* stamp. The largest group (Marschak, Helen Makower, H. W. Robinson and Goronwy Daniel) was on labour migration. Robinson was at the same time writing a thesis on the determinants of building activity. There was also an Oxford social survey, on which Elizabeth Ackroyd worked at the Institute. Richard Goodwin worked there (under the supervision of Richard Sayers, I think – Sayers having come recently to a Fellowship of Pembroke) on British money supply. His work is referred to in the first edition of that long-running classic *Modern Banking* (1938). From the autumn of 1937, Harold Wilson worked largely at the Institute as research assistant to Sir William Beveridge, who had become Master of University College, on unemployment and trade-cycle matters. Wilson was also working on his own account on historical railway statistics; he won the Gladstone Prize with an essay on that subject. George Shackle worked there, as research assistant to Henry Phelps Brown, on the recent statistics of monetary circulation in the United Kingdom. I come to his other interest presently. R. F. Bretherton worked on income-elasticity of tax yields, Walt Rostow, in a more historial vein, on (so far as I can remember) price trends in the nineteenth century, and were critical of the then standard, Layton and Crowther, quantity theory explanation given to them.

None of these activities had, as I have remarked, a strong *General Theory* flavour, though some of them were relevant to the Kahn multiplier. The investigations which, on the face of it, looked as if they might have been influenced by Keynes Mark II, were those of Edward Radice, William Blair and myself. Radice's work, culminating in his book *Savings in Great Britain, 1922–35* (1939) obviously had an indirect consumption function as well as a direct Kahn multiplier significance. He found, for instance, that the elasticity of saving with respect to real income was generally above unity, while its elasticity with respect to interest rate was apparently negative, but hard to estimate properly. This could be taken as giving support to underconsumptionist rather than overconsumptionist theories of the trade-cycle, but Radice's main concern was with the application of Frisch's confluence analysis to savings functions rather than with trade cycle theory as such.[3] The inspiration was Keynesian in a broad sense, but not very specifically *General Theory*.

William Blair and I started work in the Institute at the same time (October 1936) and quickly found that Marschak had suggested to both of us the same line of work on security prices. On being approached about this, he told us a beautiful parable about two explorers of Africa who started from the same place and discovered quite different new regions. He was, of course, quite right; Billy Blair wrote a successful BLitt thesis on *Risk, Interest Rates and Security Prices;* I, whose title was registered as *Liquidity Preference: A Study of Investment*, soon wandered into a different part of the forest.

Charles Hitch had suggested the subject of liquidity preference to me – I can hardly disclaim a *General Theory* inspiration for that. He had also interested Marschak in supervising me. I think Marschak was responsible for the sub-title. His inspiration may not have been Keynesian at all, but due to his incipient, and perhaps independent, interest in valuation and decision under uncertainty, stimulated by an article of Tinbergen's (1933) called 'The Notions of Horizon and Expectancy in Dynamic Economics'. I pursued this trail for a chapter in the mostly vain search for elements in security valuation attributable to liquidity and then decided that the balance sheets of the London Clearing Banks, despite the difficulties arising from their containing five main kinds of asset, might show interesting relations between the ratios of those assets to one another, their relative yields, and total assets held. The result is set out in 'The liquidity preference schedules of the London Clearing Banks' (1938). I persuaded myself that I had discovered such a relation, though banks to whom I was introduced were not equally persuadable – not even Billy Blair, after he went into one of the Scottish banks (alas, only briefly – he died in the El Alamein campaign). This bit of balance-sheet analysis had few direct consequences.

After that I turned back from my sub-title to my main title. (Marschak was an ideal supervisor; he always had suggestions on where I should go next, but pretended to have forgotten them if I, in fact, went somewhere else – provided that it was interesting.) I remember exactly when the obvious idea, hitherto hidden from me, of estimating a demand schedule for money, or for 'idle' money, first struck me; shortly after I had moved into All Souls in November 1937. The result along with an excursion into the Gibson Paradox, Wicksellian theory, and an ill-considered attempt to defend the latter from the Research Group's doubts on the effectiveness of interest, appeared in *OEP* No. 2, May 1939 as 'Interest, prices and the demand schedule for idle money' (subsequently reprinted in *Oxford Studies in the Price Mechanism* (1951)).

There was not much reaction to this work in the few months between its appearance in print and the outbreak of war, and when James Tobin entered the same territory in 1947–48 he seems to have done so independently. My Oxford friends, of course, had known about it before it was published, and I remember an occasion when Dennis Robertson came to address the Oxford Economics Society on some topic which led him to compare the liquidity preference approach unfavourably with that through loanable funds. Someone, in the subsequent discussion, quoted my work, and I was drawn into the argument. I do not recall that any dramatic conversion took place.

Meanwhile, outside the Institute of Statistics, important work with a Keynesian relevance was being done. Meade, after his *Introduction to Economic Analysis and Policy* (1936), proceeded to write a book on consumers' credits as an anti-depression measure. It was reviewed by Keynes in the *Economic Journal* in 1938, by which time James was in Geneva seeking to interpret current events in the new theoretical terms. The acceleration principle (with a reference to Harrod) appears in the League of Nations' *World Economic Survey* for 1937–38; the multiplier hovers discreetly in the background, but emerges more explicitly in the *Survey* for 1938–39. Harrod's *Trade Cycle* (1936) perhaps received less attention in Oxford than one might have expected, but he went on to redeem his promise to dynamise the system. I vividly remember sitting with Charles Hitch in the meeting of the Oxford Economics Society at which the warranted rate of growth, and all that goes with it, were revealed to us, some time in advance of the publication of 'An Essay in Dynamic Theory' in the *Economic Journal* (1939). George Shackle was writing his *Expectations, Investment and Income* (1938), basically a theory (or two theories) of the trade-cycle, using mainly multiplier–accelerator interactions, but with stress on expectations, rather than any mechanical linkage, as the promoters of capital stock adjustments. It must have been just after the publication of this book that he described to me, in conversation, the radically new approach to the theory of decision under uncertainty to which he was moving.

There were two main channels through which these developments, and others, from the past and from outside Oxford, were discussed; the Marschak–Opie seminar and the various meetings in the Institute. Unfortunately, I did not keep notes on seminars, so that a good deal of what went on in the Marschak–Opie meetings is hard now to recall. It was a seminar confined to selected third-year undergraduates and to postgraduate students, and the contrasting approach of its two leaders made it a particularly stimulating one. In my third year, it had discussed Wicksell's *Lectures* (1934). In the last term or two before the war, it discussed Hicks' *Value and Capital* (1939). To its not very successful discussion of the *General Theory* in the summer of 1936, with Hall in the place of Marschak (who was perhaps on leave), I have already referred.

Another seminar played a smaller part in my postgraduate years. I think I first went to it in the LSE, when it was still called the 'London and Cambridge Economic Seminar' – I did not then connect it (as I believe it was connected) with the approach made by Abba Lerner and other junior LSE economists in 1933 to the Cambridge 'circus' in an effort to bridge the Hayek/Keynes gap, and with the foundation of the *Review of Economic Studies* (the management of which excluded all senior figures in a very marked manner). Lerner was still the moving spirit at the first meeting I attended; then he left LSE. Subsequently, 'Oxford' was added to the seminar's title, and it sometimes met there. In some sense, its glory had departed, but no gathering containing Nicholas Kaldor could avoid a certain liveliness.

But for me, the seminars, classes and informal discussions at the Institute are what come back most vividly as giving the flavour of the time. A good deal of effort and discussion, of course, went into learning and applying statistical techniques. Marschak was an enthusiastic econometrician, and well in touch with the leaders of that trade. Haavelmo and Koopmans both visited the Institute in my time. Like Edward Radice I was persuaded to use Frisch's confluence analysis in both my subsequently published liquidity preference estimations – a technique not, I think, used again in this country until Richard Stone's demand function work, published in the *Journal of the Royal Statistical Society* in 1945 (which M. G. Kendall, in the discussion, took to be the first appearance here). More to the present point, however, was the acquaintance we made with the new dynamic econometrics. Sometime in the Hilary and/or Trinity terms of 1937, we worked in a seminar through most of Tinbergen's 'Annual Survey: Suggestions in Quantitative Business Cycle Theory' in *Econometrica* (1935), and it was from this, I think, that I, and no doubt others, got the first inkling of what systematic analysis can do.

Tinbergen first attempts, with little success, to turn the trade-cycle theories of Keynes and Hayek into difference or differential equation form, so as to test analytically whether, and in what conditions, they give realistic cyclical results. He then turns to the schemes of Frisch and Kalecki (both first published in 1933) and to two schemes (one long-lag, the other short-lag) of his own, and explores their properties. I was excited by this; I produced for my own satisfaction a second-order differential equation version of Hawtrey's theory (in the form of which Haberler reduces it in *Prosperity and Depression*). Tinbergen's short-lag scheme formed the basis of my first answer on the economics paper in my second, and successful, assault on All Souls in October 1937, and a simple cyclical model derived from Wicksell's relation and the 'Gibson Paradox' occurs in my 1939 *OEP* article. The appearance of this article virtually coincided with that of Samuelson's famous 'Interactions between the Multiplier Analysis and the Principle of Acceleration' in the *Review of Economics and Statistics* (1939) by which I should probably have been even more excited, but by that time my attention, like that of many others, was elsewhere; I, at least, did not become aware of it until much later.

The chief change of which I was aware in those years immediately after 1936 was that everybody started talking about dynamics. Very soon, 'dynamic' was a synonym for 'good' or 'helpful'; 'static' for 'useless', 'old-fashioned'. It is true that there were some differences of opinion about what 'dynamic' meant in economics. There was some rather pointless argument about whether values relating to more than one point of time were included, or whether rates of change of the variables were brought in – all of which amount to much the same thing, familiar from the dynamic subdivision of mechanics. There was also a school which equated 'dynamic' with 'involving expectations'. It was this school – represented, at this distance of time, most clearly by George Shackle – that had no difficulty in maintaining that the *General Theory* was dynamic, and therefore had the virtue attached to that quality. Harrod, whose schematization of the theory was clearly static, recognized the fact, and, as I have noted, proceeded to dynamize it, according to a version of the mechanical criterion. In the final phase before the war, we were all reading Hicks' *Value and Capital*, which can hardly be accused of under-emphasising expectations, except in the rather important matter of shrugging off their uncertainty. He says: 'I feel myself that there ought to be an Economics of Risk on beyond the Dynamic Economics we shall work out here ...' (1939, p. 126). This, of course, is what Shackle was even then trying to supply, and what he, in particular, understood Keynes to be acknowledging in his 1937 *Quarterly Journal of Economics* article as supremely important, and the heart of his General Theory.

Most of us, however, were excited mainly by the possibility of being definite about the course of income and employment which the difference and the differential equations of Frisch, Tinbergen and Kalecki gave us, rather than about the blank uncertainty at the centre of all decision-making. Even as I am writing this, I see that Richard Goodwin (1985), who was one of us, has just described how, when he went back to Harvard, he was full of enthusiasm for the new mathematical cycle theory, and tried to convert Schumpeter and Haberler to it. To that extent, we were perhaps, in the terms that Joan Robinson invented a generation later, 'bastard Keynesians'. Perhaps the chief evidence that this 'term of endearment' (as Robert Solow recently called it) was justified lies in Keynes' own well-known resistance, not only to Tinbergen's empirical econometrics, but to his analytical dynamic schemes as well – despite Harrod's efforts to reconcile him to them.

I do not think most of us totally ignored the importance of uncertainty. Some of us had been pretty well introduced to it through Frank Knight's *Risk, Uncertainty and Profit* (1921). For my part, I had been obliged to think a good deal about it in the course of coping with liquidity preference, and my favourite chapter of the *General Theory*, in one sense, was Chapter 12 – the only one that could be described as providing light relief. But cycles, not random variations, in total activity, were the background against which everyone had tried to understand prosperity and depression, even though some cyclical depressions were outstandingly severe, and some booms unusually feeble. The message that, because of the state of ignorance in which capital formation is decided upon, the decisions are at the mercy of trivial and irrelevant information – that 'investment is a flighty bird' (as Hicks puts it somewhere) – would not, by itself, have seemed a satisfying key to recent history. What George Shackle later dismissed rather scornfully as 'hydraulics' (no doubt thinking of the Phillips–Newlyn model, which arrived in Leeds shortly before he did) had a powerful appeal, because they explained regular fluctuations, into which exogenous factors could be understood to introduce a measure of irregularity.

The strength of this appeal derived largely from the inherent convincingness of the multiplier and the acceleration principle on which (in its more developed form, from about 1936 onwards), the new trade-cycle theory rested. That, together with the analytical precision with which it could be presented, was why this, effective demand-based, brand of theory triumphed so completely over consumptionist and related schools. I have noted how, in the early

1930s, Hayek's *Prices and Production* attracted attention which made it a serious rival to the Keynes Mark I (*Treatise* and earlier) intimations of the nature of depression. But when Keynes Mark II (*General Theory*), backed by multiplier-based cycle theory, came along, there was no real contest. Hayek published *Profits, Interest and Investment* in 1939. It is unlikely that it would have commanded general support even if it had been produced in 1931; it is in some ways more challenging to common sense than *Prices and Production* (the depression is attributed to shortening of the period of production caused by high profits, due, in turn, to a fall in real wages as consumer goods prices are driven up (relatively) in the boom). Kaldor reviewed it destructively in *Economica* in 1942. But, as it was, the intuitively much more appealing effective demand approach having received the legitimation of rigorous multiplier-accelerator theory, it had no chance.

In fact, I do not remember it being discussed at all at the time; I caught up with it only much later. After Munich, the time for high theory was running out – we had *Value and Capital* to talk about, besides our own immediate work, but, after a brief worry about the recession of 1938, the main economic cause for concern among my friends was changing from unemployment to the balance of resources between the Axis Powers and their probable opponents, and the British supply of aircraft. In the autumn of 1939, James Meade, at that time lying ill in Geneva, sent his friends some verses about economists' prognostications of the next depression, with the concluding couplet:

> The Devil laughed, and set the world at war
> To show how unrealistic theorists are.

With the war, most members of the Sub-Faculty either left Oxford or, like me, became absorbed there in wartime tasks. A new generation worked at the Institute under A. L. Bowley, who had come out of retirement as temporary successor to Marschak. This was the generation which, in 1944, published *The Economics of Full Employment*, of which David Worswick (1985), one of its authors, has recently reminded us in his 1984 Presidential Address to the Royal Economic Society. The other authors were Burchardt, Mandelbaum, Schumacher, Balogh and Kalecki. The last-named was the moving spirit, and the strong correspondence between the contents of the book and what one nowadays thinks of as immediate postwar Keynesian orthodoxy might be taken as showing how close the independent thinking of Kalecki had, indeed, been to that of Keynes. I had a peripheral connection with the Institute for the first few months of the war, but it faded away (more particularly after I went to work in London in 1943) and I do not know how far the thoughts of the Institute group stemmed from the letter of the *General Theory*, or its Harrodian/Hicksian interpretations, and how far from the Kaleckian thought, which, in any case, its author had probably adapted to some extent to a Keynesian mould. However that may be, I believe Kalecki had an important influence on what came to be regarded as postwar Keynesian orthodoxy, not least through the early economic publications of the United Nations Secretariat of which he was a member. I well remember, in 1950, hearing his distinctive voice, rarely still, penetrating the thin partitions of the former bombing-sight factory at Lake Success which was the Secretariat's first home.

Certainly the thinking of the wartime Institute group, in so far as I was aware of it at the time, either directly or through the new *Bulletin* which it published, was 'Keynesian' in a high degree, with an emphasis on income changes and relatively little regard for the price mechanism. Because the people concerned were different, one cannot take it as representing the further evolved thought of the prewar Sub-Faculty, and when, in 1951, the latters' successors republished (with some additions) what they presumably thought the cream of the first series of *Oxford Economic Papers*, they called it *Oxford Studies in the Price Mechanism*.[4] But equally, one cannot say that there was any natural break, as opposed to the artificial break of war, between the two. And the new Sub-Faculty that assembled after the war contained a blend of the two elements – Henderson, Harrod, Hargreaves, Andrews and (briefly) Hitch and Hall with Balogh, Burchardt and Worswick, together, of course with many new arrivals, though the majority of us were seeking our fortunes elsewhere.

IV

Does this narrative throw any light on the nature of the Keynesian Revolution? There are dangers in starting from a personal story of the time when one was engaged in the first, intensive, phase of becoming acquainted with one's subject, because that is a revolution inside one's head, in any case, whether what one is learning is new or old, and the revolution inside can easily be mistaken for one outside. I was just too late to be a witness of the imperfect competition 'revolution' even though I became acquainted with the crucial, Joan Robinson and Chamberlin, books only a couple of years after they first appeared. I learnt something of the developments behind them – Clapham, Sraffa, Yntema, Harrod – but I was not nurtured on Marshall's 'representative firm', and came to know about it only as a sort of historical curiosity. On the other hand, I and my contemporaries were old enough to be keenly aware of the conflict between Lloyd George's *We Can Conquer Unemployment* (backed by Keynes and Henderson in *Can Lloyd George Do It?*) and what we were given on Say's Law and general equilibrium by, for instance Cassel, and we experienced some of the struggles to resolve the conflict as current events. George Shackle and Harry Johnson later classified the economic doctrinal 'revolutions' of the interwar years in different ways.

My own feeling is that it makes good sense to distinguish only two – one in microeconomics (which, as I have just said, I was too late actually to witness), and one in macroeconomics – a term not, so far as I know, invented then. Indeed, in the 1920s there was no need for such a term because there was very little for it to describe. The general equilibrium system, if one held with such un-British devices, was all-embracing. If one did not, then, outside microeconomics, there was Say's Law, there were the concept and the measurement of the natonal income, and the implications of the consumption– investment split (which Cassel just missed making into Harrodian dynamics), there was the quantity theory of money, and there was a mixed bag of trade-cycle theories, not qualifying for inclusion in the Grand System. Experience of war-disturbed economies, violent fluctuations and persistent mass unemployment stimulated interest in all these macroeconomic odds and ends, and eventually it started a search for a more general, preferably equilibrium, theory of the level of activity which would embrace stagnation, as well as trade-cycle fluctuations. The *General Theory*, with its Kaleckian *doppelganger*, was the result of this search, but the Keynesian Revolution, especially in its practical aspect, as the source of a revolution in economic policy, was at least as much the result of thought given to what I have just called the macroeconomic odds and ends. And, in any case, there were connections between the two.

It is useful to distinguish the practical man's Keynesian Revolution from that of the theorist. The practical man's version was, essentially, acceptance of monetary and budgetary policy as instruments for correcting excess and deficiencies of effective demand. In Keynes' writing, the need to frame monetary policy so as to prevent unacceptable inflation goes back to the *Tract* (1923) or earlier; so does the doctrine that the use of monetary stringency to bring wages down is a bad idea, because it works only through depression and unemployment. The use of public investment, of a kind in itself useful, to raise employment in times of depression is endorsed in *Can Lloyd George Do It?* (1929), on grounds declared to be 'common sense', taking account of employment directly and indirectly created by the primary expenditure, with only a vague reference to secondary (multiplier) effects.

One may speculate on whether we should now be talking about a Keynesian Revolution if theorizing had stopped there. Logically, it should have happened, because the case for using monetary and budgetary policy to stabilize activity, 'playing it by ear' if no more sophisticated method is available, is a strong one, and intuitively clear. The reasons why it did not happen at once, or had not happened sooner were:

1   the tendency to maintain that all unemployment was either voluntary or due to technical progress (just like now!);
2   the 'Treasury view', which depends on failing to grasp the fact that there *are* unemployed resources;
3   the institutional limits of the time on the amount and variation of public investment, including the large extent to which it was controlled by local authorities; and
4   fears of the effect of budget deficits on confidence, at home and abroad.

An additional reason becoming effective (as it happpened) as the depression deepened, was the arrival of over-consumptionist theories (especially Hayek's), which turned the logic of demand-regulation on its head. In the not very long run, however, that line of thought would probably have been seen to be a paper dachshund, in any case, and other hindrances and inhibitions might have been overcome. We might have learned from the practical experience of depression to adopt a 'Keynesian' policy, not only without the *General Theory*, but even without Kahn's theory of the multiplier, and Keynes' name might still have been attached to it. But it might have taken a long time – it is arguable that, even in the event, it took the war to drive the lesson home.

I believe that, so far as academic opinion was concerned, Kahn's multiplier article of 1931 was immensely important. The general idea of the sequential multiplier now seems so obvious that it is hard to believe that it was not always part of economic thought; but the fact seems to be that it was a line of approach used imprecisely by laymen and shunned by professionals. Howson and Winch, in *The Economic Advisory Council* (1977) record how in the spring of 1930 even Colin Clark (abetted by A. W. Flux) shied off from estimating the secondary expenditure and employment an increase in exports would bring, on the ground that it '... would lead to assuming an infinite series of beneficial repercussions. This clearly cannot represent the case . . . '. The systematic period analysis of the results of an increment in investment expenditure provided the most striking and practically important example of short-term dynamics and shattered the professional economist's myth that only static equilibrium analysis is intellectually safe. It was Kahn's multiplier, and the schedule of propensity to consume (which, after all, is implicit in his formulation of it, as well as explicit in Keynes') that provided the basic apparatus for effective demand regulation, and were responsible for most of the applied work bearing a Keynesian label for quite a long time after the *General Theory* was published. The multiplier was important also in providing, along with some kind of investment function (of which the 'relation' or 'accelerator' was the most obvious) a basis for formal trade-cycle theories which, by their combination of rigour and intuitive appeal, drove over-consumptionist rivals out of the field. Once it was formulated, the occurrence of some sort of Keynesian Revolution, at least at the level of practical policy, was probably assured.

What, then, is the importance of the *General Theory* itself? Its primary importance for economists lies, of course, in its claim to provide a general theory of the level of actitivity in which the possibility of underemployment equilibrium is implicit. Practical men may be fairly happy with a general equilibrium theory implying full use of factors of production, even though, because of frictions and tendencies to 'hunt', that implication is not matched by reality, so long as they think they know when, where and approximately how hard to kick the economy to produce a required short-term result. This is the position into which the Kahn multiplier promised to put them. They are happier if they also have a theory of the way in which the economy 'hunts', which can in some measure be quantified; theorists demand this, too, and the new trade-cycle theories of Frisch, Tinbergen and Kalecki, unlike most rival theories, held out this promise. But theorists, in particular, were happier still to welcome a theory that claimed to explain the short-term static equilibrium level of activity in the economy, and intrigued that it gave indications that this level might be, in the long run, biased downwards from reasonably defined full employment levels – the error in the old general equilibrium theory was a systematic one, due to misspecification. For the time being, it did not matter much to them, or to the practical men, that the *General Theory* was, in most people's terms, static, and did not explain the trade-cycle as such; they would set to work to dynamize it, taking their cues from the quantifiable dynamic cycle theories recently produced.

These four stages of development – an empirically quantifiable multiplier, systematic and quantifiable cycle theories, a theory of

the short-term equilibrium level of activity, and the first step towards dynamizing it – all arrived in the 1930s. Keynes was responsible for only a part of them, albeit a bigger part, probably, than
anyone else, and to some of them he was less than welcoming. But
to those who were young and learning when these things happened,
they blended together into a heady mixture, which seemed to hold
the promise of a new and better economic world.

Notes

1. Lord Roberthall (then Robert Hall) tells me that Cassel's book was also his
   introduction to general equilibrium analysis, and came as a revelation to him.
2. This may not have been true of Cambridge. A story circulated in Oxford that it
   was only when Keynes expounded his marginal efficiency of capital there in
   February 1935, that a member of the audience pointed out the relation of that
   concept to Fisher's rate of return over cost.
3. Hugo Radice reminds me that his father Edward subsequently worked on trade-
   cycle dynamics. He published 'A dynamic scheme for the British trade cycle,
   1929–37' in *Econometrica* in 1939.
4. Edited by T. Wilson and P. W. S. Andrews (1951).

3 *The General Theory* after fifty years – why are we not all Keynesians now?

John Brothwell

Keynes wrote *The General Theory of Employment, Interest and Money* to explain to his fellow economists why the capitalist economies of the interwar period were failing to maintain full employment and to suggest means of correcting the malady. For him: 'The outstanding faults of the economic society in which we live are its failure to provide for full employment and its arbitrary and inequitable distribution of wealth and incomes' (1936, p. 372). Twenty-five years after the *General Theory* was published most economists would have agreed that he had been completely successful in his employment objective. He seemed to have accomplished a revolution in economic theory; the whole subject of macroeconomics was based on his disciples' simplifications of the *General Theory*. More significantly, there was a political consensus that Keynes had shown how to control the level of employment through fiscal (and monetary) policy; governments were committed to maintain full employment through such demand management policies and these appeared to be highly successful. It is true that unemployment in Britain had fallen from around three million to below two million by the time the *General Theory* was published, and the recovery from the Great Depression was under way. But, both in this country and the USA, the wartime full employment, obtained through massive increases in government expenditure, and the maintenance of much higher levels of employment after the war than previously had been deemed feasible, were evidence of the success of Keynesian policy and the correctness of his theory.

Today, twenty-five years further on, the world economy is struggling to recover from the worst setback since the depression of the 1930s. Unemployment in the UK is back to well over three million. Yet Keynesian demand management policy in Britain (and many other countries), together with the commitment to full employment, has been abandoned. It is ironic that, at a time when our economy and many of the other western capitalist economies are in the greatest need of Keynesian remedies, the main 'remedy' being applied is the leech of monetarism: a remedy which undoubtedly has aggravated the disease, based on an economic theory which Keynes had struggled to overthrow. The question which Joan Robinson posed as long ago as 1972 – 'What has become of the Keynesian Revolution?' – is more poignant than ever before.

The immediate cause of the abandonment of Keynesian *policies* was their failure to deal satisfactorily with the 'stagflation' of the mid-1970s, precipitated by the collapse of the Bretton Woods system and, above all, by the oil and commodity price explosions of 1973–74.[2] Policy-makers, faced with a combination of accelerating unemployment, accelerating inflation and increasing balance of payments difficulties grasped at the simple remedy proffered by monetarists – control of the growth of the money supply. But it is unlikely that the policy changes would have been so complete unless the policy-makers (and their advisers) had been 'softened up', so to speak, by the *theoretical* counterattack to the Keynesian Revolution launched by Friedman and the monetarists as early as the mid-1950s.[3] Indeed, one of the conclusions which can be drawn from the reappraisal of Keynesian economics in the late 1960s and early 1970s, induced partly by Friedman but also by the work of Keynesian economists[4] dissatisfied with the way textbook Keynesianism had developed, is that Keynes did not succeed in his objective of overthrowing the pre-Keynesian, neoclassical paradigm. In other words, for the majority of economists, there has never been a Keynesian Revolution in economic *theory*. Leijonhufvud (1983) asserted:

> Keynesian economics used to be the mainstream. Now, the younger generation of macrotheorists and econometricians regard it just as a backwater, look to Monetarism for navigable channels, and find their real white water thrills in the technically demanding rapids of Rational Expectations.

Yet there is no doubt that Keynes intended there to be a revolution in economic thinking. In the first (one paragraph) chapter of the *General Theory* he states:

> I shall argue that the postulates of the classical theory are applicable to a special case only and not the general case, the situation which it assumes being a limiting point of the possible positions of equilibrium. Moreover, the characteristics of the special case assumed by the classical theory happen not to be those of the economic society in which we actually live, with the result that its teaching is misleading and disastrous if we attempt to apply it to the facts of experience.

And, at the end of the book, he concludes:

> Our criticism of the accepted classical theory of economics has consisted not so much in finding logical flaws in its analysis as in pointing out that

its tacit assumptions are seldom or never satisfied, with the result that it cannot solve the economic problems of the actual world. (1936, p. 378)

Thus, in the *General Theory* Keynes set out to convince his fellow economists that the basic assumptions on which they had built their (rudimentary) *macro*-theory, their theory of aggregate employment and output, were wrong. I believe, however, that, in the end, he failed, and the Keynesian Revolution in *theory* never succeeded, because he did not simultaneously and deliberately discard much of neo-classical *micro*-theory (which for him meant Marshallian theory, but for many economists also embraces Walrasian theory). In particular, the *General Theory*, despite the author's 'long struggle of escape from habitual modes of thought and expression', retained a considerable amount of neo-classical marginalist value theory, and this greatly facilitated the Keynesian/neo-classical synthesis and the subsequent neo-classical resurgence culminating in the complete rejection of all Keynesian elements in the New Classical macroeconomics – and the wheel had turned full circle. The valiant efforts of Joan Robinson, George Shackle, Sydney Weintraub, Paul Davidson and the other post-Keynesian fundamentalists to proclaim and preserve Keynes' great macro-truths – especially the principle of effective demand and the likelihood of demand-deficient (involuntary) unemployment – have been undermined by Keynes' failure to purge the *General Theory* of neo-classical marginalism. He failed to realize that the neo-classical theory of employment and the neo–classical theory of value and distribution stand or fall together.

The essence of the *General Theory*

The central message of Keynes' *General Theory* is that, to understand the forces which determine changes in the scale of output and employment as a whole, it is first necessary to understand that the real world we inhabit is a dynamic *monetary* economy, moving through calendar (historic) time from an irrevocable past to an uncertain future. In the preface he states:

> A monetary economy, we shall find, is essentially one in which changing views about the future are capable of influencing the quantity of employment and not merely its direction. (1936, p. vii)

And, in Chapter 21, on The Theory of Prices, there is a key passage where Keynes distinguishes between the classical theory of stationary equilibrium and his theory of shifting equilibrium, by which he means the theory of a system in which changing views about the future are capable of influencing the present situation – the theory of a monetary economy:

> *For the importance of money essentially flows from its being a link
> between the present and the future.* We can consider what distribution of
> resources between different uses will be consistent with equilibrium
> under the influence of normal economic motives in a world in which our
> views concerning the future are fixed and reliable in all respects. ... Or
> we can pass from this simplified propaedeutic to the problems of the real
> world in which previous expectations are liable to disappointment and
> expectations concerning the future effect what we do to-day. It is when
> we have made this transition that the peculiar properties of money as a
> link between the present and future must enter our calculations. (1936,
> pp. 294–5)

He had first expounded this fundamental concept of the crucial
distinction between a monetary production economy and a real-
exchange (barter) economy in his contribution to a *Festschrift* for
Professor A. Spiethoff in 1933, 'A Monetary Theory of Production'.
Money in a monetary production economy was *not* neutral:

> [It] plays a part of its own and effects motives and decisions and is, in
> short, one of the operative factors in the situation, so that the course of
> events cannot be predicted, either in the long period or in the short,
> without a knowledge of the behaviour of money between the first state
> and the last. (Keynes, 1973, p. 408)

Rotheim (1981) shows that Keynes made much more of this
fundamental difference between an ongoing monetary production
economy (or what he also termed an 'entrepreneur' economy) and a
real-exchange (or 'cooperative') economy in discarded early drafts
of the first three chapters of the *General Theory*.[5] It is a great pity
that Keynes omitted this discussion of the distinction between a
cooperative economy and an entrepreneur economy from the published version of the *General Theory* as it would have made clearer
the different foundations, both methodological and theoretical, of
the *General Theory* compared with neo-classical economics. As it
was, the discussion of the 'essential properties' of money was rele-
gated to Chapter 17 and neglected by most economists[6] until Paul
Davidson (1972; 1977) demonstrated that the core of Keynes' theoretical contribution in the *General Theory* lay in that chapter.
Money's essential properties are (i) zero, or negligible, elasticity of
production: thus a rise in the demand for money (by individuals
wanting to defer the commitment of resources in the face of uncertainty) does not encourage entrepreneurs to employ resources in the
production of additional quantities of the money commodity; (ii)
zero, or negligible, elasticity of substitution: thus a rise in the
demand for money does not divert people into substituting other
assets, which have high elasticities of production, as a store of value.
The result is that a rise in the demand for money (and near-money
financial assets) as a store of value in an uncertain world does not

generate a demand to commit resources and Say's Law breaks down. In a dynamic, changing, uncertain world, where the future is not predictable in any probability sense (i.e. the system is non-ergodic), money, the essential medium of exchange possessing the above properties, becomes *the* liquid asset and store of wealth, which assists agents to cope with intractable uncertainty. In addition, society develops the institution of forward contracting in money terms to organize time-consuming production and exchange processes efficiently in the face of uncertainty. A complex dynamic monetary economy cannot operate without such forward contracts to cover at least the period of production. The money wage contract is the most pervasive. Modern production economies are therefore money wage contract based systems. It follows that the general level of money wages and the price level (which is mainly determined by money wages and the productivity of labour, i.e. wage costs) must be *sticky*. The neo-classical assumption of perfectly flexible money wages and prices is as unrealistic and irrelevant to a modern production economy as is its assumption of perfect knowledge (certainty). As Keynes puts it: 'In fact we must have *some* factor, the value of which in terms of money is, if not fixed, at least sticky, to give us any stability of values in a monetary system' (1936, p. 304). But this *vital* institution in a modern economy, money, is nevertheless the source of the massive market failures that can occur. It is the existence of money that breaks the investment/saving nexus; that breaks the circular flow of income and expenditure and allows unemployment to occur. Because of the peculiar properties of money, Say's Law is not applicable to a monetary economy – aggregate demand can be less than (or greater than) aggregate supply. As Keynes so vividly expresses it in Chapter 17:

> [M]oney is a bottomless sink for purchasing power, when the demand for it increases, since there is no value for it at which demand is diverted – as in the case of other rent-factors – so as to slop over into a demand for other things. (ibid., p. 231)

and,

> Unemployment develops, that is to say, because people want the moon; – men cannot be employed when the object of desire (i.e. money) is something which cannot be produced and the demand for which cannot be readily choked off. (ibid., p. 235)

So savers are enabled to accumulate stocks of money and near-money assets and, unless this is matched by investment injections, output and employment fall. On the other hand, in a growing economy, investment can exceed saving as a result of injections of new money (or running down of idle balances) and income can expand.

Davidson (1984) has summarized all this by arguing that Keynes in the *General Theory* rejected three major neo-classical axioms

1   the axiom of reals,
2   the axiom of gross substitution, and
3   the axiom of an ergodic economic world.

In his monetary production (entrepreneur) economy, the sort of world we happen to inhabit, the axiom of reals does not apply; money is *not* neutral. Money matters[7] because it affects real spending decisions. It affects them in particular via the rate of interest, which is a monetary phenomenon,[8] determined by the supply of money and liquidity preference. Also, because of the existence of money, planned spending need never be equal to, or constrained by, actual income; agents, in a monetary economy, can find resting places for savings in non-reproducible assets because the axiom of gross substitution does not apply. Real assets, producible by labour, are *not* gross substitutes for money and near-money assets in savers' portfolios; spending falls below income and Say's Law is broken. The axiom of an ergodic economic world does not apply because decision-making agents know that the future need not be predictable in any probability sense. As Hicks puts it: 'One must assume that people in one's model do not know what is going to happen, and know that they do not know just what is going to happen. As in history!' (1977, p. vii).

Such fundamental uncertainty means that private investment decisions depend upon businessmen's state of confidence ('animal spirits') in the face of 'the dark forces of time and ignorance which envelop our future', and therefore may be subject to waves of optimism or pessimism. Movements of income can easily become cumulative and swamp any hypothetical neo-classical substitution effects. Unemployment is the norm in a market-oriented, monetary production economy.[9]

In sum, Keynes, by rejecting the above three major neo-classical axioms, reverses the two main hypotheses of the neo-classical (monetarist) system. For Keynes, (1) money, via the rate of interest, is an important determinant of effective demand, real output and employment, rather than prices; (2) money wage contracts, fixed in the labour market, determine labour costs and prices, rather than employment and output; and, even so, it is social, institutional and historic factors (rather than strictly economic factors) which influence the level of money wages.

It is this second hypothesis of Keynes, implying that the labour market in a monetary production economy has little to do with the determination of the level of employment, that most starkly distinguishes his model from that of orthodox neo-classical theory. In the latter, the level of employment is determined in the labour market by the real wage moving to bring the demand for, and supply of, labour into equilibrium at full employment (or the natural rate of unemployment). If unemployment occurs, it must be because the real wage is being prevented from falling: labour has 'priced itself out of work' and such unemployment is, therefore, voluntary. For Keynes, in a monetary economy, (1) labour can only bargain to fix a money wage,[10] not a real wage; (2) even if the real wage were reduced, this would not increase the demand for labour unless it increased the effective demand for goods because, as is explained below, the neo-classical marginal productivity of labour curve is *not* the macro-demand curve for labour (Davidson, 1983). The labour market is the centre of the neo-classical theory of employment. For Keynes it is peripheral;[11] the centre of Keynes' theory of employment is the goods market. Indeed, when Keynes summarized his theory in the famous *Quarterly Journal of Economics* (1937) article,[12] he nowhere mentioned the workings of the labour market. What he did say was:

> aggregate output depends on the propensity to hoard, on the policy of the monetary authority as it affects the quantity of money, on the state of confidence concerning the prospective yield of capital assets, on the propensity to spend and on the social factors which influence the level of the money wage.

Keynes' theory of employment dispenses with the labour market: money wages, fixed in that market by the bargains reached between employers and employed, are exogenously determined (1936, p. 247). He sets out the substance of his General Theory of Employment in Chapter 3, 'The Principle of Effective Demand'. Here he deploys the two new concepts of aggregate supply and aggregate demand to show why Say's Law does not hold in a monetary economy; how income moves to bring the two into equality; how investment determines saving (and not vice versa) and how there can be a paradox of thrift:

> Thus the volume of employment is not determined by the marginal disutility of labour measured in terms of real wages, except in so far as the supply of labour available at a given real wage sets a *maximum* level to employment. The propensity to consume and the rate of new investment determine between them the volume of employment, and the volume of employment is uniquely related to a given level of real wages – not the other way round. (1936, p. 30)

And he noted: 'the essential character of the argument is precisely the same whether or not money-wages, etc., are liable to change' (ibid., p. 27).

Most of the remainder of the book is devoted to explaining this employment and output determining mechanism in more detail. Chapter 5 explains that, in a monetary economy, it is *expected* aggregate demand and supply which govern the behaviour of firms in their output and employment decisions. Short-term expectations determine current output and employment: long-term expectations govern the investment decision. (All Keynes' functional relation–ships are expectations augmented.) Since aggregate demand consists of consumption expenditure and investment expenditure, Chapters 8 to 10 discuss another new[13] concept – the propensity to consume; while Chapters 11 to 13 discuss the inducement to invest; the famous Chapter 12 ('The State of Long-term Expectation') explaining the importance of 'animal spirits' and 'spontaneous opti-mism' in the investment decision in an uncertain world and why, therefore, investment expenditure is the main source of fluctuations in output and employment. Chapters 13 and 15 demonstrate that the rate of interest in a monetary production economy is a monetary phenomenon (not the real phenomenon of orthodox theory) deter-mined by liquidity preference and the money supply and inadequate to keep planned investment and saving equal at full employment income, while Chapter 17 ('The Essential Properties of Interest and Money'), already referred to, points to money as being the ultimate source of the trouble. Finally, Chapter 18 ('The General Theory of Employment Re-stated') gathers together the threads of the argu-ment, recapitulating the argument first adumbrated in Chapter 3 and then developed in the intervening chapters; all with little or no reference to the workings of the labour market. The 'escape from habitual modes of thought and expression' (1936, p. viii), the old orthodox neo-classical theory of employment, appears complete.

The neo-classical resurgence

Why has this revolution in theory not been accepted? Why do we open macroeconomics textbooks and find the primitive phallic symbols of neo-classical monetarism dotted all over the place – vertical[14] aggregate supply curves and long-run Phillips curves? As I have indicated above, Keynes' revolutionary paradigm never took a firm hold. From the time the *General Theory* was published many of his fellow economists set about modifying it to tame it and absorb it into their orthodox framework of thought – neo-classical marginalist and Walrasian general equilibrium theory. And Keynes facilitated this process by failing to jettison neo-classical marginalism along with the three major neo-classical axioms already referred to.

The most striking (and damaging) example of this is his accep-tance of what he terms the first postulate of the classical theory of employment. It has been argued above that Keynes should have retained his original discussion of the difference between a monetary production economy and a real-exchange economy in the early chapters of the published version of the *General Theory*. Instead, he embarked upon a discussion of what he called the two fundamental postulates of the classical theory of employment. With hindsight, it is clear that he made a tactical error in criticizing the classical theory of employment in great detail in Chapter 2 before expounding his own, fundamentally different, theory in Chapter 3. But the crucial mistake was to accept the first postulate – the wage is equal to the marginal product of labour – without due qualification. He threw over the second postulate – the utility of the wage when a given volume of labour is employed is equal to the marginal disutility of that amount of employment – which underlies the classical labour supply schedule, by pointing out that labour itself is not in a position to decide the real wage for which it works:

> But the other, more fundamental, objection, which we shall develop in the ensuing chapters, flows from our disputing the assumption that the general level of real wages is directly determined by the character of the wage bargain. In assuming that the wage bargain determines the real wage the classical school have slipt [sic] into an illicit assumption. (1936, p. 13)

But this is only half the story: even if labour could determine the real wage, a reduction need not increase the demand for labour. However, Keynes went on to say:

> In emphasising our point of departure from the classical system, we must not overlook an important point of agreement. For we shall maintain the first postulate as heretofore, subject only to the same qualifications as in the classical theory: and we must pause, for a moment, to consider what this involves.
> It means that, with a given organisation, equipment and technique, real wages and the volume of output (and hence of employment) are uniquely correlated so that, in general, an increase in employment can only occur to the accompaniment of a decline in the rate of real wages. Thus I am not disputing this vital fact which the classical economists have (rightly) asserted as indefeasible. ... So long, indeed, as this proposition holds, *any* means of increasing employment must lead at the same time to a diminution of the marginal product and hence of the rate of wages measured in terms of this product. (1936, pp. 17–18)

This unnecessary concession to neo-classical marginal productivity theory has proved disastrous. The fact that Keynes accepted the first postulate has been taken to mean that he accepted the neo-classical assumption that the aggregate marginal productivity of labour curve is also the demand schedule for labour at the macro-level. But he is quite clearly *not* making that assumption. By accepting the law of diminishing marginal productivity he is simply accepting that 'an increase in employment can only occur to the *accompaniment* of a decline in the rate of real wages': and, '*if* employment increases, then, in the short period, the reward per unit of labour in terms of wage-goods must, in general, decline and profits increase.'[15] That is, the chain of causation runs *from* employment *to* the real wage, NOT, as in a demand schedule relationship, from a change in the real wage to a change in employment:

> a decline in employment, although necessarily associated with labour's *receiving* a wage equal in value to a larger quantity of wage-goods is not necessarily due to labour's *demanding* a larger quantity of wage-goods; and a willingness on the part of labour to accept lower money-wages is not necessarily a remedy for unemployment. (1936, p. 18)

For Keynes, the level of output, employment and hence the real wage is decided outside the labour market by the effective demand for goods and services, as he demonstrates in the following Chapter 3 and the remainder of the book (especially Chapter 19). But the damage was done. Keynes' acceptance of the first postulate provided a springboard for the neo-classical resurgence. It was assumed that Keynes' attack on the neo-classical theory of the labour market applied only to the supply side, and could be summed up by saying that he believed that workers suffered from money illusion, resulting in downward money (and real) wage rigidity. Unemployment becomes due solely to 'imperfections' in the labour market and Keynes' theoretical contribution is minimal.[16] Most mathematical treatments of Keynes' system, which consider the labour market along with the goods and money markets, perpetrate this error by making the demand for labour a function of the real wage.[17] Keynes himself realized later that he was hasty in accepting the first postulate and, indeed, that it was inconvenient for his own theory:

> That I was an easy victim of the traditional conclusion [of rising marginal cost] because it fitted my theory is the opposite of the truth. For my own theory this conclusion was inconvenient, since it had a tendency to offset the influence of the main forces which I was discussing . . . (1939, p. 40)

Here Keynes is emphasizing that, to accept that the real wage must fall as employment rises is likely to obscure his argument that the fall in the real wage is the *consequence* of the rise in employment and not the *cause*.

Keynes' acceptance of the first classical postulate is only one of several instances of his failing to break away completely from orthodox theory, thereby jeopardizing his attempt to overthrow it. His acceptance of the first postulate (the wage is *equal* to the marginal product of labour) is part and parcel of his overall acceptance in the

General Theory of the neo-classical axioms concerning competitive firms; that they are price-taking profit-maximizers, equating expected price to short-run rising marginal cost. In short, he accepted the basic concepts of constant returns technology and marginal productivity theory. Now it may be true that the essence of his theory does not depend upon the type of industrial market structure assumed (*pace* Weitzman and Kaldor);[18] and it was a remarkable achievement to demonstrate that, even in a highly competitive economy of small, price-taking firms, involuntary unemployment could occur.[19] But this was another needless concession to orthodoxy which misled many economists into thinking that Keynes accepted the microfoundations of the Walrasian general equilibrium system and was simply pointing out the various types of market imperfection in the real world – particularly in the labour market – which could result in market failure and disequilibrium. The Clower/Leijonhufvud 'reappraisal' of Keynes went down this cul-de-sac;[20] both of them at first trying to relate Keynes to Walras, though Leijonhufvud (1981) eventually decided that the link to Marshall was more apposite. It is strange that Keynes, who saw the deficiencies of the classical theory of employment at the macro-level so clearly, did not incorporate into his theory of a monetary production (entrepreneur) economy a realistic theory of the firm; a theory of the firm based on realistic assumptions of constant average variable cost, decreasing average total cost, *with output limited by demand*, and price set by a mark-up on prime cost in an uncertain oligopolistic market.[21] This would have provided micro-foundations compatible with his macro-theory and incidentally supplied a further reason for 'sticky' prices in a monetary economy. Moreover, it is much more convincing to construct Keynes' aggregate supply curve on the micro-foundation of demand-constrained, price-making imperfectly competitive firms, operating under conditions of excess capacity, than to construct one on the basis of price-taking, perfectly competitive firms. There is no doubt that the macroeconomics of Keynes and oligopolistic competition complement each other, just as perfect competition is integral with the Walrasian general equilibrium system. Kalecki, by assuming from the start imperfect competition and mark-up pricing in uncertain, oligopoly markets, succeeded in integrating the analysis of prices and the analysis of effective demand much more convincingly than Keynes. By discarding marginal productivity theory and substituting his own 'degree of monopoly' theory of income distribution, he also arrived at a simple explanation of effective demand, without the rather weak[22] Keynesian concept of the consumption function (Robinson, 1977; Sawyer, 1982). For Kalecki, the overall relation of national income to consumption is strongly affected by its distribution between wages and profits. In effect, wages are consumed and gross profits (and therefore savings) are determined by capitalists' spending on gross investment and consumption.

It is fascinating to find that Bertil Ohlin (in an unpublished section of an article submitted in 1937 to Keynes in his capacity of editor of the *Economic Journal* and commenting on the *General Theory*) likewise attacked Keynes' acceptance of the first postulate and assumption of perfectly competitive firms:

> What is really startling, however is that Keynes ... without explanation accepts the crude form of marginal productivity *in terms of physical units*. ... Unfortunately, the relation of this 'orthodox' physical marginal productivity theory to the aggregate supply and demand function analysis is not explained. ... In the case of an increase in the sum total of purchases in the country, e.g. through large public works, the employers – being able to sell more goods at the same price – will hire more men at the same wage rates. There is no reason, in a period of large surplus capacity, why this should raise the costs of living. Hence employment will increase without any reduction in the real wage. The fact that the orthodox economists came to the contrary conclusion is due to the fact that they tacitly assumed either some kind of monetary stability which excludes the primary increases in monetary demand, or assumed 'perfect' competition. In this as in some other respects Keynes does not seem to me to have been radical enough in freeing himself from the conventional assumptions. When reading his book one sometimes wonders whether he never discussed imperfect competition with Mrs Robinson. (Keynes, 1973, Vol. XIV pp. 195–6)

Keynes, in his editorial comments, replied rather obtusely:

> I have not been able to make out here what you are driving at. The reference to imperfect competition is very perplexing. I cannot see how on earth it comes in. ... In this section I feel unrepentant, or rather I have no clear idea what it is you are really driving at. I have always regarded decreasing physical returns in the short period as one of the few incontrovertible propositions of our miserable subject! (ibid., p. 190)

But, as shown above, he changed his mind two years later (Keynes, 1939).

The close link between the macroeconomics of Keynes, with its accent on unemployment as the norm, and the theory of the firm in imperfect competition with its accent on demand-constrained output and excess capacity, must not lead one into the trap of thinking that it is the breakdown of competition (for whatever reason) which is the ultimate cause of unemployment. Reference has already been made to the fallacious imperfectionist argument that the basic cause of unemployment is price and wage rigidity. Another version of 'imperfectionism' is Weitzman's (1982) thesis that the ultimate source of unemployment equilibrium is increasing returns. Kaldor (1983) has surprisingly accepted this,[23] but it betrays complete ignorance of Keynes' thesis that the ultimate source of unemployment lies in the fact that Say's Law does not apply to a monetary economy. Weitzman commences his article by recapitulating the discredited argument of Clower and Leijonhufvud that insufficient aggregate demand is caused by

> a failure to coordinate the desired consumption and production plans of all agents because the unemployed lack the means to communicate or make effective their potential demands. ... There is an atmosphere of frustration because the problem is beyond the power of any single firm to correct, yet would go away if only all firms would simultaneously expand output.

This naive hypothesis is refuted simply by noting that, if the marginal propensity to consume is less than unity, *unless investment rises to match the extra saving generated at the higher level of income*, firms would be unable to sell the increased output. Davidson *et al.* (1985) have no difficulty in demonstrating that the ultimate cause of insufficient aggregate demand (which Weitzman admits is the cause of 'persistent involuntary underutilisation of the major factors of production') is the beakdown of Say's Law in a monetary production economy, *not* increasing returns in combination with short-run expectations of spoiling the market (if output were to increase). In the real world there is always a threat of a lack of effective demand, independent of the existing returns to scale or the degree of competition. Involuntary unemployment is a demand problem not a supply (technological) problem. Even if the unemployed could turn themselves into one person 'mini-firms' in a strict constant returns-to-scale world (which they cannot in an increasing-returns world) there would still be the likelihood of unemployment as long as it was a world in which savers wished to hold their wealth in the form of non-producible liquid assets.

In the neo-classical system the analysis of output and employment is part and parcel of the theory of value and distribution – marginal productivity theory. Employment and the distribution of income are simultaneously determined (Eatwell and Milgate, 1983). Thus it is not surprising that Keynes' efforts to overthrow the neo-classical theory of employment have been vitiated by his failure to purge the *General Theory* of marginalist value theory. The disastrous consequences of his acceptance of the classical postulate that the wage is equal to the marginal product of labour have been discussed; Garegnani (1983) suggests that Keynes' concept of the marginal efficiency of capital likewise made it easier to return to the traditional theory. The Cambridge Capital Controversy and the work of

Joan Robinson, Garegnani *et al.* (1966) has completely discredited the marginal productivity theory of value and distribution:

> The principle that the proportions in which the factors are employed vary with the prices of their services, so as to give rise to demand functions of these services, can in fact be deduced from the conditions of equilibrium in production only if the quantities of the factors can all be defined independently of the system of prices. But this *cannot* be done when one of the factors is the value of the magnitude 'capital'. (Garegnani, 1983, p. 39)

The concepts of an aggregate production function and the marginal products of capital (and labour) in a real world of heterogeneous capital (and largely fixed technical coefficients of production) are meaningless. There is evidence in the *General Theory* that Keynes was critical of the concept of the marginal *product* of capital: 'It is much preferable to speak of capital as having a yield over the course of its life in excess of its original cost, than as being *productive*' (1936, p. 213).

Be that as it may, Garegnani's criticism of Keynes is misplaced since Keynes' marginal efficiency of capital concept is *not* the same as the marginal product of capital – the return to a process of capital deepening. Textbook treatments of the investment decision usually fudge the difference between the neo-classical theory of investment (in which a fall in the rate of interest induces capital *deepening* until the marginal product of capital is equal to the rate of interest) and Keynes' theory. In Keynes' marginal *efficiency* argument, if a fall in the rate of interest leads to the investment project being *ex ante* profitable, the entrepreneur expands his whole production process (plant, machinery, *labour* and other inputs). This has nothing to do with *substitution* between capital and labour – there is no reason to assume a change in technique.[24] The fall in the rate of interest raises the demand price of capital (compared to supply price) just as does an improvement in the flow of expected returns. Both lead to capital *widening* – an expansion with fixed factor proportions. Thus although Keynes' marginal efficiency theory needs some tidying up (and the stock/flow problems sorted out) it is a necessary building-block in any sensible theory of investment.

The fact that Keynes' marginal efficiency of capital concept is related to capital widening (rather than deepening) makes it easily reconcilable with accelerator theories of investment. Thus Harrod (1939) was able to explore the long-period implications of Keynes' theory by marrying the 'acceleration principle' with Keynes' 'multiplier' theory. Starting with the correct capital:output ratio (presumably where the marginal efficiency of capital equals the rate of interest), if producers expect a particular increase in demand (increase in the expected returns from expanding their whole capacity to produce, which means an increase in the marginal efficiency of capital) they will be induced to invest – the acceleration principle. There will be an expected rate of growth of the system which keeps aggregate demand equal to aggregate supply with capital and output expanding in fixed proportions (capital widening) – Harrod's warranted growth rate. Now Keynes' theory of employment has been criticized as being solely a short-period theory of capacity utilization; might not the system tend to full employment (full capacity) in the long period? Keynes thought not:

> ... we oscillate, avoiding the gravest extremes of fluctuation in employment and in prices in both directions, round an intermediate position appreciably below full employment and appreciably above the minimum employment a decline below which would endanger life. (1936, p. 254)

But obviously, his sketchy treatment of the long period in the *General Theory* leaves him open to the charge that his theory of unemployment equilibrium is not fundamentally different from the orthodox theory, but simply indicates the various imperfections, frictions and rigidities which prevent the system from converging on full employment in the longer run (Eatwell, 1983). Harrod rescues Keynes from this charge by placing the principle of effective demand in a long-run setting. He demonstrates that Keynes' belief about the long-period behaviour of the economy is likely to be correct. Deploying his concepts of the warranted, actual and natural growth rates, he argues that developed capitalist market economies are likely to fluctuate around a growth path well short of full employment, because the warranted path is unstable and the warranted growth rate most of the time exceeds the natural (full employment) growth rate, so that there will be chronic Keynesian demand-deficient unemployment. In a dynamic monetary production economy, moving through historic time from an unalterable past to a perfidious future, unemployment is likely to be the norm.[25] Solow (1956) provided the (predictable) neo-classical response showing that, in an artificial, timeless, non-monetary, single-composite commodity, ergodic world, a perfectly operating market mechanism would ensure full employment growth.

Although Keynes' marginal efficiency of capital concept is different from the neo-classical marginal product of capital, there are instances in the *General Theory* where he fell into the trap of thinking of the accumulation of capital in static marginal productivity terms. This is especially the case where he discusses the likely future euthanasia of the rentier:

> ... I should guess that a properly run community equipped with modern technical resources of which the population is not increasing rapidly, ought to be able to bring down the marginal efficiency of capital in equilibrium approximately to zero within a single generation. (1936, p. 220)

However, the most notorious examples of not just his failure to escape from, but indeed his acceptance of, neo-classical marginal productivity theory are in Book VI, 'Short Notes Suggested by the General Theory'. In the Notes on Mercantilism:

> Regarded as the theory of the individual firm and of the distribution of the product resulting from the employment of a given quantity of resources, the classical theory has made a contribution to economic thinking which cannot be impugned. It is impossible to think clearly on the subject without this theory as part of one's apparatus of thought. (1936, p. 340)

And later on, in the Concluding Notes:

> But if our central controls succeed in establishing an aggregate volume of output corresponding to full employment as nearly as practicable, the classical theory comes into its own again from this point onwards ... then there is no objection to be raised against the classical analysis of the manner in which private self-interest will determine what in particular is produced, in what proportions the factors of production will be combined to produce it, and how the value of the final product will be distributed between them. (1936, p. 378)

No wonder Joan Robinson declared:'there were moments when we had some trouble in getting Maynard to see what the point of his revolution really was, but when he came to sum it up after the book was published he got it into focus' (1973, p. 170). She was referring, of course, to the 1937 *Quarterly Journal of Economics* article.[26]

Conclusion

A Keynesian revolution in economic thinking never took place. Keynes failed to convince the majority of his fellow economists that orthodox economics was at fault and should be thrown over in favour of his *General Theory*. The main reason for this was that not even Keynes could escape completely from the old ideas; he failed to realize that the neo-classical theories of output, employment, value and distribution are inseparable and needed to be discarded *in toto*. In particular, by accepting the first classical postulate (the wage is equal to the marginal product of labour) he seemed to be accepting the neo-classical marginal productivity theory of factor prices and distribution with its implication that the marginal product of labour curve is the demand curve for labour at the macro-level. This, more than anything else, paved the way to the Keynesian–neo-classical synthesis.

It is sometimes argued that the first step on the way to the synthesis was Hicks' (1937) IS–LM analysis. Now there are many criticisms that can be made of 'Islamic Keynesianism'. By neglecting the aggregate supply schedule, and concentrating entirely on aggregate demand, it left Keynesians without a satisfactory theory of the price level, and therefore of inflation, when stagflation struck.[27] It exaggerates the stability of the system and it is easy to underestimate the degree of interdependence of the IS and LM schedules. It is often used as a vehicle for propagating the fallacious 'imperfectionist' argument that unemployment is ultimately the result of *money* wage rigidity.[28] However, we know that Keynes approved of it (Hicks, 1973) and although it is now less popular with its begetter (Hicks, 1980–81) I would argue that, on the whole, IS–LM has assisted, rather than hindered, the acceptance of Keynes' theory. Provided the IS–LM model is 'expectations augmented', in the spirit of Keynes and we remember that the schedules are mere straws in the winds of uncertainty (Brothwell, 1975; 1976) it is a useful tool for getting to grips with Keynes' theoretical framework.

No! The real disaster occurred (Chick, 1983) when a neo-classical production function and labour market analysis were added to the IS–LM model. By attempting such a Keynesian–neo-classical synthesis, Patinkin (1958) in effect only succeeded in draining the model of its Keynesian content. Instead of employment being determined by aggregate demand and supply in the *goods* market, the labour market becomes the prime determinant of employment *if* the marginal product of labour curve is treated as the demand curve for labour. Keynes' gratuitous acceptance of the first classical postulate has been (wrongly) deemed to justify this step. Focusing on the labour market, it appears that the cause of unemployment is that the real wage is too high rather than that aggregate demand is too low. Keynes is submerged and we have reverted to neo-classical (now New Classical) macroeconomics and monetarism. In the famous closing passage of his book Keynes said:

> Practical men, who believe themselves to be quite exempt from any intellectual influences, are usually the slaves of some defunct economist. Madmen in authority, who hear voices in the air, are distilling their frenzy from some academic scribbler of a few years back. (1936, p. 383)

Only if the madmen in authority distil their frenzy from Keynes' academic scribblings of fifty years ago will their policies help rather than hinder the path of output and employment.

Notes

1. A condensed version of this chapter is to be published as an article in the *Journal of Post-Keynesian Economics*. The author is grateful to Arthur Brown, Paul Davidson, Geoff Harcourt and Tony Thirlwall for their comments on a draft.

2. Keynes' *theory*, on the other hand, can explain stagflation much more satisfactorily than can monetarism. This is because it comprehends cost-push inflation, unlike monetarism which assumes inflation is caused essentially by excessive increases in the money supply (demand-pull). Keynes emphasises that the wage-unit can be regarded as the essential standard of value:

   > And the long-run stability or instability of prices will depend on the strength of the upward trend of the wage-unit (or, more precisely, of the cost-unit) compared with the rate of increase in the efficiency of the productive system. (1936, p. 309)

   See also below p. 49, and Brothwell (1982).
3. Friedman's 'New' Quantity Theory was published in 1956.
4. Robert Clower, Axel Leijonhufvud, Paul Davidson and Sydney Weintraub in the USA and Joan Robinson, Nicholas Kaldor and George Shackle in the UK.
5. Which only came to light when they were discovered in a laundry basket at Keynes' country house, Tilton, in 1976 (Keynes, 1979).
6. Lerner is a notable exception. See T. Scitovsky, 'Lerner's Contribution to Economics', *Journal of Economic Literature*, Vol. XXII, December 1984.
7. It is paradoxical that money is neutral for monetarists and therefore does not *really* matter!
8. Not the real, technologically and psychologically determined, phenomenon of neo-classical theory.
9. As explained further below, pp. 57–9.
10. And since any particular group of workers who consent to a reduction of money wages relatively to others will suffer a relative reduction in real wages, this is a sufficient justification for them to resist it. Keynes stresses this as a further reason for money wages possessing the (essential) property of 'stickiness' (1936, p. 14).
11. Fender (1981) claims that Keynes' major criticism of the classical theory of employment is that the labour market may not be stable and therefore fail to clear. But this does not go far enough. Keynes' main point is that, in a monetary production economy, the classical labour market mechanism is inoperative since its 'demand curve', the marginal product of labour curve, is not a demand curve at all!
12. 'Holy Writ' for all true Keynesians.
13. New, because it is impossible to conceive of such a function until one has abandoned the notion that the system always finds its equilibrium at a *single* level of income – full employment.
14. All the erections occurring, of course, at the natural rate!
15. 1936, p. 17: my emphasis.
16. This, of course, is the argument underlying the so-called 'Pigou effect' critique of Keynes' unemployment equilibrium. Note that the Pigou or real balance effect argument, which purports to show that Keynes' unemployment equilibrium depends upon the assumption of rigid *money* wages, is very different from the neo-classical explanation of unemployment – *real* wage rigidity. The argument that if *money* wages (and therefore prices) were flexible the 'Keynes' effect' (via the impact of rising real balances on the rate of interest and investment) and/or the 'Pigou effect' (via the effect of increasing real balances on wealth and consumption) would restore full employment is fundamentally different, since it accepts Keynes' basic hypothesis that employment depends on effective demand rather than the real wage. The argument is nevertheless fallacious for at least three reasons. First and foremost, the neo-classical assumption underlying it (perfectly flexible money wages and prices) is incompatible with the operation of a monetary production (entrepreneur) economy. Such an assumption in effect *demonetizes* the system; money loses its store of value function and becomes simply a neutral medium of exchange. Second, the nominal value of the stock of financial assets (which depends on expected future cash flows) cannot remain unchanged. Even in the case of bank

money, a coordinated fall in money wages and product prices will induce the collapse of the nominal value of the banking system's assets, so that with unchanged nominal liabilities, there will be widespread bankruptcies of banks, and the stock of nominal bank money (most of the money stock) will decline. Third, within the private sector, for each creditor whose real wealth is rising there is a debtor whose real obligations are rising. If, as is likely, the debtor goes bankrupt again the nominal value of financial assets will fall but, more significantly, with widespread bankruptcies not only will real investment fall, offsetting any rise in real consumption, but firms will be going out of business altogether on a scale which must cause employment to shrink and potential full employment capacity to decline.

17. Yet another example of the use of mathematics in economic theory causing confusion rather than enlightenment.

18. See below, pp. 56–7.

19. Chick (1983, p. 25) claims that, by taking the small firm as his model, Keynes strengthened his argument by meeting the neo-classical theory on its own ground. Only the assumption of perfect knowledge was changed. But, since the crux of his attack on classical theory was that its postulates are 'applicable to a special case only' and the characteristics of this special case 'happen not to be those of the economic society in which we actually live', it seems rather perverse to make unrealistic assumptions about the nature of the representative firm.

20. As did Barro and Grossman (1971) with their 'General Disequilibrium Model' and Malinvaud (1977) with his quantity-constrained approach. All assume that disequilibrium is due to temporary wage and price rigidity and that, given time, prices will adjust and the Walrasian general equilibrium be attained.

21. That such ideas were known to him is revealed in his 1939 article:

> Indeed, it is rare for anyone but an economist to suppose that price is predominantly governed by marginal cost. Most businessmen are surprised by the suggestion that it is a close calculation of short-period marginal cost or of marginal revenue which should dominate their price policies. They maintain that such a policy would rapidly land in bankruptcy anyone who practised it. (1939, p. 46)

And, in any case, he must have been aware of the work of Joan Robinson (1933) and Chamberlin (1933).

22. As Joan Robinson (1977) points out, Keynes relies upon a psychological law that men are disposed to increase their consumption as their income increases, but not by as much as the increase in their income. 'Men' and 'incomes' are undifferentiated. By separating 'men' into workers and capitalists and income into wages (all consumed) and profits (mainly saved), Kalecki provides a more convincing explanation of the overall relation between income and consumption.

23. He suggests, 'Keynes would have been very grateful for Mr Weitzman's support had it been available to him.'

24. Such as might be induced by a change in the *price of machines* relative to the wage rate.

25. Davidson also provides a Keynesian long-period theory of employment (1972, Chapter 5).

26. See above, p. 5 and note 12.

27. This is also a major defect of Samuelson's (1939) model as summarized in his famous 45° line diagram.

28. The 'Pigou effect' argument; see above note 16.

4 Did Keynes have the answer to unemployment in the 1930s?

Michael Collins[1]

It is commonplace to portray the state of economic thinking in the interwar period as one of crisis. Donald Winch stresses two aspects: the crisis of self-confidence within the economics profession, and the crisis of public credibility

> The failure of economists to agree on diagnosis or remedies, and the ineffectiveness of those remedies that were advocated or tried, helped to undermine the authority of the profession. Consciousness of this fact brought about a state of crisis.[1]

It was the persistence of mass unemployment that starkly questioned the validity and relevance of much contemporary economic analysis. In their theoretical posturing most economists still worked on the assumption that full employment was the normal or equilibrium state in a capitalist economy. The presence of some cyclical unemployment was usually permitted in formal analyses but by its very nature this was a temporary affair, the possibility of long-term, persistent unemployment was rarely recognized. But reality flatly contradicted such assumptions. From the end of the postwar boom in 1920 until the outbreak of World War II in 1939, official unemployment rates rarely fell below 10 per cent – one million – of the insured labour force; experience in the 1930s was worse than the 1920s; and much worse in the cyclical downturns of 1920–1, 1929–32 and 1937–38. Some disruption had been anticipated at the end of World War I and the subsequent readjustment to peacetime conditions, but as the years passed and the one million unemployed remained, hopes of a spontaneous market recovery waned. Concern turned to the failings of the market economy, with mass unemployment and its eradication becoming the central issue. Its continuation for two decades highlighted the failure of economists to provide a convincing explanation, or solution. Herein lay the crisis: 'Many economists began to realise that they could not argue indefinitely that unemployment would not exist if only the world were a different place from the one in which they actually lived.'[2]

If by 'crisis' is meant a 'turning-point' then the analogy has been considered by many as being particularly apt. At least until the 1970s it was common for textbooks to present the inability of orthodox economics to provide a practical solution to unemployment as a malaise from which the economics profession did not recover until there had been a fundamental shift away from forms of analysis rooted in neo-classical tradition. The shift, of course, was towards Keynesian economics with its emphasis on macro-analysis and its optimism about the prospects for effective economic intervention by the state. The publication of *The General Theory of Employment, Interest and Money* in 1936 provided the crucial theoretical underpinning for this transformation, and wartime experience during 1939–45 was greatly to increase public expectations about the future level of economic and social provision by the state. By the late 1940s/early 1950s not only was Keynesianism the new orthodoxy within the economics profession but more popularly – for politicians and the public at large – there was a revolution in how the state's economic responsibilities were perceived. The bounds of legitimate state intervention were irrevocably loosened and the air of fatalism which had permeated interwar governmental attitudes towards unemployment had, by then, been largely dispelled. If some doubts remained there was a keenness to recognize the government's new responsibilities:

> The Government accept as one of their primary aims and responsibilities the maintenance of a high and stable level of employment. ... In submitting proposals for an extension of State control over the volume of employment, the Government recognise that they are entering a field where theory can be applied to practical issues with confidence and certainty only as experience accumulates and experiment extends over untried ground. ... Today, the conceptions of an expansionist economy and the broad principles governing its growth are widely accepted by men of affairs as well as by technical experts in all the great industrial countries. But the whole of the measures here proposed have never yet been systematically applied as part of the official economic policy of any Government. In these matters we will be pioneers.[3]

This optimism owed much to the acceptance of Keynes' economic analysis, the *General Theory* supplying the *raison d'être* for state intervention and Keynes' national income accounting techniques providing the means by which the new policies could be implemented. This shift in the parameters of economic policy – the marked change in what was considered feasible and desirable within a free enterprise democracy – has been seen as the most important policy outcome of the Keynesian Revolution. The discipline of economics had recovered from its interwar fatalism and was now able to offer a more hopeful prospect of the future.

Thus, went the tale told in the textbooks of the 1950s, 1960s and early 1970s.[4] The accepted assumption was that modern (post-1945) economic analysis had the means by which to avoid large-scale unemployment, and the great regret was that the conversion to Keynesianism came too late to affect policy in the interwar years.

Fifty years on from the publication of the *General Theory*, a much less sanguine view is taken of the Keynesian revolution in economic policy. Today the economics discipline faces a crisis of credibility similar to that of the 1920s and 1930s, only this time it is the Keynesian orthodoxy under attack. The inability of successive governments in the 1970s and 1980s to cope with the twin problems of high rates of inflation and unemployment has been particularly important in undermining general confidence in the efficacy of economic management. The re-emergence of mass unemployment from the late 1970s – with an average of 12 per cent (some 2.9 million) of the labour force without work in 1981–85 – has forced a broad reappraisal of Keynes' contribution to both economic theory and policy. Part of this reappraisal has been a reconsideration of the appropriateness of Keynes' policy prescriptions for the unemployment of his own time. The reappraisal has arisen on three fronts: from those who doubt Keynes' analysis on theoretical grounds; from empirical work testing the validity of some of Keynes' assumptions, or measuring the likely impact of his policy proposals; and from a deeper examination of the historical record either as a result of new data becoming available or, more significantly, with greater access to the private and public records of the period.

The fiftieth anniversary of the publication of the *General Theory* provides a suitable opportunity to bring together many of the diverse pieces of work on Keynes' policy prescriptions, to survey them and assess the degree to which they qualify any claim that Keynes had the answer to mass unemployment in the 1930s.

I

Figure 4.1 plots two different series for the rate of unemployment over the period as a whole. Series 1 has been compiled by Charles H. Feinstein as the 'percentage of total employees unemployed'.[5] Series 2 is that used by contemporaries and refers only to workers within the National Insurance scheme which provided for some 60 per cent of the labour force.[6] This second series shows the number of insured workers registered as unemployed, expressed as a percentage of the total number of workers in the scheme. Feinstein's data produce a lower average rate of unemployment – 9.1 per cent

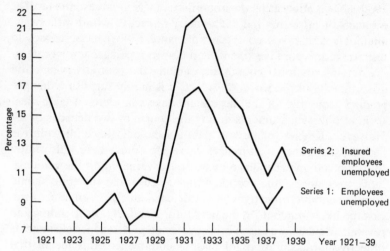

Source: *C. H. Feinstein,* National Income, Expenditure and Output of the United Kingdom, *1855–1965 (Cambridge University Press, 1972), p. T128.*

Figure 4.1 Percentage unemployed (annual average) 1921–39

as opposed to 12 per cent for the insurance series during the 1920s; and 12.8 per cent as against 16.5 per cent for the 1930s – because in addition to insured workers they include such uninsured groups as central and local government employees, railway and public utility workers, and non-manual workers earning over £250 per annum; workers who were much less susceptible to unemployment. Even so, both series reveal the gravity of the unemployment problem between the wars – the rate of unemployment was much worse than during the three decades following World War II. Both series also faithfully reflect two characteristics of interwar unemployment: the sharpness of cyclical fluctuations, especially in the downturns of 1920–21, 1929–32 and 1937–38; and the chronic nature of the problem, with unemployment remaining at over 1 million (about 10 or 8 per cent depending on the series) even at cyclical peaks.

Such was the scale of the problem Keynes faced. During the period he advocated a variety of policy changes which he thought would significantly ameliorate unemployment. Thus in the 1920s, he favoured sterling devaluation, with his 'The Economic Consequences of Mr. Churchill' administering a stinging reproof for official policy which re-established a fixed exchange rate regime on the basis of the pre-World War I parity of £1:$4.86.[7] During the early 1930s he was advocating the imposition of a general revenue tariff as a means of offsetting the deflationary impact of world-wide recession.[8] He also favoured the maintenance of low interest rates to encourage private investment[9] and he was a persistent advocate of greater international cooperation among the central bankers and governments of the world.[10] In fact, it is hardly surprising that the leading economist of the day should have considered a wide spectrum of policy instruments during the course of two decades or so. However, Keynes' name has been associated, above all, with the use of fiscal policy to stimulate aggregate demand. In full fruition this involved an acceptance by central government of the responsibility to 'manage' the economy in the sense that the state should adopt economic objectives, monitor economic performance, forecast the likely outcome in the near future, and alter its spending and revenue in such a way as to bring projected performance closer to its objectives. In conditions of mass unemployment this meant that the government should increase its expenditure, more especially through greater capital spending. Any subsequent deficit in the Chancellor's budget should be no bar to increased expenditure and, in fact, Keynes argued that it would be only temporary as the rise in investment led to more jobs, higher tax receipts and fewer welfare payments.[11] It was these two policy prescriptions – central government deficit financing and increased public investment – that most clearly divided Keynes' policies from the way of thinking of the chief policy-makers and policy advisers of the period; and it is on these two that most of the recent reappraisals have concentrated.

This paper surveys these reappraisals, looking first at a group of empirical studies which has tried to calculate the magnitude of economic dimensions considered critical to the success of Keynes' policies. Such studies have estimated the size of the public expenditure multiplier and drawn conclusions as to the likely income and employment consequences of a given injection of public investment. Another theme in recent reappraisals is the importance of economic constraints inhibiting the effectiveness of a central government boost to aggregate demand. Emphasis is placed on the limits imposed by Britain's dependence on export sales, by the long-term nature of structural change occurring within the economy and by the regional concentration of much of the unemployment. The importance of administrative and political constraints have been yet another theme. Finally, some recent work on the years between the wars has sought to discredit Keynes by adopting different theoretical stances as the basis of statistical analyses of 'the cause' of unemployment, but this is referred to only briefly.

II

During the 1930s there was no great reliance on statistical analysis in the debate over the use of public expenditure to ameliorate unemployment. Much more attention was paid to the likely *direction* of the impact of budget deficits or public works proposals; there were very few attempts to elicit the *magnitude* of that impact. In retrospect, many of the critical issues are indeed ones of magnitude. Awareness of this and the refinement of statistical techniques and computer facilities has led to a number of latter-day calculations of the effects of ignoring Keynes' advice on fiscal policy. The common feature of these studies is that they do not depend upon explicit assumptions about the theoretical underpinnings of Keynes' proposals, though they generally take his hypotheses as given and try to measure the effects of his proposals.

Roger Middleton has recalculated the size of the central government fiscal balance over the period, 1929–39.[12] To do this he has reorganized official data to provide a consistent set of accounts, producing two series with which to assess the thrust of fiscal stance. Both series are plotted in Figure 4.2. The first is the actual budget

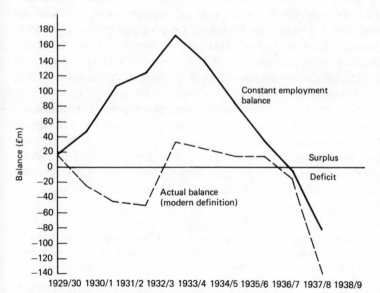

Source: Roger Middleton, *'The Constant Employment Budget Balance and British Policy 1929–39,'* Economic History Review, *2nd ser., 34 (1981).*

Figure 4.2 Central government budget balance (actual and constant employment measures), 1929/30–1938/39 (£m).

balance compiled on the basis of modern national accounting definitions. This reveals a budget balance that was highly sensitive to business-cycle fluctuations. The main reason was the high elasticity of unemployment rates to cyclical changes in national income, so that when the economy went into recession, as in 1929–32, unemployment rose sharply, causing a fall in tax revenues and a rise in social security payments; and the converse happened as the economy recovered from 1932/33. With such a high-cycle sensitivity the budget balance is likely to move in a stabilizing manner (running into deficit during economic recession, and into surplus during recoveries) independent of any conscious, or discretionary, action by the government. In fact, during the period governments were ostensibly committed to balancing the budget – with current expenditure more or less equalling current revenue – so that the non-discretionary changes brought about by business cycle fluctuations were able to have their effect on the *ex post* balance. Thus, on the basis of the series for the actual balance in Figure 4.2 it appears that the impact of the fiscal balance was counter-cyclical over most of the 1930s. The budget ran into deficit, 1930/31–1932/33, when the economy was going through the Great Depression, and moved back to surplus, 1933/34–1936/37, when national recovery was underway. In other words, despite the Treasury's oft-repeated objective of maintaining a balanced budget, economic circumstances prevented this objective being achieved – central government budgets were essentially stabilizing or counter-cyclical, no matter the stated intention of policy-makers.[13]

Middleton, however, is highly critical of using the 'actual balance' series to assess fiscal stance. To him a more appropriate measure of the discretionary impact of the budget is a cycle-adjusted or 'constant employment' budget balance. He devises such a budget in order 'to distinguish the budget's influence on the economy from the economy's influence on the budget'.[14] Therefore, he produces

> the budget balance that would result (with the same tax rates and public spending plans) if private sector demand was just sufficient continuously to maintain activity at a constant rate of unemployment. It is thus a measure of the budget balance which would have occurred had there been no deviation of economic activity from its trend path.[15]

As this series 'extracts' from the actual balance the effects of unemployment in raising expenditure on unemployment benefit and the effects of falling profits and more bankruptcies, short-time working and redundancies on tax income, it is hardly surprising that the constant employment budget balance provides a wholly different interpretation of the course of government fiscal stance during the 1930s. As Figure 4.2 shows, this balance was in surplus throughout the entire period, 1929/30–1936/37, only falling into deficit under the impact of increased defence expenditure at the end of the decade. Moreover, the size of the surplus increased, year on year, throughout 1929/30–1933/34 and, thus, reinforced the recessionary movement in national income. Also as the size of the surpluses declined after 1933/34 (during economic recovery), Middleton concludes that for the 1930s as a whole fiscal stance was deflationary and destabilizing (pro-cyclical).

Middleton's use of the constant employment balance has been criticized on a number of grounds,[16] but for the present assessment of Keynes' policies the important finding is that Keynes was correct to view contemporary budgets as deflationary and, therefore, damaging to employment opportunities. It has sometimes been argued that the tight fiscal policy of the 1930s may have helped to keep interest rates low and may have helped maintain conservative business confidence,[17] but to Middleton the degree of discretionary fiscal contraction was so great as to overwhelm any beneficial effects. There is strong collaboration for this view from Terence Thomas who independently calculated the size of a cycle-adjusted balance for the years 1927–38: '... the policy of the government – whether they knew it or not – was strongly contractionary, and became more so as the slump worsened.'[18]

In themselves measurements of the budget balance indicate only the direction of fiscal stance. In order to assess the impact on income and employment an estimate of the government expenditure multiplier is needed. In an article published in 1983, Mark Thomas makes such a calculation.[19] Thomas is interested in the impact of the rearmament programme in the second half of the 1930s, but within a discussion of Keynes' employment policy increased government expenditure on arms, of course, could be viewed as a substitute for more public works – a parallel exercise undertaken for different reasons. Thomas uses a social accounting matrix – a type of input–output matrix permitting sectoral analysis – to assess the effects of increased defence expenditure. By the late 1930s the arms programme was making a significant dent on the unemployment figures. Thus according to Thomas, by 1937 the programme was providing 1.8 million jobs at a time when unemployment was 2.4 million. From these results Thomas draws the general conclusion that: 'The success of rearmament in creating employment ... leads us to view the eschewment of fiscal policy in the thirties as a missed opportunity for the economy.'[20] Here is clear support for Keynes' position that increased public expenditure (from the early 1930s) on capital projects other than arms, would have markedly improved the level of unemployment.

However, some of Thomas' own detailed results greatly qualify this general inference. First, he uses his social accounting matrix to estimate the size of the long-run government expenditure multiplier and produces a figure of about 1.6 for the years, 1935–38. This figure of 1.6 is low compared to what Keynes seems to have had in mind during the period (a figure in the range of 2–3[21]) although it is close to the pioneering estimate made by Bretherton, Burchardt and Rutherford.[22] According to Thomas, then, there were reasonably strict confines to the multiple impact of increasing government investment. Moreover, Thomas' sectoral analysis highlights the structural and regional nature of unemployment in the period and he acknowledges that this could have further restricted the overall impact of an expansionary fiscal policy. Indeed, a detailed simulation that he conducts concludes that increased government expenditure on construction would have had less of an impact on unemployment than the same expenditure on arms because of the latter's close linkages with producer-goods sectors which were responsible for much of the long-term unemployment in the regions. Finally, he further qualifies his optimism about the likely effects of a fiscal stimulus by accepting a point made by Keynes at the time, that some action would have been necessary to protect the balance of payments.[23]

These general conclusions are similar to those of a separate study by his namesake, Terence J. Thomas.[24] T. J. Thomas' research addresses itself explicitly to quantifying the impact in the 1930s of an increase in government expenditure unmatched by revenue. To do this he uses a fourteen-equation econometric model, based on modern Keynesian theory. The model is used to produce estimates for a number of critical coefficients, including 'the multiplier'. An important result is that the long-term standard government multiplier was of the order of some 1.5 (and of about 1.3 in the shorter term) – again, significantly lower than Keynes envisaged, and of a similar magnitude to another recent estimate made by Sean Glynn and P. G. A. Howells.[25] The small size of the multiplier was due to the large degree of leakages from the initial income stimulus, partly to the high marginal propensities to save and import, but also as a result of inbuilt budget stabilizers; in particular, the fact that a rise in employment would reduce the size of any budget deficit through the consequential increases in tax revenues and falls in unemployment insurance payments (Middleton's point).

As a counter-factual case study, Thomas uses his econometric model to estimate the employment consequences of the government having adopted the public works programme proposed by the Liberal Party in the election of 1929. These proposals were for increased expenditure of about £100 million per annum on capital projects (mainly roads) and they were proposals that won the explicit support of Keynes.[26] Thomas assumes this increased expenditure would have been maintained for five years, 1929–33, and concludes that the reduction in unemployment arising from the programme would have been in the range 329–359,000 over the years 1931–33, at a time when actual umemployment stood at 3.1–3.4 million. His conclusion is that the potency of increased public investment would have been greatly restricted in the period. Moreover, it was not merely a matter of magnitude (i.e. that Lloyd George's programme should have been larger) for Thomas' simulation shows that serious balance of payments constraints would have operated as rising domestic income pulled in more imports. He also assumes that there would have been (unestimated) inflationary consequences.

III

This emphasis on the practical limitations to government-induced job creation was, in fact, a common feature of the contemporary debate. From the late 1920s, policy advisers in the Treasury and Bank of England were fond of stressing the structural nature of unemployment and the importance of sectoral rigidities. Amongst professional economists, too, it was common to point to supply rigidities which could either nullify or severely limit the effect of a demand stimulus. The commonly stated rigidities were the failure of real wages to fall in the face of trade union power and/or the operation of dole payments for the unemployed; the mismatch of skill and location in the supply of and demand for labour; and the immobility of capital stock locked into industries facing long-term contraction of their markets. Many socio-economic surveys highlighted the uneven spread of unemployment, underlining the dependence of certain towns and regions on the ill-fortunes of industries undergoing long-term decline – of Lancashire on cotton; of Wales, Scotland and the North on coal; of the ports on shipbuilding and commerce; and of Scotland and the North-East on iron and steel. Regional and structural decline were major components of unemployment between the wars. As the Royal Commission on the Distribution of the Industrial Population found:

> The more highly specialised an industrial area and the skill of its workers, the more difficult it becomes to adapt it to occupations of entirely different types, and when an area that has concentrated over a long period mainly on one form of specialised industrial activity and that

activity, for international or other reasons, encounters a severe and prolonged depression, the consequences to the workpeople and indeed to the population of the area as a whole are likely to be disastrous. At no time has this been more vividly illustrated than during [the interwar period] when certain industrial areas of the country ... have suffered intensely because of the steep decline in the industries on which ... they had concentrated. Many large enterprises in those areas such as shipbuilding yards, steel works, engineering works, textile mills and coal mines were abandoned, unemployment reached an unprecedently high level [and] local minor activities such as shops and small businesses were forced to close down because of the reduction in purchasing power of the inhabitants ...[27]

Above all, in the period it was W. H. Beveridge who analysed the data in such a way as to emphasize the diverse nature of unemployment.[28] In a series of articles in *Economica* (1936–37), he provided a detailed breakdown of Ministry of Labour unemployment data, drawing the general inference that: 'It is as fallacious to speak of "unemployment" in general as to speak of "labour" in general, without distinguishing between different industries and different types of unemployment.'[29] In particular, he emphasized the strong sectoral and regional disparities in both the incidence and duration of unemployment.

The export staples of coal and other mining, cotton and other textiles, shipbuilding and pig iron production accounted for a disproportionate share of the total, while other sectors such as electric cables, motor vehicles, printing and commerce and finance fared much better. For instance, the average unemployment rate, April–September 1936, was 12.9 per cent, but it was as high as 31.4 per cent for shipbuilding, 23.6 per cent for coalmining and 15.6 per cent for cotton; whereas it was relatively low at 3.9 per cent for commerce and finance, 6.3 per cent for motor vehicles and 6.6 per cent for electric cables. Beveridge saw much of the explanation in the chronic contraction of export demand for particular industries and as these industries tended to be highly localized, the economic fortunes of whole towns or regions suffered. It was for this reason that there were great regional differences in unemployment rates. Table 4.1 summarizes Beveridge's regional figures.

Unemployment rates were high everywhere, but it is clear that mass unemployment was particularly bad in the North and Wales, the areas most heavily dependent on the staple industries. Moreover, Beveridge emphasized the chronic nature of this regional unemployment by showing that since 1929 (when figures first came available) the duration of unemployment had increased and that long-period unemployment (of one year or more) was heavily concentrated in the regions with the higher rates of unemployment.

Table 4.1   Regional distribution of unemployment, average percentage rate, 1929–36

London	8.8
South-eastern	7.8
South-western	11.1
Midlands	15.2
North-eastern	22.7
North-western	21.6
Scotland	21.8
Wales	30.1
Great Britain	16.9

Note: The data refer to insured persons, aged 16–64.
Source: Sir William Beveridge, 'An Analysis of Unemployment', *Economica*, n.s. vol. 3 (1963), p. 379.

Thus, in June 1936 some 9 per cent of unemployed men in London and the South-East were suffering from long-period unemployment, but this was true of 30 per cent in Scotland and 37 per cent in Wales.[30]

The thrust of Beveridge's analysis in the 1930s, therefore, was to stress the diversity of the problem. By 1944 he was prepared to accept Keynes' thesis of a general deficiency of demand as offering part of the explanation, but he still believed that the structural and regional nature of the problem called for more than an acceptance by government of the responsibility to maintain demand and to counter cyclical recessions:

> The reduction of unemployment to a harmless minimum requires, therefore, measures of three kinds; measures to ensure sufficient steady demand for the products of industry; measures to direct demand with regard to the labour available; measures to organise the labour market and to assist the supply of labour to move in accord with demand.[31]

Emphasis on the complexity of unemployment and the degree to which this would have limited the impact of a fiscal stimulus – reasons why the multiplier was small – has been another theme of recent reassessments of Keynes' proposals. A series of articles by Alan Booth, Sean Glynn and P. G. A. Howells has revived many of the points made by Beveridge.[32] These authors criticize all contemporary economic theorists, including Keynes, for seeking a monocausal explanation for unemployment. They are particularly critical of Keynes for conducting the debate in terms of a closed economy when, in fact, a great many of the UK's problems arose from its relationships with the rest of the world. In essence Keynes' approach was too simplistic. Following Beveridge, these authors see unemployment as a multiple problem, comprising frictional, cyclical and structural unemployment, with the last two accounting for the bulk of the problem. They accept that a fiscal boost along the lines suggested by Keynes, if carried through with some skill, could have offset the fall-off in demand during the recessions but they feel it would have done very little to tackle the underlying, non-cyclical unemployment which was 'essentially structural and frictional and, in its worst manifestations, highly regional'.[33]

Booth *et al.* repeat Beveridge's emphasis on the disproportionate concentration of unemployment among a number of large industrial sectors heavily dependent on export sales. These industries had been facing increasing overseas competition from the turn of the century but wartime disruption added seriously to their problems. In particular, they suffered from wartime inflation, the breakdown of pre-war international commercial and financial arrangements, and from the lurch towards trade restrictions in world markets. The geographical concentration of these industries seriously compounded the social effects of unemployment but this regional aspect also had important implications for economic policy. Following the argument of the Royal Commission on the Industrial Population, Glynn and Booth argue that the depressed regions were caught in a vicious spiral whereby high unemployment and low profitability of the export staples had multiplier effects on local income growth which, in turn, inhibited the development of alternative investments in those regions. At the same time, of course, they acknowledge that the Midlands and South-East were much more prosperous, with a greater concentration of industries such as motor vehicles and electrical goods which were responding to rising domestic consumption. They thus revive the concept of a dual economy, with depressed local regions where the multiplier effect of any national income injection would have been very low or even negative, and expanding regions enjoying relatively low unemployment rates and higher growth of real incomes. To Booth and Glynn this duality created a major policy dilemma:

> The traditional British industrial economy, based on the staple export industries, faced a severe cost problem resulting in classical unemployment which could be solved unilaterally only by deflation and wage reductions; whereas the potential growth industries required reflation and rising consumer demand to generate expansion and development. This industrial problem tended to become translated into a regional problem, since performance in all industries tended to be poorer in the depressed areas.[34]

It is for this reason that they reject both these aggregate, or monolithic, policy prescriptions as unrealistic for the period. Instead, they prefer a much greater interventionist approach, concluding that the advocates of fiscal expansion, 'but particularly Keynes himself, did not give enough attention to the need for *ad hoc* regional and industrial policies as a means of easing the structural problem.'[35] But even here pessimism pervades. A fiscal stimulus backed by a regional policy geared to encouraging new investment into the depressed regions may have achieved more than what actually occurred, but they do not think *any* unilateral action by the UK would have been successful. They opine that greater international cooperation was essential, but not forthcoming in the period.

It should be said that Booth and Glynn's criticisms of Keynes' naivity are in danger at times of erecting an Aunt Sally. It is rather unrevealing, for instance, to attack the *General Theory* for being too abstract – it was after all a theoretical work! In his article with Howells, Glynn shows greater awareness of this and somewhat alters the focus of his criticisms. Here he accepts that Keynes was aware of the complex nature of unemployment between the wars. Indeed, further examination of Keynes' work makes it clear that he was also aware of many of the constraints highlighted in recent articles. Thus, in 1943 he was acknowledging that: 'It is quite true that a fluctuating volume of public works at short notice is a clumsy form of cure and not likely to be completely successful ... the amount one can do in the short period is likely to be meagre.'[36] He also accepted that structural and regional unemployment had been important in the 1930s and its existence would reduce the size of the multiplier (to perhaps less than 2, he thought), although he continued to stress the importance of a general deficiency in demand. 'I should say that in almost every year of the ... decade there was a deficiency of effective demand, the actual level of unemployment being the result of a combination of this and of structural unemployment.'[37] In addition he had doubts about Britain's ability to succeed unilaterally, especially if the USA should go into a slump.[38] Also, by the time of the Second World War he was emphasizing the importance of *maintaining* a high and stable level of demand, a recognition that it would be much more difficult to engineer a recovery from a position of sharp deflation. Nevertheless, it is still true that Keynes retained a high degree of optimism over the efficacy of his proposals and to this extent it remains justifiable to highlight their limited application to the real economy of the 1930s – limitations played down by the conventional Keynesian wisdom of the post-1945 period. But it is a criticism with which Keynes himself may have partially agreed.

Very recently others have taken up a position close to that of Keynes. Thus, W. R. Garside and T. J. Hatton have condemned the pessimism about the feasibility of the options available to British governments in the 1930s, although they have had to recognize the low size of the estimated public expenditure multiplier and the constraining influence of the balance of payments.[39] These authors suggest that during the 1930s a 'moderate' fiscal expansion could have had important beneficial effects if the authorities had taken action to ease the external constraint by depreciating the international value of sterling. However, even this modest and qualified support for a Keynesian approach has had to acknowledge that other non-economic barriers stood in the way of implementing such a policy.

IV

Another main doubt emphasized in recent literature has been that, irrespective of the economic merits of Keynes' proposals, they greatly underestimated the importance of administrative and political constraints. The most obvious hurdle was the stated opposition of Treasury officials responsible for advising ministers on policy, an opposition which was upheld by the leading political figures who formed governments at the time. In historical shorthand this opposition has become known as the 'Treasury view'. Economic advisers within the Treasury have justifiably been portrayed as conservative in outlook, as defenders of the status quo against such reformist proposals as those advocated by Keynes. The Treasury view encompassed many aspects of *laissez-faire*, non-interventionist ideology and Gladstonian budget tradition.[40] A brief listing of some of the more relevant tenets held by Treasury officials readily displays the hostile policy environment in which Keynes had to promote his own suggestions.

Most generally, there was a fundamental trust in the efficiency of the market mechanism, with the concomitant belief that the state should avoid interfering in the operation of that mechanism. Thus, high taxes were perceived not only as politically unpopular but also as damaging to the workings of the market. There was a great emphasis on fiscal discipline, which lauded balanced budgets and sought reductions in the National Debt. Suggestions of large deficit budgets and a wholesale public works programme were, therefore, anathema.

Specific opposition to public works included arguments over relevancy, 'crowding-out' in financial markets, the effects on business confidence and administrative impracticability. Thus, the relevance of extra public expenditure on such as road-building was seriously questioned by those who perceived unemployment as resulting largely from the loss of export markets or from uncompetitive production costs at home – public works were essentially beside the point. Leading Treasury officials prescribed to the view that if the state should increase its own borrowing to increase spending, then this would deny capital to the private sector and, so, have little or no overall impact on employment levels. Middleton argues that such a view need not depend upon concepts of a fixed and fully employed stock of available funds. He shows that Treasury arguments were more sophisticated in part, emphasizing that if increased public borrowing was not matched by an increase in the stock of money then this could adversely affect business confidence, raising market anxieties which, in turn, could increase cash balances and push up interest rates.[41] Higher interest rates would depress private borrowing, the overall effect being a substitution of private borrowing by public, but perhaps with no net increase in total investment or employment. The adverse effect on business confidence was also stressed in its own right. It was argued that in a world in which balanced budgets and minimum state intervention were accepted as desirable norms, a rising budget deficit or public investment programme could seriously undermine confidence both at home and abroad, leading to capital flight, hoarding and, thus, greater unemployment. Finally, another important Treasury criticism was that public works programmes of the sort supported by Keynes were unrealistic in terms of scale and practical implementation: there were not enough viable schemes and/or the necessary administrative and financial resources were unavailable.

All in all, these arguments added up to a formidable battery to shoot down any proposals for an expansionary policy. As Winch notes: 'The objections raised against additional State capital expenditure could be made against *all* active remedies for unemployment except wage-cuts.'[42] Keynes himself accepted that the launching of a large-scale public works programme could create 'practical' difficulties, but he was optimistic about overcoming them.[43] Also the question of business confidence was to the core of much of his own reasoning over the cause of unemployment but he felt, of course, that the best hope of restoring business confidence lay in a recovery of aggregate demand.[44] Finally, he scathingly dismissed the Treasury's 'crowding-out' arguments at a time of unemployment:

> The argument is certainly not derived from commonsense. No ordinary man, left to himself, is able to believe that, if there had been no housing schemes in recent years, there would, nevertheless, have been just as

much employment. . . . [The] argument is not only implausible, it is also untrue.[45]

It is important to recognize, however, that the Treasury was not opposed to the use of public works, *per se*. Public works had a long lineage in British unemployment relief programmes and, in fact, during the 1930s these were used on an unprecedented scale, providing perhaps half a million jobs.[46] Moreover, recent examination of unpublished public records suggest that Treasury officials were prepared to use public expenditure in a Keynesian-type manner as a counter-cyclical measure. For instance, a study of the Economic Advisory Council (1930–39) by Susan Howson and Donald Winch has shown that exposure of civil servants to the views of the Council members, who included Keynes, helped prepare the ground for the more general acceptance of the responsibility for economic management after the Second World War.[47] By the late 1930s leading Treasury officials could countenance the use of public investment, first to moderate the boom of 1936–37, and then, to offset the recession of 1937–38.[48] Middleton's researches also suggest a greater responsiveness to new ideas than may have been anticipated from the traditional presentation of the Treasury view.[49]

But in terms of accepting the use of public investment and the conduct of fiscal policy as central tools of economic management, such softening of the Treasury line was exceedingly marginal. George Peden and Alan Booth have specifically addressed the question of how leading Treasury personnel responded to the new expansionist ideas and they conclude that the traditional picture of the Treasury as conservative defenders of the status quo is essentially sound.[50] Indeed, the thrust of the most recent comments has been to question whether the permanent senior officials in the Treasury were converted to Keynes' unemployment policies even by the close of the Second World War.

At the time Keynes was in no doubt that he had so converted the civil servants, for of the internal report on employment produced under the auspices of Richard Hopkins, Permanent Secretary of the Treasury, and serving as the basis for the 1944 White Paper on Employment, he said: 'I am in general sympathy with the line taken in this Report and with its recommendations. It is, indeed, an outstanding State Paper which, if one casts one's mind back ten years or so, represents a revolution in official opinion.'[51] And many historians have echoed this sentiment. Charles Feinstein, for instance, believes that the adoption of a national income accounting framework for the presentation of the budget of 1941 – the first 'Keynesian' budget – also confirms the extent of the Treasury's conversion during the war:

The adoption of this approach was of enormous significance. It not only endorsed Keynesian theories of the relevance of fiscal policy, but also accepted the government's responsibility for the management of aggregate demand. This was a far-reaching departure from the traditional view . . .'[52]

However, through the use of public records that have become available to wider scrutiny only recently, Peden and Booth show that talk of a 'Keynesian Revolution' within the Treasury is somewhat misplaced. They suggest that the Treasury continued to drag its feet, leaning against the Keynesian wind. For instance, Treasury officials agreed to the Keynesian aspects of the 1944 White Paper on Employment only after great pressure from an influential group of economists inside the War Cabinet Secretariat. Booth shows that these economists (Meade, Stone, Fleming, Tress and Robbins) came under Keynes' influence and that they had continually to argue their case in order to win concessions from the Treasury. Nor were they wholly successful by 1944 with, for instance, the prominence given in the White Paper to balanced budgets reflecting the continuing strength of traditional Treasury ideas. Booth's use of internal records reveals that

> on every occasion at which employment policy was seriously considered by the wartime administration, the Keynesians and the Treasury were on opposite sides . . . [T]he White Paper was a compromise, in which Keynes's views on the budget were watered to gain Treasury support.[53]

In fact, he thinks it was not until 1947 that the Treasury first adopted Keynesian demand-management policies. At that time there was full employment and threatening inflation, direct economic controls were being relaxed and monetary policy was in abeyance. Fiscal policy was the main instrument available and it was not till then that budgetary policy was presented within a Keynesian demand-management framework.

Others have gone even further in stressing Treasury conservatism. Robert Skidelsky feels that the Treasury's opposition to an expansion of the state's role was motivated by a fear of socialism; and, of course, in the 1930s the examples overseas of both national socialism and soviet socialism were anathema to Treasury knights.[54] But even within the British political tradition, J. D. Tomlinson and N. Rollings doubt if the Treasury was converted even by the year chosen by Booth – 1947.[55] Tomlinson in particular stresses that as inflation was the problem in 1947 there was no sharp break with Treasury fiscal tradition in seeking a budget surplus to deflate demand. He wonders whether the response would have been so sanguine if they had been considering the adoption of a budget deficit to tackle unemployment. Moreover, as full employment was to be experienced for the next 25 years, Tomlinson feels that the traditional Treasury commitment to balanced or surplus budgets was never really challenged – there may never have been a 'Keynesian Revolution' inside the Treasury.

It is not necessary to deny that the Treasury were ever converted to Keynes' views to recognize the hostile policy environment in which Keynes was promoting his unemployment policies in the 1930s. Winning acceptance for such an expansionist programme was always going to be an uphill battle: a struggle to persuade, to educate, to convince public opinion of the need to widen the parameters of legitimate government responsibility. In the event, it was to be the rigour of another world war that provided the necessary social and political catalyst to tip the balance in favour of state economic management.

So, the hostility of those in charge of the policy-making machine was in itself a major impediment to the adoption of Keynes' unemployment proposals during the 1930s. However, recent studies of the Treasury suggest also a second constraint which, if accepted, is fundamentally more damaging to Keynes' case – namely, that there was much credence in the Treasury's charges of administrative impracticability. In other words, even if the counter-factual had happened and Keynes had won the political argument, success would have still been significantly impaired by administrative and practical constraints.

Middleton makes the important point that while public expenditure was growing on trend between the wars, the power of the state to influence aggregate demand was still relatively small.[56] As a proportion of GDP total public expenditure rose from 11.1 per cent in 1924 to just 15 per cent in 1937. Moreover, central government accounted for only a small share of total public sector investment. It was the local authorities with their expenditure in such areas as housing and roads that provided the bulk of public investment. Thus, over the period 1929–32, only 3.4 per cent of Gross Domestic Fixed Capital Formation was directly attributable to central government and 26.5 per cent to local authorities. To the extent, therefore, that Keynes' proposals depended upon increased investment by central government a tremendous expansion in scale would have been necessary in order to have had any significant impact on demand and unemployment. Within this context it is easier to understand the Treasury's scepticism about finding enough worthwhile schemes and about its own ability to launch and supervise them.

According to Middleton, the alternative of operating an expansionary public works programme through the local authorities would have met another set of important obstacles. The local authorities, of course, had their own elected representatives, their own source of finance (local rates) and a jealously guarded tradition of independence from Whitehall. Middleton emphasises the difficulties this would have created:

> Although economic policy was formulated at the centre, the British financial system had evolved in such a way as to limit the channels through which central government might operate its fiscal policies: neither the Treasury nor Parliament directly controlled local expenditure either on current or capital account, this despite the increasing importance of central governments. Local authorities had not become simply the spending agencies of central government.[57]

The effective implementation of a public works programme on an unprecedented scale would have called, therefore, for both major reforms of the administrative machinery and a significant shift in the constitutional relationship between central and local governments. Once again, the question of scale is seen to be important – the existing administrative machinery may have been able to cope with a modest public investment programme but not with a massive one. Of leading politicians in the period, Lloyd George and Oswald Mosley came closest to advocating the necessary wholesale reforms, but the charge against economic theorists such as Keynes is that they greatly underestimated the scale and nature of the administrative changes needed. Experience under the Labour government of 1929–31 shows that even where the political commitment to increase capital expenditure existed, administrative constraints imposed serious delays on implementation.[58] How much more difficult would it have been to implement a *radical* increase in public investment?

And, as has been shown, recent estimates conclude that a radical increase would have been essential if a serious impact was to be made on unemployment. On the basis of T. J. Thomas' econometric findings, Alec Ford suggests that in order to reduce unemployment by one million within a period of four years, public expenditure would have had to rise by over 50 per cent.[59] Glynn and Howells reach a similar conclusion.[60] The administrative and practical constraints were real ones. This is not to deny that a conservative bureaucracy will use the argument of feasibility in order to avoid sharp changes in existing practices and, of course, the war was to show that such changes could indeed be forced through. The truth is that unemployment was never given anything like the political priority given to national defence and – here Keynes is open to criticism – Keynes himself did not directly address the important issue of how to bring about the radical administrative and political reforms that would have been essential to the effective implementation of his policies in peacetime.

V

Another fundamental issue on the viability of Keynes' proposals is, of course, whether or not the theoretical model of the economy which underlay the Treasury's objections was closer to the truth than Keynes' model. This is not the subject of the present essay but it must be acknowledged that as Keynesian economics has continued to come under fire in the current theoretical debate, the Treasury's stance has tended to win more sympathy. To date, though, there have been very few attempts to apply explicitly non-Keynesian models to the problem of interwar unemployment.[61] Two exceptions should be noted. Daniel K. Benjamin and Lewis A. Kochin have denied the possibility of a general deficiency of demand in the period and have tested a rival explanation of non-cyclical unemployment.[62] They conclude that much of the non-cyclical unemployment was a direct result of the disincentive effects of a lax and generous system of unemployment benefits. Another attack on the Keynesian thesis has come from Michael Beenstock, Forrest H. Capie and Brian Griffiths.[63] These authors have emphasized the importance of supply-side factors, in particular arguing that rising unemployment between 1929 to 1931 was the result largely of a rise in real wages, and the subsequent recovery from 1932 was a consequence of a fall-off in the growth in real wages. Both these approaches have drawn considerable flak,[64] but they do serve to illustrate the extent to which Keynes' views of the period are under attack. As the consensus on the analysis of current unemployment has evaporated, so too has consensus on the interwar years. Old doubts have been resurrected and new calculations and reappraisals have fuelled these doubts.

VI

The fact that Keynes' prescriptions were never tried between the wars left intact the hope that if mass unemployment should ever threaten again, then democratic governments should be able to respond effectively through an expansionary fiscal programme. Recent experience has gravely damaged that hope. Moreover, as this chapter has shown, there are now serious doubts as to whether interwar governments could have effectively taken action of the sort suggested by Keynes. Almost all commentators (to varying degrees) believe that an expansionary fiscal policy would have been of some benefit but, more importantly, most stress that there was much truth in the scepticism of Keynes' contemporary critics. The impact of

Keynes' measures would have been greatly restricted in the absence of a radical increase in political will to institute both administrative reforms and to interfere more directly in the workings of the economy. Keynes had seemed to offer a middle way between unfettered capitalism and state socialism – a middle way which was to be readily embraced by the consensus politics of the 1950s and 1960s – but the general assessment of recent historical reappraisals is much less optimistic. Interwar experience suggests that when capitalist economies are faced with mass unemployment either government relies on piecemeal palliatives in the form of dole payments, temporary employment schemes and the like; or, if fiscal expansion is to be introduced, success requires that it be on a sufficiently large scale and that it be accompanied by direct intervention to protect the balance of payments (e.g. tariffs, devaluation, restrictions on capital flows) and a determination to impose the necessary administrative transformation. Twentieth-century history shows that British society could organize itself effectively in times of war, but the experience of the interwar period shows no such determination in tackling mass unemployment in peacetime.

These conclusions are not new, of course. In 1944 W. H. Beveridge argued:

> Experience in peace has shown that the desire of men who are already above want to increase their profits by investment is not a strong enough motive or sufficiently persistent in its action to produce a demand for labour which is strong enough and steady enough. Experience of war has shown that it is possible to have a human society in which every man has value and the opportunity for service, when the motive, power and direction of economic activity are given not by private interest, but by collective determined pursuit of a common good.[65]

Beveridge's criticism of the government's White Paper on Employment was, in effect, an attack upon Keynes. To Beveridge 'the seriousness of the disease [was] the extent of the past failure of the unplanned market economy',[66] and he called for much greater state direction of private investment as the cure for future unemployment.

Notes

1. Winch (1969), p. 186.
2. Ibid.
3. HMSO (1944), pp. 3 and 26.
4. For instance Youngson (1968, Appendix); Phillips and Maddock (1973, ch. 8); Stewart (1967) and Aldcroft (1970).
5. Feinstein (1972), pp. 217–23, T128.
6. Garside (1980, ch. 2), HMSO (1971), pp. 16–18.
7. 'The Economic Consequences of Mr. Churchill', in Keynes (CW, Vol. IX, pp. 207–30).
8. 'Mitigation by Tariff', ibid., pp. 231–44.

9. *The General Theory of Employment, Interest and Money*, in Keynes (CW, Vol. VII, pp. 374–77).

10. For instance 'The Means to Prosperity' (1933), in Keynes (CW, Vol. IX, pp. 335–66). See also Keynes (CW, Vol. XXIV) especially 'The Loan Negotiations', pp. 420–628.

11. For a considered discussion of budget deficits, see 'Memo to Sir Wilfred Eady: "Maintenance of Employment. The Draft Note for the Chancellor of the Exchequer"' (10 June 1943), in Keynes (CW, Vol. XXVII, pp. 352–57).

12. Middleton (1981) and (1985, ch. 7).

13. The main exception to the counter-cyclical movements in the actual balance was the late 1930s when defence expenditure put the budget into deficit not only in the recession year, 1937/38, but even more strongly in the following year when the economy entered a general recovery.

14. Middleton (1981), p. 266.

15. Ibid.

16. Broadberry (1984), and Middleton's reply (1984).

17. Richardson (1967), pp. 211–22 argued on the basis of contemporary budgetary figures that fiscal policy was not counter-cyclical in its direct income effects but nor was it too destabilizing and, in fact, restoration of a balanced budget after 1931 would have had favourable confidence effects.

18. Thomas in Floud and McCloskey (1981), p. 335.

19. Thomas (1983).

20. Ibid., p. 571.

21. 'Memo to Sir Wilfred Eady' (3 September 1942), in Keynes (CW, Vol. XXVII, pp. 311–12); and 'Means to Prosperity' in Keynes (CW, Vol. IX, p. 343).

22. Bretherton, Burchardt and Rutherford (1941), especially pp. 312–16.

23. 'Mitigation by Tariff', in Keynes (CW, Vol. IX, pp. 231–44).

24. Thomas (1975).

25. Glynn and Howells (1980), especially pp. 34–41. Here it is estimated that the value of the multiplier was about 1.3.

26. 'Can Lloyd George Do It?', in Keynes (CW, Vol. IX, pp. 86–125).

27. HMSO (1940), p. 87.

28. Beveridge (1930; 1936; 1937a and b; 1944).

29. Beveridge (1936), p. 370.

30. Beveridge (1937a), pp. 7–8.

31. Beveridge (1944), p. 109.

32. Booth and Glynn (1975; 1983); and Glynn and Howells (1980).

33. Booth and Glynn (1975), p. 629.

34. Booth and Glynn (1983), p. 337.

35. Booth and Glynn (1975), p. 631.

36. 'Memo to J. E. Meade' (27 May 1943), in Keynes (CW, Vol. XXVII, p. 326).

37. Quotation from 'Memo to Sir Wilfred Eady' (10 June 1943), in Keynes (CW, Vol. XXVII, p. 352). Also see 'Memo to Sir Wilfred Eady' (3 September 1942), in Keynes (CW, Vol. XXVII, pp. 311–12); 'Memo to J. E. Meade' (25 April 1943), in Keynes (ibid., pp. 322–23); and Peden (1980, pp. 11–12, 14).

38. 'Letter to Sir William Beveridge' (16 December 1944), in Keynes (CW, Vol. XXVII, pp. 380–81). In a postscript to this letter Keynes revealed his own thoughts on possible postwar employment levels: 'No harm aiming at 3 per cent unemployed, but I shall be surprised if we succeed' (p. 381).

39. Garside and Hatton (1985). See also Glynn and Booth's reply (1985).

40. A short summary appears in Youngson (1968), pp. 294–96. For more detail see Winch (1969), pp. 118–22. A more recent appraisal appears in Middleton (1985).

41. Middleton (1985, ch. 8).

42. Winch (1969), p. 122.

43. For instance, see 'An Economic Analysis of Unemployment' (1931), in Keynes (CW, Vol. XIII, p. 364).

44. *The General Theory*, in Keynes (CW, Vol. VII, passim).

45. 'Can Lloyd George Do It?', in Keynes (CW, Vol. IX, p. 116).
46. Glynn and Howells (1980), p. 34.
47. Howson and Winch (1977).
48. Ibid., pp. 134–48. Also see Booth (1983), p. 113.
49. Middleton (1982).
50. Booth (1983); Peden (1980; 1983; 1984).
51. 'Note ... on the Report of the Steering Committee' (1944), in Keynes (CW, Vol. XXVII, p. 364).
52. Feinstein (ed.) (1983), p. 13. The same view is expressed in R. S. Sayers '1941 – The First Keynesian Budget', reprinted in the same volume, pp. 107–17, and in Dow (1968), p. 1.
53. Booth (1983), p. 116.
54. R. Skidelsky, 'Keynes and the Treasury View: The case for and against an active unemployment policy, 1920–39', in Mommsen (ed.) (1981), pp. 167–87.
55. Tomlinson (1981; 1984); Rollings (1985).
56. Middleton (1982), especially pp. 65–70 and (1983).
57. Middleton (1983), p. 356. Also, see Bretherton *et al.* (1941) pp. 175–76.
58. Middleton (1983), pp. 360–61.
59. Alec Ford, 'Unemployment: Lessons of the Inter-War Years', in Cowling (1984), p. 13.
60. Glynn and Howells (1980), p. 42.
61. Barrett and Walters (1966) made an early assessment of the relative merits of regression equations employing, first, monetary variables and, then, Keynesian autonomous expenditure items to explain movements in consumption. The results suggested the autonomous expenditure items provided a better explanation.
62. Benjamin and Kochin (1979).
63. Beenstock, Capie and Griffiths (1984).
64. On Benjamin and Kochin, see Collins (1982), Cross (1982), Metcalf, Nickell and Floros (1982), Ormerod and Worswick (1982) and Hatton (1984). On Beenstock *et al.*, see Dimsdale (1984) and Worswick (1984).
65. Beveridge (1944), p. 274.
66. Ibid.

5 Inflation, unemployment and the Keynesian wage theorem

Rodney Crossley

Introduction

Keynes did not work out fully any one theory of money wage inflation, but left sketches of several that varied according to the circumstances considered. It is consistent with this eclectic view that no characteristically Keynesian model has subsequently been found to account for all the wage behaviour observed since 1940, when his most explicit model appeared in *How to Pay for the War* (Keynes, 1940a). The model relied on what would now be regarded as very unsophisticated price expectations on the part of trade unionists, namely a single period-lag of wage behind price change, though the Keynesian emphasis on wage bargaining left open the possible impact on inflation of an exogenous change in trade union expectations about the growth of real wages, even if trade unions had not yet arrived at the fully rational exploitation of economic data and models that some recent theory ascribes to them. Keynes was well aware that unsophisticated price expectations might be modified under higher rates of inflation. That such a qualitative change in the formation of expectations seems in the event to have been deferred for a full twenty years, until the late 1960s or even the mid-1970s is one reason for recasting the model now in terms of what might be regarded as the next higher level of expectations sophistication, which is a simple adaptive scheme, within the same basic framework from *How to Pay for the War*.

Consistent with the historical relativity of Keynes' approach, this model may have been overtaken more recently by others with higher-order expectations schemes. A second reason for attempting to develop the model of *How to Pay for the War* is that it provides an alternative view of the Phillips curve over the period when it seems actually to have existed, with the features that the primary line of causation runs from the rate of inflation to the level of unemployment, rather than the opposite stressed in the Phillips curve literature, and collective bargaining plays a key role in the determination of the inflation rate. Such a model, it will be argued, is more consistent than the well-established Lipsey–Phillips ration-alization (Phillips, 1958; Lipsey 1960), of the Phillips curve as a labour market adjustment process, with Keynes' earlier view on wage determination set out in the *General Theory* (1936), and described by Hicks as the Keynesian *Wage Theorem* (Hicks, 1974).

In outline (see (4.7) below), we suppose that the main line of causation runs from the real wage to the level of unemployment. The numerator of the real wage is the outcome of bargaining over money wages by a trade union movement whose expectations of price changes are adaptive rather than fully rational. The denomi-nator of the real wage is governed by changes in the money supply, which is simply assumed to be determined exogenously by govern-ment monetary policy. We do not explore the nature of the mechan-ism which guarantees so effective a monetary control, nor take up the objections to treating the aggregate labour demand function simply as a marginal productivity schedule. It also lies beyond the scope of the present paper to ask how the outcome would differ if the behaviour of either party were made to depend automatically upon the observed or expected unemployment level that results.

It is not to be expected in a macro-model that the cause of inflation can be attributed to wage bargaining alone. The trade union movement as a whole sets the money wage level, but the government is assumed to validate the wage increase, more or less completely, by an expansion of the money supply. Consequently, the inflation process in any one period looks very much like a tug-of-war between the trade unions and the central bank. This model would be unstable without an important measure of conservative behaviour on the part of the unions and an attempt is made to locate this possibly temporary behaviour. Moreover, any departure from an exact validation, more or less, determines a new real wage level and hence a different rate of unemployment if we follow Keynes in assuming a classical whole economy labour-demand curve. Before formalizing a Keynesian wage bargaining model, we consider briefly the theory of *How to Pay for the War*, and the implications of the Keynesian *Wage Theorem*.

Wage determination in *How to Pay for the War*

In terms of the income-expenditure model of *How to Pay for the War*, Keynes saw the main problem of wartime finance as the reconciliation of the claims of private consumption with the special production demands of the war. During World War II inflation had shifted the distribution of full employment income towards profits, and thereby raised the average savings propensity, without the need for severe fiscal intervention. In the labour market the reduction in the real wage had on the whole not led to policy negating (rational expectations) reactions such as fully compensating wage claims or the simple bidding up of money wages due to the excess demand. No doubt this was partly due to the special restraints operating under wartime conditions, so that the expectations of real wages gain were temporarily negative. But by the late 1930s the quite different idea of money illusion had also appeared in the *General Theory* in the sense that a sufficiently modest increase in prices might be sustainable, without compensatory wage claims, to cause a fall in unemployment through the consequent cut in real wages.

For Keynes in 1940, however, this simple relationship had come to depend on monetary growth rates. In a letter quoted by Trevithick, 'Everyone, including the Trade Unions, has become index-number conscious. Wages will pursue prices with not so lame a foot. And this new fact means that the old type laissez-faire inflation is no longer to be relied upon.' Rather than rely on money illusion, Keynes wrote, in *How to Pay for the War*, that 'wage adjustments and the like take time ... It is these time lags and other impediments that come to the rescue ... Wages and other costs will chase prices upwards, but nevertheless prices will always ... keep 20 per cent ahead.' Full indexation might be achieved through collective bargaining, in short, but the same institution caused it to be applied with a lag. Consequently, a wedge could still be driven between price and wage *levels* through an appropriate choice of the inflation *rate*.

This was a proposed use of price inflation as a policy instrument that went well beyond what was subsequently called validation, and as Trevithick notes, the reliance on an institutional lag meant that the required price inflation was a continuing process rather than the once-for-all change in the price level envisaged in the *General Theory*. Moreover, if trade unions had learned something about indexation over the interwar period, they could continue to learn more so the likelihood was that the institutional lag would progressively shorten. Even today, however, many unions continue to bargain for compensating price increases with a lag, and it seems sensible, if we are to follow Trevithick's observation that this is not what money illusion has come to mean in neo-Keynesian theory, that we should regard such behaviour as implying simplicity essentially in the expectations scheme, in which last year's price increase is taken as the prediction for the forthcoming one. That in turn allows the model of *How to Pay for the War* to be reformulated with expectations schemes of which the Keynesian version is simply a special case.

Despite the large volume of exegetical work subsequently

published, the point seems to have been overlooked that this Keynesian model already contains the elements of a Phillips curve construction, though it is a very different account from that given either by neo-Keynesians working with a labour market adjustment process (see below) or by Tobin's suggestion that there exists a dynamic counterpart, in terms of money wage changes, to the original static concept of money illusion (Tobin, 1967). Suppose that Keynes was right in estimating the required lead of prices at about 20 per cent, but that monetary and fiscal policy has had only a moderate success in hitting this target over a succession of years. In addition, assume that individual labour market participants react in a neo-classical manner on both demand and supply sides to these institutionally-determined prices and wages. In years of overshoot, a high rate of rise of prices will cause real wages to be temporarily too low, with the consequence of severe excess demand in the labour market, measured by a very low rate of unemployment. Conversely, an undershoot will produce more moderate inflation with a somewhat higher rate of unemployment; and all of this variation will occur within a range of what we now consider to be fairly full employment. A model of unemployment and inflation resulting from such behaviour is given in a later section.

The Keynesian wage theorem
Certain difficulties arise in reconciling such a model of inflation with the views on wage determination set out in the *General Theory*. As several commentators have pointed out (Hicks, 1974; Artis, 1981) it has become habitual to suppose – incorrectly – that the *General Theory* makes a sharp distinction between two states of the economy, at less than full and at full employment, respectively, and to ascribe different wage determination mechanisms to these two regimes, viz. administration by collective bargaining, and the bidding up of wages by excess demand in the labour market. But if price changes induce money wage changes with a lag, it cannot be satisfactory to treat wage determination as a wholly exogenous outcome of collective bargaining, since price changes are likely to become an instrument for controlling unemployment via the real wage, and conversely that same intervention undermines the theory that money wages simply move to clear the labour market at full employment.

From the discussion in *How to Pay for the War* it is clear that Keynes was anxious that conditions of over-full employment should not, in effect, cause a regime switch from the model he was describing, but this possibility was envisaged mainly as a breakdown in the essentially conservative way in which wages were administered with a lag. Since unemployment fell as low as 0.7 per cent at the peak of wartime demand it seems that the administrative process turned out to be fairly robust. We can perhaps conclude that as between widely differing employment levels, analysis of wage determination should focus on the way the collective bargaining process operates, including the partial inducement of wage changes by prior price changes.

It is instructive to compare the Keynesian argument with that of the quantity theory in its reformulation by Friedman and others (Friedman, 1968). From the standpoint of high theory, what this restatement does is to re-establish the quantity theory as the dynamic adjunct to the Walrasian set of general equilibrium equations. If there is disequilibrium in two or more markets, the excess demand equations will cause relative prices to change, but when equilibrium is reached absolute wages and prices can rise (or, in principle, fall) in the same proportion as the change in the quantity of money without having real effects. It was also a major principle of Keynes – a principle that Hicks has called the *wage theorem* – that just such a neutral change in money wages and prices could also occur under certain conditions in his system without disturbing the real configuration of the economy. It was on the basis of this theorem that he argued that cuts in money wages would not have the beneficial effects on unemployment that others were predicting at that time. As Hicks has written: 'when there is a general (proportional) rise in money wages, says the theorem, the *normal* effect is that all prices rise in the same proportion – provided that the money supply is increased in the same proportion (whence the rate of interest will be unchanged).'

It follows that the money wage level was not in general constant at less than full employment, as textbook expositions often imply. It might be rising or falling and the important points about it are three. First, as already noted, it was given autonomously from outside the macro-system as the outcome primarily of collective bargaining. Second, the various components of the Keynesian system were independent of money wages. That was why Keynes deflated by the money wages index and why the textbook expositions having started from a constant wage level should go on to show that under certain conditions a change in the wage level will make no difference.

The proposition that money wage changes make no difference, even in a closed economy, has of course been very hard to swallow in its application to the post-war years, and in particular the Phillips curve evidence shows that the *wage theorem* cannot have held in a strong form even for the conditions broadly characterized by validation that Keynes was writing about. Given any particular level of unemployment, it was clearly not the case that the money wage change was variable over a wide range. What we had come to believe as the surviving form of the *wage theorem* was that for each particular level of unemployment there was one rate at which wages and prices could rise proportionately, and neutrally – a sort of quasi-equilibrium as Hansen (1970) has called it – which was theoretically the dual of Keynesian unemployment equilibrium, and that was the rate read off the Phillips curve. The fact that, over certain periods at least, what we observe in the Phillips curve is a schedule of wage changes against a schedule of employment levels may find an explanation, as suggested later, in the largely implicit assumption by Keynes that the strength and policy of the trade union movement is relatively fixed over the short run. Shifts in the Phillips curve may then be associated with changes on the institutional side.

Thirdly, the *wage theorem* gives a dynamic role to exogenous wage change that is in some ways strikingly similar to the growth of the money supply in the quantity theory. Provided the wage change is validated by an equal proportionate change in the money supply, there is no change in the real configuration of the economy. The result is more general than the quantity theory by virtue of its extension to unemployment states, but also much narrower in requiring exact validation. Since money wages do not themselves respond immediately and fully to a price change, a departure from exact validation allows, for example, a movement towards fuller employment if prices are raised by more than wages. If, in the extreme case, money wages were fully indexed and subject to no autonomous component of wage change, price and wage change would always be the same as that of the money supply, and the Keynesian *wage theorem* would simply extend the dynamics of the quantity theory to unemployment conditions.

It is also an important feature of the *wage theorem* that Keynes makes price changes depend on the change in the money supply and this proposition is maintained in the argument below. If g_M is the growth rate of the money supply, that is, we adopt the price equation

$$g_P = g_M \qquad (2.1)$$

rather than the equation widely used in econometric work reflecting

$$g_P = g_W \qquad (2.2)$$

an hypothesis that prices are set by mark-up over unit labour costs. This allows abstraction from interest rate changes (and corresponding changes in the composition of final demand); but equally importantly, it links price levels directly with the policy variable M so that their changes may themselves become a policy variable, as envisaged in *How to Pay for the War*.

Market-clearing wage changes

Consider first the alternative model of market-clearing money wage changes and excess demand (Phillips, 1958; Lipsey, 1960), and for simplicity assume that the dynamic adjustment process applies at the level of the whole economy labour market. Assuming continuously differential market demand (q_L^d) and supply (q_L^s) functions for labour in the neighbourhood of the equilibrium real wage μ with the real wage W/P as argument, the first order Taylor expansions about μ give

$$q_L^d(W/P) = q_L^d(\mu) + (W/P - \mu)q_L^{d'}(\mu) \tag{3.1}$$
$$q_L^s(W/P) = q_L^s(\mu) + (W/P - \mu)q_L^{s'}(\mu) \tag{3.2}$$

so that $q_L^x \equiv q_L^d - q_L^s = [q_L^d(\mu) - q_L^s(\mu)] + [q_L^{s'}(\mu) - q_L^{d'}](\mu - W/P)$
$$\tag{3.3}$$

consequently if $q_L^x = 0$ when $W/P = \mu$ (the equilibrium real wage) then:

$$q_L^x = (q_L^{s'}(\mu)q_L^{d'}(\mu))(\mu - W/P)$$
$$= \alpha(\mu - W/P) \tag{3.4}$$

say, where $\alpha > 0$

Adding a Samuelson-Walras adjustment function gives:

$$(W^{.}/P) = \beta.q_L^x = \alpha\beta(\mu - W/P) \tag{3.5}$$

where $\beta > 0$ and we should note (compare Lipsey, 1960) that it is the absolute rate of change of W/P that appears on the left-hand side of equation (3.5). The transformation to a Phillips curve follows from setting out the proportional derivative (growth rate):

$$W/P(g_w - g_p) = \alpha\beta(\mu - W/P)$$

which reduces to

$$g_w = g_p + \kappa\left(\frac{\mu}{W/P} - 1\right) \tag{3.6}$$

where $\kappa = \alpha\beta$, the speed of response when excess demand is measured in terms of real wage disequilibrium.

This is the wage change equation implied by neo–classical general equilibrium theory. In particular, since real wages are adjusted, g_p enters with a unitary coefficient (again, compare Lipsey, 1960). Because expressions like $\kappa(\frac{\mu}{W/P}-1)$ will also appear in the sequel it is worthwhile to note that this is a simple rectangular hyperbola in W/P, bounded from below at $-\kappa$. Moreover since:

$$\kappa(\frac{\mu}{W/P} - 1) = \frac{\beta}{W/P}q_L^x, \qquad (3.7)$$

the expression (3.6) for the growth of money wages is non-linear in W/P and hence in unemployment u even if unemployment is assumed to be a linear (negative) index of the excess demand for labour.

Assuming a neo-classical labour market, $\kappa(\frac{\mu}{W/P}-1)$ transforms monotonically to $f(u)$, some strictly decreasing function of unemployment, and in consequence:

$$g_W = g_p + f(u) \qquad (3.8)$$

Hence for the *wage theorem* to be satisfied, in conjunction with this equation, $f(u)$ must vanish so that W/P must be at the equilibrium level μ, from which we conclude that the market clearing version of the Phillips curve is not generally compatible with the *wage theorem*.

However, the adjustment function (3.5) does not preclude sufficiently flexible wages and prices for $g_W = g_p$ at all times, so that $f(u)$ instantaneous, that provides a motivation for setting:

$$g_W = g_p e + f(u) \qquad (3.9)$$

as a short-run model. In conjunction with the hypothesis that expected *growth rates* adapt exponentially, that is:

$$\dot{g_p}e = \pi\{g_p - g_p e\} \qquad (3.10)$$

this is Friedman's wage equation. When the price equation (2.2) above is added:

$$g_p = g_W \qquad (3.11)$$

the eventual convergence of $g_p e$ on g_p from (3.10) leaves as the simultaneous solution of (3.9) and (3.11):

$$f(u) = 0 \tag{3.12}$$

and at the root of this equation, $\bar{u}$, say, inflation cannot depend upon the level of unemployment.

A strong wage bargaining model

At the opposite extreme of neo-classical market-clearing wage movements is the notion that money wages are set, monopolistically, by a strong trade union movement which need not fear apparent unemployment consequences because there is a national policy commitment to full employment.

Suppose then that wage negotiators set themselves a target real wage level λ, where $\lambda > \mu$. We assume that the current price level is not known when the money wage is negotiated and accordingly write:

$$W(t) = \lambda \, P^e(t) \tag{4.1}$$

where the expected price *level* $P^e(t)$, is taken to be an exponentially weighted moving average of past price *levels*:

$$\dot{P}_e(t) = \delta \, \{P(t) - P_e(t)\} \tag{4.2}$$

The assumption that expectations are adaptive in levels rather than growth rates turns out to be critical and it raises the question to be explored below whether there is an implied adaptation of growth rates, as well, at least asymptotically. (With the more usual assumption of adaptation in terms of growth rates (e.g. Friedman, 1968) there has been surprisingly little discussion of the converse problem of what is implied about the behaviour of expected levels.)

We also make the strong assumption that this relation holds for all t, so there is no need to follow Sargan (1964) in specifying a catch-up or error adjustment term arising from failure to hit the target in say $t - 1$. This does not necessarily make irrelevant to the empirical validity of equation (4.1) the considerable number of models estimated by Sargan (1964; 1980) and others (Henry, 1981) of the so-called real wage resistance type since Sargan introduces the definition of the expected proportional price change r as

$$r_t \equiv \ln P_t^e - \ln P_{t-1}$$

which can be shown to lead necessarily to an equation with a catch-up term:

$$g_W(t) = r_t + g_\lambda(t) + \ln\left(\frac{\lambda_{t-1}}{W_{t-1}/P_{t-1}}\right) \tag{4.3}$$

Consequently, any model correctly specified by equation (4.1) in conjunction with a correct expectations function can be set out in Sargan's form (4.3) with an appropriate restriction on the meaning of r.

Differentiating (4.1) with respect to time, assuming λ is constant and substituting for $P_e(t)$ from (4.2) gives:

$$\dot{W}(t) = \lambda \, \delta \, \{P(t) - P_e(t)\} \qquad (4.4)$$

and on division by $W(t)$, and rearrangement, we obtain

$$g_W(t) = \frac{\dot{W}(t)}{W(t)} = \delta \left(\frac{\lambda}{W(t)/P(t)} - 1 \right) \qquad (4.5)$$

This expression may be compared directly with the right hand side of the neo-classical equation (3.6) and its graph appears in Figure 5.1.

We assume that while money wages are set by the trade union movement aiming at the target real wage λ individual actors on both sides of the labour market respond as in the neo-classical labour market. Consequently, since a high real wage is associated with high unemployment, and conversely, under these assumptions, equation (4.5) predicts a stable relation of the Phillips type, between the rate of money wage inflation and the rate of unemployment.

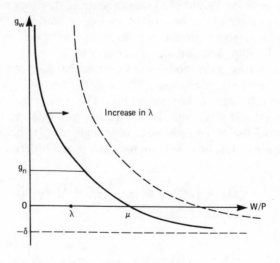

Figure 5.1

According to equation (4.5), the rate of money wage inflation will be positive if the real wage falls below the target level, and the government has a choice then between accepting rather mild inflation with unemployment up to the possibly quite high level given by setting the real wage equal to the target λ, or a higher rate of inflation that will reduce unemployment by pushing down $W(t)$ which is geared to $P^e(t)$ which in turn lags behind $P(t)$. The key element in this story is that it is possible for $g_p(t) = g_pe(t)$ while $P \simeq P_e$. Indeed, it is easily seen that P and P_e must differ for any non-zero value of a steady growth rate g_p:

From
$$P_e(t) = \delta\{P(t) - P_e(t)\}$$
$$P_e(t) \,(\delta + g_pe(t)) = \delta P(t)$$

and
$$P_e(t) = \frac{\delta\,P(t)}{\delta + g_p^e} = \frac{1}{1 + g/\delta}P(t)$$

so that
$$P_e < P \text{ for } g_pe = g_p = g \text{ say} \qquad (4.6)$$

Moreover for constant g,

$$P_e(t) = \frac{1}{1 + g/\delta} = \frac{-g/\delta}{eP(t)} = P(t - g/\delta)$$

for small g/δ so that the lag of P_e and W behind P is proportional to the rate of inflation.

From equations (4.1) and (4.5) we can write $g_w(t)$ either as equal to $g_p^e(t)$ or as a function of the level of unemployment, but not both together. This is some ground for suspecting misspecification in both Lipsey–Phillips and Sargan-type equations.

The prime mover in the model is however neither $g_p^e(t)$ nor u_t; it is the actual rate of price inflation $g_p(t)$. If $g_p(t)$ rises, the real wage falls because $P_e(t)$ lags further behind $P(t)$. That reduces unemployment and $g_w(t)$ and $g_p^e(t)$ both rise to equality with $g_p(t)$, subject to examination of the non-steady state behaviour of $g_p^e(t)$ below. As between steady states, however, we have the casual ordering:

$$g_p(t) \rightarrow g_p^e(t) \rightarrow g_w(t) \rightarrow \delta\{\frac{\lambda}{W(t)/P(t)} - 1\} = \psi(u_t) \qquad (4.7)$$

A diagram of $g_p(t) = g_w(t) = \delta(\frac{\lambda}{W(t)/P(t)} - 1)$ should strictly speaking have g_p and g_w on the horizontal axis, since g_p is the independent variable, but for the purpose of comparison with Phillips curve diagrams it is convenient to put it the other way round, and bear in mind that the function involving W/P can be written equivalently in terms of unemployment.

Given the non-linearity of (4.5), the relation predicted is one that has more curvature than the simple hyperbola shown in Figure 5.1 if Lipsey's comments on the non-linear relation between unemployment and excess demand are accepted. Although Lipsey found a significant coefficient of U^{-2}, and an increase in curvature between periods when there was apparently both an increase in trade union density and the induced component of wage change, this evidence is only indirectly relevant because in the present model unemployment is a dependent variable.

With this model, the wage theorem holds at any real wage level and it can be summarized from equations (4.1) and (4.6) as the relation

$$\frac{\lambda}{1 + g/\delta} = \frac{W}{P} = f(u), (f' < 0) \tag{4.8}$$

which holds in a steady state, i.e. with constant price inflation g and fully adjusted adaptive expectations. If we now add the monetary hypothesis that $g = g_M$ (2.2 above), the model is closed, giving a long-term trade-off, provided the target real wage λ remains constant. This is what was meant earlier by a conservative element in the behaviour of wage negotiators. For a given g_M, on the other hand, an exogenous rise in the target real wage λ will cause unemployment to rise. If the policy of validation is sustained it follows from the wage theorem $g_p = g_w$ that $g_p - g_p^e = g_\lambda$ which will generally only be possible with an accelerating value of g_p. This formalizes the 'tug of war' between the trade unions and the monetary authorities, and is explored further in the concluding section.

The derived adjustment function

Since in this model individual responses to the real wage are not abolished by its joint administration by collective bargainers and the monetary authorities, we can derive the relation implied between g_w and excess demand q_L^x and compare it with that normally used since Lipsey (1960) to represent a Phillips curve with a market-determined wage. It will be recalled that in the latter case, g_w is usually taken to be a simple proportional function of q_L^x. Those who have written about the possibility of cost-push in a general equilibrium setting, however, have conjectured that the function may have a positive intercept on the g_W axis (Hansen, 1970), and that it may be non-linear. No theoretical basis is available for these conjectures.

We assume: $q_L^x = \alpha(\mu - W/P)$ from (3.4) above

$$= \alpha\,\mu - \alpha\,\lambda\frac{P^e}{P}$$

$$= \alpha\left(\mu - \frac{\lambda}{\delta + g}\,\frac{\delta}{\delta + g}\right) \text{ using (4.6)} \qquad (5.1)$$

Consequently, for $q_L^x = 0$:
$$g = \delta\left(\frac{\lambda}{\mu} - 1\right) > 0$$

which gives a positive intercept, that is, some inflation even in market equilibrium, as a result of union policy. In addition, the non-negativity of P_e and P, in the expression

$$P_e = \frac{\delta}{\delta + g}P$$

together with $\delta > 0$, implies that g has the lower bound $-\delta$. This suggests that strict downwards rigidity in money wages applies not to levels but to growth rates. As $g \to -\delta$, $-q_L^x$ (i.e. unemployment) becomes infinitely large. For $g_W \to +\infty$, on the other hand, $q_L^x \to \alpha\,\mu$ because excess demand is bounded from above at the level corresponding to a zero real wage.

$$\text{At } g_W = 0, q_L^x = \alpha\,(\mu - \lambda) < 0 \qquad (5.2)$$

The general appearance of this function is shown in Figure 5.2.

The dashed line AB is Lipsey's version of the Samuelson-Walras adjustment function, and in comparing the two it should be borne in mind that they have opposite directions of causality. More fundamentally the curve derived as the implied adjustment function describes alternative long-run steady states, whereas AB describes a transient relationship. In addition, the dashed line AB assumes static money illusion.

Subject to these points, Figure 5.2 suggests that it is impossible for the labour market to be simultaneously in price and quantity equilibrium. If we want full employment, the system has to inflate at least at the rate given by the intercept $g = \delta\left(\frac{\lambda}{\mu} - 1\right)$. If the market is left to find its own level, on the other hand, with a non-validatory monetary policy, it will drift into a Keynesian disequilibrium, whose full description is seen to involve the inflation rate as well as the unemployment rate.

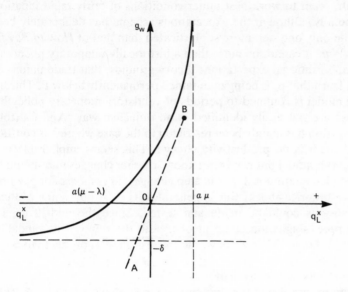

Figure 5.2

In the absence from this model of productivity change and import price changes, the candidate for description as the natural rate of unemployment, at $\alpha(\mu - \lambda)$, depends directly on the power and policy of wage-bargainers. Comparing the speed of adjustment envisaged in the two models (the slopes of the adjustment functions), it is obviously possible that for a certain range of values of the excess demand for labour – around medium positive levels, say – the rate of money wage inflation may actually be less under the collective bargaining than the market regime. But given the non-linearity of the derived adjustment function, at a sufficiently high level of positive excess demand, the bargaining regime must eventually have the higher rate of inflation, and the divergence between the two is especially marked under conditions of depressed aggregate demand.

The evidence from econometric studies for a non-linear relation between g_w and q_L^x is mixed, and several problems require further theoretical discussion before a satisfactory direct test can be devised. The model shows how price inflation stimulates the demand for labour by reducing the real wage. That has a close family resemblance to the proposition in monetary theory that inflation reduces the demand for cash balances and thereby stimulates aggregate demand at least temporarily. The latter effect, and perhaps both, seem to work best under conditions of fairly rapid inflation. Secondly, although the expectations scheme has deliberately been made only one step more sophisticated than that of *How to Pay for the War*, it cannot be more than a historically temporary phenomenon, on rational expectations theory grounds, that trade unions do not learn that p_e is being maintained permanently below P. Thirdly, the model is confined to periods of validatory monetary policy but these are not easily identified in an objective way. And fourthly, discussion has mainly been restricted to the case where λ is constant and there is no productivity change. This seems implausible in a long-run model but we do not know whether changes in λ should be modelled continuously, or in step changes, in response for example to an oil price shock. But in general, it is clear how some of these extensions could be made and tested. Since the mid-1970s, for example, stagflation could involve both the removal of validation and a relative rise in λ above the trend growth of productivity.

Non-steady state behaviour

Suppose that the system summarized in (4.8) has been at a particular level of $g_p(t)$ for some time, and $g_p(t)$ then rises to a higher level because of an increase in g_M. There is now a mathematical complication, because we want both P^e to follow P, and $g_{p_e}(t)$ to follow $g_p(t)$; the question now is whether the adaptive mechanism for the first carries over into a convergent adaptive mechanism for the second.

This adjustment of the expected price level is written in (4.2) above as:

$$\dot{P}_e(t) = \delta\{P(t) - P_e(t)\}$$

Therefore, $g_{P_e} = \delta(\dfrac{P}{P_e} - 1)$ ⁣ (6.1)

and, $\dot{g}_{P_e} = \delta \dfrac{P}{P_e}(g_P - g_{P_e})$

$$= (\delta + g_{P_e}(t))(g_p(t) - g_{P_e}(t)) \qquad (6.2)$$

For a step-change in g_p between steady values $g_p(0)$ and $g_p(t)$, this is a non-linear first-order differential equation of the Bernoulli type. To obtain the solution it is convenient to introduce some change of notation as follows:

Write $P(t) = p$ and $P_e(t) = q$ and let the rate of growth of P be g for $t < 0$ and k for $t \geqslant 0$. Then:

$$\dot{q} = \delta(q - p) \tag{6.3}$$

Write $p = \alpha e^{kt}$ $t \geqslant 0$

Then: $q + \delta q = \alpha\delta e^{kt}$ from (6.3) $\tag{6.4}$

with: $q = ae^{kt} + be^{lt}$

where a and b are constants of integration,

then: $\dot{q} = ake^{kt} + ble^{lt} \tag{6.5}$

Comparison with (6.3) gives:

$$a(\delta + k) = \alpha\delta \text{ and } b(\delta + 1) = 0,$$

so the general solution is

$$q = \frac{\alpha\ \delta}{\delta + k}e^{kt} + be^{-\delta t} \tag{6.6}$$

For $t < 0$, p has grown at the rate g, consequently

$$q = \delta p/\delta + g \qquad \text{at } t = 0$$

Hence $\dfrac{\alpha\ \delta}{\delta + g} = \dfrac{\alpha\ \delta}{\delta + k} + b$

So that $b = \dfrac{\alpha\delta(k - g)}{(\delta + k)(\delta + g)} \tag{6.7}$

Substitution in (6.6) gives:

$$q = \frac{\alpha\ \delta\ e^{kt}}{\delta + k}\left[1 + \frac{(k - g)e^{-(\delta+k)t}}{(\delta + g)}\right] \tag{6.8}$$

Therefore:

$$\dot{q} = \frac{\alpha\delta\ ke^{kt}}{(\delta + k)}\left[1 - \frac{\delta(k - g)e^{-(\delta+k)t}}{k(\delta + g)}\right] \tag{6.9}$$

So

$$g_{P_e} = \dot{q}/q = k\ \frac{1 - \dfrac{(k - g)}{k(\delta + g)}\ e^{-(\delta+k)t}}{1 - \dfrac{(k - g)}{(\delta + g)}\ e^{-(\delta+k)t}} \tag{6.10}$$

At $t = 0$, this reduces to $g_{p_e} = k$ as required, and for large $t > 0$ a close approximation is

$$g_{p_e} = \dot{q}/q = k - (k - g)\frac{(\delta + k)}{(\delta + g)}e^{-(\delta+k)t} \rightarrow k \qquad (6.11)$$

as required.

Consequently, g_{p_e} converges on g_p, but is it an unusual feature of the process that the convergence is very much faster for large values of g_p (see (6.2) above). In a wage equation of the Lipsey-Phillips type, with g_{p_e} substituted for g_p, this would cause the coefficient of g_{p_e} to rise at higher rates of inflation, even though that estimatng equation is mis-specified from the point of view of the present model. Several recent studies have found evidence of this effect.

Equally, at very low values of g_p, the convergence of g_p (and hence of g_w) on g_p is extremely slow. This is a possible formulation of those conditions of extreme stickiness in money wages from which Keynes apparently concluded that for very low g_p, induced changes in money wages could be neglected in the short run. Other implications follow. If the economy moves towards generally higher levels of employment, the (clockwise) Phillips curve loops that represent adaptive price expectations in non-steady-state behaviour will become attenuated by the reducing response of g_{p_e} to falling g_p. Similarly, the non-linearity of this response will introduce a bias in the coefficient of g_p in any econometric study which uses g_p as a proxy for g_{p_e}, unless all the positive and negative movements happen to sum to zero.

The instability of mixed (autonomous and induced) inflation
By an obvious extension of the induced inflation model (e.g. starting again at (4.1)), we can write:

$$g_w(t) = g_\lambda(t) + g_{p_e}(t) \qquad (7.1)$$

and interpret $g_\lambda(t)$ as the autonomous growth rate of the parameter λ, previously taken to be zero, and now assumed to be a positive constant.

If it is desired to maintain a particular level of unemployment, the condition $g_w = g_p$ must be satisfied. In conjunction with (7.1), however, this implies:

$$g_p(t) - g_{p_e}(t) = g_\lambda(t)$$

which cannot be sustained for any constant g_p, since g_{p_e} converges on that constant value as shown in the last section. Hence the rate of inflation must accelerate, to maintain a given level of unemployment.

Substituting for $(g_p(t) - g_{P_e}(t))$ in equation (6.2) above,

$$\dot{g}_{P_e}(t) = (\delta + g_{P_e}(t))g_\lambda(t) \qquad (7.2)$$

Therefore $\dot{g}_{P_e}/g_{P_e} = \{1 + \dfrac{\delta}{g_{P_e}}\} g_\lambda \to g_\lambda$ from above, as t increases
$$\text{without limit} \qquad (7.3)$$

Thus g_{P_e} accelerates and so does g_W: while monetary policy must be so conducted that g_p also accelerates both to induce the acceleration of g_{P_e} and to match that of g_W. g_{P_e} adjusts to the acceleration rate necessary to make $g_W = g_\lambda + g_{P_e}$ equal to g_M and g_p. For that adjustment in g_{P_e} to be made, however, it is clear that g_p (and hence g_M) and g_{P_e} must all accelerate and their proportionate rate of acceleration depends primarily on g_λ, the autonomous component. In effect, the model decomposes, to a first approximation, with monetary expansion explaining the rate of inflation, and autonomous wage push its acceleration.

Conclusion
Some years ago, it was customary among Keynesians of a neo-classical inclination to explain how, with a given (and constant) money wage, a small rise in the price level might be engineered to reduce the real wage, in order to underpin in the labour market an expansion of the aggregate real demand for good that was simultaneously taking place, as illustrated for example in the income-expenditure diagram. This paper has retold this story with the difference that the collective bargaining system also gives the growth rate of money wages, so that a government pursuing a higher employment policy is obliged to push the rate of price inflation ahead of that of money wages. This process implies a non-linear relationship between money wage growth and unemployment, as an explanation of the empirical Phillips curve, if the response of trade unions to price change – at least in the 1950s and 1960s is better characterized by an adaptive than a rational expectations scheme. In effect, therefore, adaptive expectations serves the same function as money illusion in the earlier story, encountering the same logical objections while enjoying more empirical plausibility. Further discussion of this point seems to require both a more general formulation of what is meant by adaptive expectations, and the much overdue investigation of whether the Keynesian surmise was correct that sectional wage bargaining may in any case produce some group

irrationality through the composition of individual rationality. For these and related further issues, however, an appropriate framework would seem to require some version of the treatment adopted here of the trade union movement and the monetary authorities as joint administrators or even bargainers over the wage-price system; neither equal in power or intent at any one time, nor necessarily single-minded or aggressive, but clearly interdependent in their joint effects as illustrated here in terms of unemployment.

6 The Great Recession 1974–84: Is a 'Keynesist' approach plausible?

Michael Surrey

> The idea then of causation must be derived from some *relation* among objects; and that relation we must now endeavour to discover. I find in the first place, that whatever objects are considered as causes or effects are *contiguous*. ... Though distant objects may sometimes seem productive of each other, they are commonly found upon examination to be linked by a chain of causes ... (David Hume, *A Treatise of Human Nature*, Book I, part III, section 2)

Introduction

It is commonplace to assert that the 1950s and 1960s were a period when the Keynesian analysis was vindicated and when government policies based on that analysis succeeded to a large extent in stabilizing employment at a high level. It is now almost as commonplace to claim that the experience of the period since 1970, and more particularly since 1974, has shown the Keynesian approach to have been false at worst or irrelevant at best. Alternative modes of analysis have been proposed, and widely accepted by policy-makers, to fill the policy vacuum left by the supposed death of the Keynesian approach. These have included the (interconnected) theories of 'natural' rates of unemployment and output, of the monetary causes of inflation, of the importance of the level of real wages as a direct determinant of employment, and of 'supply-side' economics.

The argument of this essay is that the UK experience suggests that Keynesian analysis has proved *insufficient* for a full explanation of postwar developments – significantly so in the 1950s and 1960s and dramatically so in the last decade – but that it is neither irrelevant nor, *a fortiori*, false. The analysis which stemmed directly from the *General Theory* needs radical extension of its general philosophy if it is still to be regarded as plausible but its wholesale rejection is not warranted by events. The key questions are:

1 Is the core of the argument of the *General Theory* still plausible as *part* of the explanation of developments in the UK economy?
2 Can this core be extended in ways consistent with the Keynesian tradition in order fully to account for these developments?

I The 'Keynesian Revolution' and 'Keynesist' economics

In the 1960s there was a good deal of discussion about the relationship between 'Keynesian' economics and 'what Keynes really said (or meant to say)' (see notably Leijonhufvud, 1968; and Clower, 1965). This essay is not concerned with that dispute but with the question of whether the analytic approach outlined in the *General Theory* can be extended to cover the problems generated in a smallish open economy which is prone to inflation (as well as to cyclical unemployment) in ways wich can legitimately be said to be 'in the Keynesian tradition of analysis'. This last is a clumsy phrase: I shall borrow a useful distinction used by some political theorists between Marxian and Marxist analysis. The former relates to the analysis and exegesis of Marx's own works, the latter to later developments of the same broad approach. Thus one may take the kind of analysis of Leijonhufvud, Clower *et al.* as 'Keynesian', while our purpose is to explore analyses of, notably, the problems of open economies, of inflation and of the interconnections between fiscal and monetary policy which can properly be said to be 'in the Keynesian tradition' – which are, that is to say, 'Keynesist'.[1]

The first task is, therefore, to find a test, or a series of tests, for what is to count as 'Keynesist'. Keynes' attack on neo-classical orthodoxy had four main prongs. First and foremost, there was the rejection of the view that in the absence of market 'imperfections' output and employment had unique 'equilibrium levels'; secondly (which comes indirectly to much the same thing), an attack on the orthodox account of the role of money and the determination of the rate of interest; thirdly, acute examination of various directions of causality in the system; and finally, a largely veiled but insistent feeling that the supply/demand/price basis of neo-classical analysis was fundamentally and systematically inappropriate at the macro-level.

The 'Keynesian Revolution' has often been taken to comprise only the first two of these.[2] Because of this, it did not prove difficult for the proponents of the 'neo-classical synthesis' to accommodate both the consumption function and the Keynesian analysis of liquidity preference and the rate of interest without abandoning the general precepts of marginalism and the self-correcting nature of disequilibrium (see, for example, Modigliani, 1944). In this view the *General Theory* dramatically widened the scope of macroeconomic analysis by providing coherent accounts both of the monetary determination of the rate of interest and of the determination of the aggregate level of employment when total output was variable not fixed. But this represented an extension, not a rejection, of the orthodox analytic system, albeit a radical one. It needed only relatively minor further amendments – the real balance effect and, later, the vertical Phillips curve – for neo-classical orthodoxy to reclaim its lost ground even in respect of the ultimate 'exogeneity' of the levels of income and employment. 'Keynesian' economics was reduced to the economics of the short run when 'inflexible' money wages might – perhaps for a protracted period – prevent orderly market adjustment to the 'natural' levels of output, employment and unemployment.

But if Keynes' analysis was merely a 'special case' of the neo-classical analysis, why did he write of a 'General Theory'? What of his 'long struggle to escape' from orthodox theory (CW, Vol. VII, p. viii); why that 'it may well be that the classical theory represents the way in which we would like our economy to behave. But to assume that it actually does so is to assume our difficulties away' (p. 34); why that '[the classical theory] is wholly unable to answer what effect on unemployment a reduction in money wages will have. For it has no method of analysis wherewith to tackle the problem' (p. 260); and so on? Unless these are to be interpreted as mere hyperbole, Keynes' attack on neo-classical analysis must have been more fundamental than simply an attack on its scope. There can be no 'long struggle of escape' from a system which one ends up extending. Our argument is that Keynes did in fact show that the supply/demand/price system is systematically wrong as a basis for macroeconomic theory, but that he was only partially successful in adumbrating a solution. Nevertheless, an examination of two key elements in the argument of the General Theory will give some idea of the real, or latent, Keynesian revolution.

The theory of interest
Keynes' criticism of what he took to be the 'classical' theory of the rate of interest has two elements. First, he pointed out that the schedule relating savings to the rate of interest neglects the impact on savings of changes in income and, secondly, since income in turn depends on the level of investment, the savings and investment schedules logically cannot shift independently:

> The classical theory of the rate of interest seems to suppose that, if the demand curve for capital shifts or if the curve relating the rate of interest to the amounts saved out of a given income shifts or if both these curves shift, the new rate of interest will be given by the point of intersection of the new positions of the two curves. But this is a nonsense theory. For the assumption that income is constant is inconsistent with the assumption that these two curves can shift independently of one another. If either of them shift, then, in general, income will change; with the result that the whole schematism based on the assumption of a given income breaks down. (CW, Vol. VII, p. 179)

Keynes' argument can be concisely put using modern terminology: the savings schedule is *mis-specified* (it omits an important variable) and when it is correctly specified, the simultaneous r/I/Y/S system becomes *under-identified*.

In formal terms, the correctly-specified system is:

$$I = f(A, r)$$
$$S = f(Y, r)$$
$$I = S$$

where A represents autonomous expenditure and/or the 'state of expectation'. But this system cannot be solved for the two fundamental endogenous variables, r and Y, in terms of the single exogenous variable, A. All that can be derived is a relationship showing for a given value of A, the level of Y following from a *given* level of r. Since the purpose of the analysis was to determine r, this relationship (the egregious IS curve) is scarcely helpful on its own.

Keynes' objection, however, amounts to more than this. Not only is the system as a whole indeterminate, but both the S/r and the I/r schedules individually are under-identified. In graphical terms, this implies that *no meaning whatsoever* can be attached to points on either the savings schedule or on the investment schedule other than the single 'observed' point representing the realized conjunction of S, I and r. This is Keynes' point about the need to be able to hypothesize *independent* shifts in the two schedules. If the investment schedule can shift – for example, because of autonomous changes in expectations – while the savings schedule remains fixed, then the points of intersection of the two schedules will trace out, or *identify*, the savings schedule. And conversely, if the saving schedule could shift without any change in the investment schedule, then the intersections would trace out, or *identify*, the investment schedule. It is clear why identification is of such central importance to econometricians: the process described above is necessary if empirical estimates of the schedules are to be obtained. But the problem is a fundamental one in theory too: if the points defining a schedule cannot *in principle* be observed, its theoretical foundation is in question.

Here, then, is the source of the 'long struggle to escape'. It is so unexceptionable at the microeconomic level to draw a downward-sloping demand curve (for instance), without pausing to doubt whether or not it is, in principle, possible to observe the response of quantity demanded simply to price, that it is not easy to see that at that macroeconomic level this process may be *systematically* illegitimate.

Keynes' own solution to the identification problem is to provide an independent account of the determination of the rate of interest. Once r is determined in this way, the system becomes identified. More formally, we have the conventional Keynesian model underlying the IS–LM analysis:

$$I = f(A,r)$$

$$S = f(Y,r)$$

$$M_d = f(Y,r)$$

$$M_s = M$$

$$I = S$$

$$M_d = M_s$$

In this model, there are two fundamentally endogenous variables, Y and r, and two exogenous variables, A and M. The investment, savings and demand-for-money functions are each exactly identified. The crucial new element in the system is the introduction of a fresh exogenous variable, the supply of money. It is important to note (see below) that matters are once more confused in a 'Keynesian' way if the supply of money is itself to be regarded as an endogenous and not an exogenous variable.

The theory of unemployment

The same approach by way of *identification* can be used to throw light on the other major point of attack of the *General Theory* – the question of how unemployment can persist despite a freely flexible 'price of labour'. The argument in the *General Theory* is less clearly set out than in the case of the I/S/Y/r nexus. Once again, it is the endogeneity of Y together with the independence of the demand for labour on Y as well as (or instead of) on the level of the real wage which causes problems for the neo-classical analysis. At the *micro* level, Keynes agrees, a fall in the wage will stimulate employment:

> In any given industry we have a demand schedule relating the quantities which can be sold to the prices asked; we have a series of supply schedules relating the prices which will be asked for the sale of different quantities on various bases of cost; and these schedules between them lead up to a further schedule which ... gives us the demand schedule for labour in the industry relating the quantity of labour to different levels of wages ... (CW, Vol. VII, pp. 258–9)

Keynes points out that the implicit *ceteris paribus* clause embracing conditions in all other industries amounts to assuming an unchanged level of aggregate effective demand: at the macro-level this cannot be assumed, and the attempt to reason from the micro-level to the macro-level by simple aggregation fails. The argument is guilty of a *logical* fallacy.

The argument can be translated very simply into modern terminology. In this part of the model we have three endogenous variables, the level of output, Y, the level of employment, N, and the level of the real wage, w/p. For these three endogenous variables we have only two behavioural equations: a production or employment function relating Y and N, and a profit-maximizing condition which brings the real wage w/p into equality with the marginal product of labour (the slope of the production function, dY/dN). The system is thus irremediably under-identified and it can be identified only by assuming Y to be exogenous (the neo-classical, and demonstrably invalid, assumption) or by providing an independent account of how Y is determined (the Keynesian solution by way of the consumption function). Once Y is independently explained, the system becomes identified and quite straightforward: the level of employment is given by the production function, and profit-maximization delivers the 'appropriate' real wage (or, given the money wage, the 'appropriate' price level). The workings of the system are plain. Suppose that there is a cut in the general level of money wages. It may well be that each (myopic) entrepreneur plans to hire more labour and increase output. The increased employment will increase aggregate demand but, because of the savings leakage, by less than aggregate production. Stocks will accumulate, prices will be cut and employment and output will fall back. Since neither the level of fixed investment nor the propensity to consume has changed, the final real equilibrium will be that ruling prior to the cut in money-wages, save only that *nominal* wages and prices will be uniformly lower.

As Keynes was quick to admit (ibid., pp. 262–5), the *indirect* effects of the reduction in wages and prices could, in various ways, tend to stimulate employment (most importantly through competitiveness effects on net exports in an open economy and through the real balance effect on consumption). (See Patinkin, 1965, chs 13 and 14.) And the 'neo-classical synthesis' depended on the demonstration that full employment was logically attainable in this way, given a sufficient fall in money wages. This partial rehabilitation of the neo-classical *result* (that flexible prices will ultimately restore full employment) did not, however, rehabilitate the neo-classical *analysis*, by which the imbalance between supply and demand in the labour market should be corrected *directly* by an adjustment of price (in this case, the real wage). The so-called 'neo-classical synthesis' thus evaded rather than answered the *logical* basis of Keynes's fundamental critique.

The inference that it is the problem of identification which lies at the heart of Keynes' attack on the neo-classical method of analysis has far-reaching implications. Put baldly, the contention is that the analysis of problems in a supply/demand/price framework is liable to systematic under-identification at the macro-level of analysis. It is in general impossible *in principle* to observe the appropriate supply and demand schedules in the way which identification requires, and it follows that analysis based on them will be vacuous.

If it was indeed this general presumption of under-identifiability in macroeconomic theory based on supply and demand analysis which Keynes intuitively suspected, most of his almost apocalyptic references to the inadequacy of the neo-classical analysis become understandable. The latent Keynesian Revolution becomes a completely fundamental one, since it calls into question the sufficiency of the supply and demand starting-point in every area of macro-economic analysis. This goes far beyond the question of whether the absence of a Walrasian auctioneer is crucial, for it is concerned with whether the very notion of market-clearing price (or vector of prices) is even in theory valid.

The market-based neo-classical approach has three crucial steps. First, there is a price at which supply and demand will be equal. Secondly, imbalance between supply and demand *can* (*ceteris paribus*) be eliminated by an appropriate change in price. Thirdly, imbalances between supply and demand *will* be eliminated by the operation of market forces. Clower and Leijonhufvud concentrated on the rejection of the third of these steps as constituting the 'Keynesian Revolution'. It is our contention that the really fundamental character of the Revolution intended to be wrought by the *General Theory* lay in the rejection by Keynes of the prior and still more fundamental second step. Put briefly, if supply and demand schedules cannot be separately identifiable (in the technical sense), the notion of a 'gap' between them is vacuous and the presence or absence of an auctioneer to make market signals 'effective' simply does not arise.

If, as we have suggested, Keynes' scepticism about the classical approach amounted to a general presumption that models in this mould are systematically under-identified and incapable of yielding any conclusions at all at the macro-level, his otherwise cryptic remarks about the total irrelevance of the classical analysis, and about a struggle to escape, become understandable. An 'intuition' that the orthodox analysis was indeterminate at the macro-level must have been profoundly worrying – and not a worry which was resoluble by piecemeal tinkering for the sake of 'realism'. On such a fundamental view, there clearly could not be a 'neo-classical synthesis'.

And yet the revolution petered out, abandoned even by Keynes himself by the time of *How to Pay for the War* (1941), and of the Bretton Woods and Washington Loan negotiations (1944–46). Was he persuaded that he had been wrong in the *General Theory*, or was he simply unable to carry through the revolution into new fields, of inflation and of international economics? Our view is that the second of these is the case: the arguments used in Keynes' analysis of inflation and those which underpin the essentially free-trade foundations of the 1944–46 arguments simply do not stand up to the kind of critique sketched by the Keynes of 1936.

The argument of *How to Pay for the War* is brief, to the point of being cursory. The problem which Keynes was addressing was that the enormous increase in government spending and employment associated with the outbreak of war would lead to excess (and effective) aggregate demand. Keynes argued that unless private consumption was reduced,

> It follows that the increased quantity of money available to be spent in the pockets of consumers will meet a quantity of goods which is not increased ... Some means must be found for withdrawing purchasing power from the market; or prices must rise until the available goods are selling at figures which absorb the increased quantity of expenditure, – in other words the method of inflation. (p. 10)

Now this is certainly not 'Keynesist' in the manner of analysis of the *General Theory* nor, indeed, is it a coherent basis as it stands for a theory of inflation. The 'increased quantity of money available to be spent' presumably means increased money *income* as output rises to its full-employment level; beyond that point, a fixed real income faces a supply of consumer goods which is constrained by government pre-emption of resources. The analysis then assumes without question that there will be an 'equilibrating' rise in prices, but it is not explained how this brings real demand and real supply back into balance. A 'Keynesist' analysis would, as a matter of course, explore the response of money wages to the price rise and the question of whether the implicit aggregate demand and aggregate supply schedules would or would not shift – the question of identification again. These questions are simply not explored in the (admittedly polemical) *How to Pay for the War*.

In the Bretton Woods and Washington Loan negotiations of 1944–46, Keynes seems to have adopted without question a series of propositions and policy prescriptions whose justification is clear only in terms of neo-classical analysis. But the foundations of international trade theory are immediately vulnerable to precisely the kind of attack launched in the *General Theory* against the classical theory of the rate of interest. Put succinctly, in a two-country world, identification of each country's offer curve requires that shifts in the other's offer curve do not alter its own. This logically cannot be so, once the dependence of the demand for imports on the level of domestic demand as well as on the terms of trade is admitted and full employment is not assumed. In such a case, there is a foreign-trade multiplier: the two countries' levels of demand and output are mutually dependent and the offer curves cannot shift independently of each other. At a stroke, this makes orthodox trade theory vacuous. In particular, without a 'Keynesist' reconstruction there is no longer a simple presumption in favour of free trade as against 'managed' trade. The implications hardly need spelling out.

A 'Keynesist' critique of the neo-classical approach to trade theory would begin by noting the apparent logical problem involved in constructing each country's offer curve on the basis of hypothetically varying terms of trade. Exactly analogously with the construction of hypothetical supply and demand schedules, identification in this case requires that as one offer curve shifts independently of the other, the latter is *identified* by successive intersections.

The difficulty with such a model of trade between two countries from a 'Keynesist' point of view is that

(a) the import functions are mis-specified by ignoring the dependence of imports on domestic income as well as on relative prices, and

(b) that once this dependence is recognized, the system becomes under-identified.

The parallel with the example taken earlier from the *General Theory* is at once apparent. A change in one country's offer curve, for example, will take place if there is a shift in domestic investment. But the increased demand for imports raises the other country's exports and, consequently, its income. In turn, this alters its own demand for imports. Thus the two countries' offer curves can no longer shift independently: the analysis founders by being under identified.

The way is, however, open for a reconstruction of international trade theory along 'Keynesist' lines. This can be done by way of the 'foreign-trade multiplier' though it is fair to say that a full formal reconstruction of trade theory which recognizes both income and price influences on trade flows, consumption, production and employment has not yet been offered. In its absence, we should clearly be at the very least sceptical about the logical foundations of conventional trade theory and policy prescriptions.

in this case nor in the case of inflation did Keynes himself carry on the 'Keynesist' approach. Once he left the academic world at least partly behind, he seems to some extent to have let the old orthodoxy take hold again and to have been unwilling to carry through the radical approach of the *General Theory* to fresh areas of analysis. It is important to see this not as a reconversion to orthodoxy but as a reflection of the inability even of Keynes to hold, unaided, to the need for a complete rethinking of macroeconomics in the face of the pressures of public involvement in the urgent problems of war finance and postwar reconstruction. It is an extraordinary irony that the world would probably have been a better place if Keynes had spent the last ten years of his life in King's instead of in Whitehall. There were many to carry out the incorporation of *ersatz* Keynesianism into public policy but none to develop and extend the real theoretical revolution of 1936.

We have argued that the essence of the Keynesian Revolution revolved round questions of identification and that in solving these problems Keynes had to introduce three crucial elements: the consumption (savings) function, the demand for money, and the demand for labour as a derived demand. Taken together these elements are sufficient to demolish Say's Law and, in consequence, the logical basis of both neo-classical theory and 'natural rate'/New Classical theories of the recent past. In widening Keynes' analysis to provide a 'Keynesist' account of the problems of an open, inflation-prone managed economy, we need to provide extensions to Keynes' more limited analysis of a closed, fixprice economy. These extensions should satisfy the criteria of identifiability (and consequential questions of endogeneity, exogeneity and causality) and the looser but equally important proposition that because the market model generally fails the identifiability test, quantity reactions to changes in exogenous variables will generally be more powerful than price reactions.[3]

Exports and imports
Here the Keynesist tradition is quite straighforward. Just as consumption (savings) depends on both income and a relative price term (the interest rate), so exports (imports) will depend on the appropriate demand terms (world trade/domestic national income). There is a presumption that income elasticities will be fairly high and price elasticities fairly low.

Inflation
We have already noted that Keynes' account of the labour market leads to the belief that the real wage is determined by the demand for labour rather than the reverse. Thus a change in the money wage will lead to a change in the price level (given the level of

employment). It follows that any analysis of inflation in which unit wage costs determine prices can legitimately be thought of as Keynesist. This is so however the change in money wages comes about – whether autonomously or through some form of the augmented Phillips curve. More generally, unit costs will in an open economy include import unit costs (and so both world prices and the exchange rate) and, with active government fiscal policy, indirect tax rates.[4]

Thus any account of inflation which focuses on the determination of money wage (and other) unit costs can be called Keynesist. Conversely, theories such as monetarism are clearly anti-Keynesist for precisely the reason stated earlier: they rely on a direction of causality in the labour market which Keynes showed to be *logically* invalid.

Fiscal and monetary policy

It was argued earlier that the exogeneity of the money supply was essential for Keynes to develop a fully identified (determinate) theory of interest rates. Clearly that is not the case. The change in the money supply is dependent in part on fiscal policy for it is equal to the government deficit *less* net sales of bonds to the non-bank private sector:

$$\Delta M_s = (G - T) - \Delta B$$

This poses no great problem, however, for together with a money demand equation

$$M_d = f(Y, r)$$

(which is implicitly a demand-for-bonds equation) and the market clearing condition, the system is complete. To be sure, monetary and fiscal policies are no longer independent but that is not to say that the system is under-identified.[5]

We may conclude, then, that there does exist a comprehensive body of Keynesist analysis which is logically sound and in principle capable of explaining contemporary developments in economies such as that of the UK. We can now, at last, look at the Great Recession of 1974–84 through those Keynesist spectacles.

II The proximate causes of the Great Recession

In this section we first try to assess how deep the recession has been and, secondly, try to isolate and quantify the major autonomous and policy changes which caused it. These exogenous factors are those consistent with the 'Keynesist' analysis adumbrated in section I. If this exercise is judged to be successful, the

Keynesist approach is vindicated. If it is not, then there is truth in the accusation that Keynesist analysis is shown to be at least insufficient and possibly falsified by the UK experience.

One way of approaching the second of these questions would be to perform extensive simulation studies with one or more of the large econometric models of the economy. There are, however, some difficulties. First, the models differ quite significantly amongst themselves: we do not have a unique, neutral, 'nearest the truth' model on which to rely (see Wallis *et al.* (1984); on related issues see Artis (1983)). Secondly, these models are now typically so big that there is a severe 'wood and trees' problem: major lines of causation are often extremely difficult to discern and identifiability complex to the point of impossibility.[6]

There is thus a strong case for using a much simpler, broad-brush, approach. This involves trying to assess the quantitative contribution of each exogenous factor to the total shortfall in demand and output – these are the *proximate* causes of the shortfall (i.e. before allowing for the multiplier and feedback effects which ensue). The first question, however, is to assess the scale of the recession.

Measuring the depth of the recession

In 1974 the number of unemployed (excluding school-leavers) stood at 560,000 or 2.4 per cent of the working population. By 1984 this figure had risen to 3,050,000, or 11.2 per cent respectively (CSO, 1986, p.99). In order to analyse the proximate causes of the rise it is first necessary to estimate how much higher total output would have had to have been in 1984 to have kept unemployment at the 1974 level. This entails two steps: first, how much extra employment would have been needed to stabilize unemployment as officially computed (i.e. excluding non-claimants)? And secondly, how much higher would output have had to have been to generate the required increase in employment?

The relationship between employment and unemployment is complicated by the fact that the official figures are based on the numbers claiming unemployment benefit. This differs from the concept of demand-deficiency unemployment for a variety of reasons: for example, it excludes those available for work but ineligible for benefit (for instance, a large proportion of married women, long-term involuntary unemployed who have become discouraged from active search) and fails to take account of possible 'distortions' caused by special employment measures. On the other hand, it includes those who receive benefit but would not normally be regarded as unemployed because of demand deficiency – structural and frictional unemployment. Nevertheless, empirical estimates generally suggest that rather more than a unit increase in employment is needed to reduce the (measured) unemployment rate by one unit. The National Institute model of the UK economy, for example, puts the relationship at –1.05 (National Institute, 1984, eq. 7.6).

There is some disagreement about the elasticity of employment with respect to output. In the non-marketed public sector, where output is conventionally estimated from employment indicators, the elasticity is usually imposed at unity. In the private sector, some models similarly impose a unit long-run elasticity to reflect the assumption of constant returns to scale. When the relationship is estimated freely, however, the elasticity is generally found to be in the range 0.6–0.8 (Wallis *et al.*, 1984, ch. 4.3) For the economy as a whole, an elasticity of 0.75 seems to be a reasonable assumption.

Between 1974 and 1984, the level of unemployment rose by just under 2.5 million, suggesting that employment would have had to have been some 2.6 million, or nearly 10 per cent higher than it actually was in 1984 to have kept unemployment at the 1974 level. Correspondingly, GDP would have had to have been nearly 13 per cent or some £27 billion (at 1980 prices) higher. This, then, is a rough estimate of the size of the shortfall from the 'full-employment' level of output associated with the recession.

The required growth rate over the decade was, on that basis, 2.0 per cent per annum compared with the actual growth rate (excluding oil production) of 0.8 per cent. This is not inconsistent with the casual observation that between 1981 and 1984 the actual growth rate of GDP (again excluding oil) of 2.2 per cent per annum just failed to stabilize unemployment (allowance must be made for lags).

Factors contributing to the Great Recession
If the Keynesist model outlined earlier is correct then it should be possible to identify as proximate (i.e. pre-feedback) causes of the recession of the last decade the following: changes in 'autonomous' expenditure – public sector consumption, investment and transfers, private sector investment and exports – and changes in behavioural parameters – tax rates, the import propensity and the savings ratio. The comparison to be made is between what actually happened and a counterfactual construction consistent with the preservation of full employment.

In the previous section it was shown that real GDP in 1984 would have had to be some £27 billion above its actual level to keep employment at its 1974 level. As a benchmark we therefore scale up the 1974 expenditure and the income data by the implied real growth rate of 2.6 per cent per annum (including oil) and compare these hypothetical full-employment, or potential, figures with the out-turns. In the case of the four kinds of (loosely) autonomous expenditure – private and public fixed investment, government current expenditure on goods and services, and exports – this is a straightforward projection. In the case of the propensities to save, to tax (indirectly and directly), to transfer current income from the public to the private sector

Table 6.1 Proximate autonomous contributions to 1984 GDP shortfall

£m	1974	1984(act.)	1984(pot.)	Shortfall (£m)	(%)
Ipv	31,895	39,704	41,081	1,377	7.5
Ig	10,277	5,687	13,237	7,550	41.3
Gc	43,296	50,689	56,577	5,888	32.2
X	52,755	68,528	67,948	–580	–3.2
%					
s	11.9	11.7	11.9	20	0.1
ti	15.7	23.0	15.7	10,618	58.1
td	20.2	20.5	20.2	627	3.4
tr	10.3	13.9	10.3	–7,522	–41.2
m	19.9	21.9	19.9	289	1.6
				18,276	100.0

Notes

Ipv   Private sector gross fixed investment (£m 1980).

Ig   Public sector gross fixed investment (£m 1980).

Gc   General government current expenditure in goods and services (£m. 1980).

X   Exports of goods and services (£m 1980).

s   Personal sector saving as % personal disposable income.

ti   Taxes on expenditure less subsidies as % consumers' expenditure.

td   Personal sector taxes on income plus National Insurance, etc. contributions as % total personal income.

tr   Current grants to personal sector as % total personal income (corrected for unemployment change).

Source   1985 Blue Book.

and to import, the 'contributions' to the shortfall represent and change in the relevant propensity (1974–84) multiplied by the appropriate actual 1984 base.

A number of features stand out from the table. First, the major shortfalls in demand were attributable to the increase in indirect taxes and to government expenditure (public sector investment fell by 45 per cent during the decade and current spending rose by only just over $1\frac{1}{2}$ per cent per annum). On the other hand, transfer payments to the personal sector from general government rose sharply (even after adjusting unemployment benefit and short-term social security for the rise in unemployment). Secondly, and perhaps surprisingly, the figures suggest that the supposed world trade recession played no part whatsoever in the UK recession – exports grew at almost exactly the potential growth rate of GDP against a background of total growth of 4 per cent per annum and trade in manufactures of over 5 per cent per annum. Nor did the small rise in the UK's propensity to import contribute significantly. The analysis shows beyond reasonable doubt that the recession can be attributed to government fiscal policies and to them alone.

Taken together, these proximate causes of the relative fall in demand between 1974 and 1984 account for some £18 billion out of the total estimated shortfall of around £27 billion. But the various elements contributing to the £18 billion shortfall do not allow for multiplier effects. The simple Keynesian multiplier in the present context is approximated by $1/(s+ti+td-tr+m)$ which, taking rough average values, would be $1/(.12+.23+.20-.12+.20) = 1/0.63 = 1.59$. And $1.59 \times £18$ bn $= £28$ bn, remarkably close (given the roughness of the arithmetic) to the overall shortfall of £27 billion.

It seems, then, that a Keynesist analysis of the most unreconstructed sort is entirely adequate to explain the underlying causes of the recession in 'real' terms. What, though, of inflation – the policy problem which ostensibly dominated policy strategy throughout the decade? An ultra–Keynesist, with his inbuilt suspicion of market-based models, might be very sceptical about the theoretical foundations of the Phillips curve, based as it is on the presumption that in the 'labour market' the relevant 'price' (the money wage) will adjust according to excess supply/demand (as proxied by unemployment).

The clearest way to tackle the question is to take an augmented Phillips curve wage-price model of an open economy with an active indirect tax policy and explore the implications of an unemployment influence tending to zero. In algebraic form we can posit:

$$w = \alpha - \beta U + \lambda p_{-i}$$
$$p = (1 - \gamma)(w - q)_{-j} + \gamma pm + \delta t_i$$

where w = change in money, p = change in price level, pm = change in import prices, t_i = change in indirect tax rates, q = underlying productivity trend, γ = proportion of import prices in final prices and i and j are unspecified lags.

Solving for the reduced-form price equation, we find

$$p = \alpha(1-\gamma) - \beta(1-\gamma)U_{-j} + \lambda(1-\gamma)p_{-i-j} + \gamma pm + \delta ti$$

Let us assume for convenience that $i+j = 1$. Then as $\lambda \to 1$ (wage-bargainers fully compensate for inflation),

$$p \to \alpha(1-\gamma) + \beta(1-\gamma)U_{-j} + (1-\gamma)p_{-1} + \gamma pm + \delta t_1$$

and as $\beta \to 0$,

$$p \to \alpha(1-\gamma) + (1-\gamma)p_{-1} + \gamma pm + \delta t_1$$

So on this 'extreme Keynesist' view of the inflationary process, the rate of domestic price inflation depends solely on the rate of change of (sterling) import prices – which, of course, is determined by changes in the exchange rate as well as by changes in the world prices – and changes in indirect tax rates.

It is an easy matter to obtain 'extraneous' estimates of γ and δ. Taking 1980 as the base year and the total final expenditure deflator as the most general indicator of overall UK prices, we have:

1980(£m)		%
Total final expenditure:	287,729	112.0
–Indirect taxes less subsidies:	–30,765	–12.0
=TFE at factor cost:	256,964	100
of which:		
Imports of goods and services:	57,718	22.5
Home costs	199,246	77.5

Thus import and net indirect tax costs contribute in the ratios of 22.5:12.0 or 65:35. We may therefore construct a variable $(0.65pm + 0.35ti)$ in order to explore the degree to which this accounts for changes in inflation during the recession.[7]

Given the naivety of the calculations the results are surely striking.

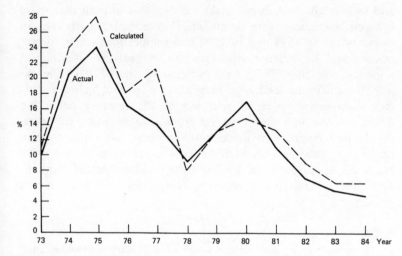

Figure 6.1 Total final expenditure deflator 1973–84: actual and calculated (% change p.a.)

(see Figure 6.1) Three factors in particular stand out. First, the general pattern in the inflation rate over the decade was predicted with considerable accuracy. Secondly, the implicit constant term in the equation (at about $1\frac{3}{4}$ per cent) seems a reasonable estimate of the growth of labour productivity. Thirdly, the sharp fall in actual as opposed to calculated inflation in 1977 (and the apparent 'catch-up' over the next three years) is entirely consistent with econometric assessments of the Social Contract and its aftermath (see, for example, Henry and Ormerod (1978)).

III Summary and conclusions

This essay has sought to show that an analysis based entirely on what I have termed 'Keynesist' principles – the explicit arguments of the *General Theory* together with extensions into the fields of foreign trade and, especially, inflation – is entirely capable of explaining economic developments in the UK during the Great Recession of the last decade. In particular, there are no grounds for asserting, as politicians from all parties have done, that we have learned that 'we cannot spend our way out of recession' (Callaghan, 1976), and there are no grounds for believing that the rate of inflation has anything *directly* to do with the level of unemployment or the thrust of fiscal policy.

Of course the recession has not been homogeneous. Our comparison simply between 1974 and 1984 as the latter year was and as it might have been masks the fact that in particular years different influences were dominant. For example, sharp rises in world prices in 1974 and in 1980 had implications for both real activity and for inflation while rises in indirect tax rates played a similar role in 1975–77 and, notoriously, in 1979–80. The extent to which the exchange rate was an indirect policy instrument (interest rate policy and use of the reserves being the direct instruments) also changed from year to year. But even the limited comparison made here between two isolated years serves to show that the UK recession, far from showing the Keynesist approach to be irrelevant to problems of the modern, open and inflation-prone economy, vindicates it in every major respect.

Notes

1. The common term 'post-Keynesian' is ambiguous – it could as well mean 'after' Keynes in the sense of 'after Keynes had been discredited'.
2. Indeed, the crude income/expenditure cross model of early (American) Keynesians took account of only the first.
3. This is not to suggest that Keynes was unaware of these problems but, in the circumstances of the time and given the need to present the already complex argument as clearly as possible, it made sense to keep the central argument as simple as possible.
4. Note that neither an augmented Phillips curve nor money wage autonomy is necessary: if the level of unemployment plays no role in wage-bargaining (an extreme Keynesist position), all that follows is that import prices (and other non-wage factors) determine the rate of domestic inflation (see pp. 121–3 below).
5. This can be shown algebraically but the manipulations required are too lengthy and tedious to reproduce here.
6. In practice, econometric modellers tend to assume the absence of under-identified equations on the grounds that in the models as a whole, the number of exogenous variables considerably exceeds the number of behavioural equations.
7. The import price variable is actually $(0.5 \, pm + 0.5 \, pm_{-1})$ to allow for lags.

7 Keynesian economics: The road to nowhere?
Bill Gerrard

Introduction

Economics in the last fifty years has been mainly Keynesian economics, inspired by Keynes' *General Theory*. Keynes challenged classical theory, the then prevailing orthodoxy in economics. Classical theory concluded that the economy tends automatically to a position of full employment if the price mechanism is free to operate in all markets. Keynes claimed to have broken away from this orthodoxy by showing that it is possible for involuntary unemployment to occur without any automatic tendency to recovery.

Keynesian economics has been an attempt to understand and elaborate on Keynes' claim, coupled with the development of appropriate policies to overcome involuntary unemployment. But within Keynesian economics, there have been and still are many deep divisions over just exactly what causes involuntary unemployment. Many Keynesians have tried to understand Keynes from the standpoint of classical theory. This is what I would call *mainstream Keynesianism* – Keynesianism that remains firmly wedded to the *market-theoretic approach* of classical theory but arrives at Keynesian conclusions. Mainstream Keynesianism is the search for the 'missing link' that reconciles the existence of involuntary unemployment with the market-theoretic approach.

Over the years there have been many attempts to provide the Keynesian missing link – the IS–LM model, the neo-classical synthesis, the disequilibrium and neo-Walrasian analyses, and the recent work on imperfect competition and imperfect information. Yet all these varied contributions can, I believe, be interpreted as a coherent research programme in which each new phase of development flowed from the perceived deficiencies of the previous phase. The object of this paper is to elaborate on this interpretation of mainstream Keynesianism and to offer an evaluation of the contribution of mainstream Keynesianism to the development of economic thought.

Keynesianism phase I

The IS–LM model

The IS–LM model is the starting-point for mainstream Keynesianism. The IS–LM model was developed by Hicks (1937) as an attempt to clarify the General Theory. It captured the essential change in the 'style' of economic theory that Keynes had instigated. Classical theory takes a 'bottom-up' approach, concentrating on the determination of prices and physical quantities within individual markets. The focus is on the micro-level, on the behaviour of rational economic agents. The macro-results of classical theory, such as full-employment equilibrium and the neutrality of money, are clearly derived from its micro-foundations. Keynesian economics, on the other hand, focuses directly on the macro-level, dealing with the determination of aggregate monetary flows.

The IS–LM model analyses the demand-side of the economy in terms of three aggregate behavioural relationships:

1   the consumption (or savings) function;
2   the investment function; and
3   the demand for money function.

Given these three functions, the level of money income and the rate of interest are determined such that the goods and money markets are in equilibrium simultaneously.

On its own, however, the IS–LM model is inadequate for an analysis of unemployment. The reason lies in the change to the macro-style of theory. The IS–LM model derives the equilibrium level of aggregate *money* income. But the level of employment (and unemployment) depends on the level of physical output, i.e. *real* income. To move from monetary flows to employment levels it is necessary to determine the composition of money income in terms of physical output and nominal value. Without a solution to this 'transformation problem' the IS–LM model cannot analyse unemployment. Hicks bridged the theoretical gap between the aggregate monetary flow and the level of employment (what could be called the 'Keynesian dichotomy') by the assumption of a fixed money wage. Given this assumption, it follows that the level of money income and the level of employment are positively related. Hence a position of full employment is associated with a particular level of money income. This creates the possibility of an unemployment equilibrium in which the demand-side of the economy is in equilibrium at a level of money income below that necessary for full employment.

The Hicksian IS-LM model views the General Theory as an inversion of the classical vision of the economy in which the supply-side drives the whole system. In the IS–LM model, the supply-side exerts no causal influence in the determination of the level of employment. Instead, the level of employment is entirely consequent on the demand-side. This implies two fundamental breaks with the method of classical theory. First, the economy is no longer seen in purely market-theoretic terms since there is no labour market. The money wage is assumed to be exogenously given rather than being determined by the forces of demand and supply. Secondly, there is now an element of *sequentialism* introduced into the theoretical structure. The classical theory of general equilibrium is concerned with the *simultaneous* determination of all prices and quantities. In the IS–LM model this simultaneity is retained only with respect to the demand-side. The supply-side outcomes (i.e. output and employment levels) are now entirely consequent on the demand-side rather than being co-determinate.

The methodological innovations of the IS–LM model were never made explicit. Instead the 'Keynes v. the Classics' debate centred on the theoretical implications of Keynes. The obvious 'innovation' of Keynes is the multiplier, the notion that investment and saving would be brought into equilibrium by changes in the level of money income. In classical theory any change in aggregate demand would be completely offset by the automatic movement of the appropriate price, namely, the rate of interest. In Keynesian theory, however, any change in aggregate demand would create a reinforcing multiplier effect through the consumption function.

But, according to Hicks's analysis, the consumption function is not incompatible with classical theory. Indeed, it follows directly from the micro-analysis of consumer behaviour under budget constraints. The consumption function falls into the background in classical theory because the level of money income is fixed by the money supply via the quantity theory of money. The existence of a multiplier effect requires the possibility that any given money supply can be associated with various equilibrium levels of money income. It is precisely just this possibility that is denied by the quantity theory of money, but is created by liquidity preference, the notion that the demand for money depends partly on the rate of interest.

Liquidity preference prevents the rate of interest from automatically adjusting to the natural rate, thus ensuring the sufficiency of aggregate demand. Liquidity preference introduces monetary factors into the determination of the rate of interest. This destroys the classical dichotomy and creates the possibility that the equilibrium rate of interest may not be the natural rate of interest (now defined as that rate of interest which generates a level of investment equal to the level of savings that is associated with the full employment level of money income).

For Hicks then, the crucial innovation in the *General Theory* is liquidity preference. But, as Hicks points out, liquidity preference is not really an innovation of Keynes. It can be seen as an extension of the Cambridge demand for money function which had already been proposed most notably by Lavington. Whereas the original Cambridge demand for money function considered money only in its role as a means of exchange, liquidity preference introduces money's other role as a store of wealth. On this view, the importance of Keynes lies in his being the first to appreciate the significance of this development. A similar conclusion is drawn on the multiplier effect which, although highlighted by Keynes, had been proposed originally by Kahn.

The view of Keynes that emerges from Hicks is very much that of an economist making a 'great leap forward' in the development of classical theory. In theoretical terms, the 'leap forward' consisted of the development of liquidity preference and its consequences, coupled with the macro style of presentation. That Hicks saw Keynes as wholly within the orthodox tradition is evident from his argument that Keynes' theory is just a special case of what Hicks called the 'Generalised General Theory', of which classical theory and so-called Treasury view are other special cases. In effect, all that Keynes is seen to have done is to give a sophisticated elaboration of the problems of demand-side maladjustment, particularly those created by the influence of monetary factors on the rate of interest. The extreme case of this occurs when the demand for money becomes infinitely elastic with respect to the rate of interest when the economy is in a liquidity trap. This possibility is what Hicks terms 'Mr Keynes' Special Theory'. Later, Keynesians also considered demand-side maladjustment caused by investment being interest-inelastic.

The difference between the form of the classical and Keynesian analyses of demand-side maladjustment due to the Keynesian introduction of liquidity preference leads to a crucial difference in consequences. Whereas in classical theory there exists an automatic tendency for the rate of interest to adjust to ensure a return to a full employment equilibrium (in the absence of any supply-side problem), there is no such tendency in the Keynesian theory. Following on from this, the importance of Keynes' theoretical contribution lies in its provision of a justification for the need for systematic government intervention to ensure sufficient aggregate demand to maintain full employment. This policy implication became the very essence of Keynesianism. Furthermore, this *necessity* for demand management became associated with the *need* to use fiscal policy especially if the economy is caught in a liquidity trap and/or investment is interest-inelastic. In both these circumstances monetary policy is rendered completely ineffective and there is no crowding-out effect to reduce the effectiveness of a fiscal expansion.

The neo-classical synthesis
The IS–LM model focuses on the demand-side of the economy with the employment implications of any demand-side equilibrium being derived by using a fixed money-wage assumption to bridge the 'Keynesian dichotomy'. From the orthodox point of view, this assumption is the crucial weakness of the IS–LM model since, in effect, it removes the entire supply-side of the economy from the analysis. Thus the orthodox theorists viewed the IS–LM model as only a partial equilibrium analysis which had to be extended into a general equilibrium analysis by introducing the labour market. This is exactly what Modigliani (1944) did in his paper 'Liquidity Preference and the Theory of Interest and Money'. The consequences were inevitable:

> It is usually considered as one of the most important achievements of the Keynesian theory that it explains the consistency of economic equilibrium with the presence of involuntary unemployment. It is, however, not sufficiently recognised that, except in a limiting case . . ., this result is due entirely to the assumption of 'rigid wages' and not to the Keynesian liquidity preference. (Modigliani, 1944, p. 65)

Bringing the labour market back into the model returns the analysis to its classical market-theoretic form. If the labour market is competitive there is a tendency for the real wage to adjust to ensure full employment. The substantive Keynesian innovation is the introduction of liquidity preference which alters the process whereby sufficient aggregate demand is generated. Given that the rate of interest is now influenced by both real and monetary factors it is possible that, at the existing aggregate price level, the equilibrium rate of interest may not be the natural rate. To compensate for this, it now falls on the aggregate price level to adjust to ensure the sufficiency of aggregate demand. If there is a lack of aggregate demand the price level tends to fall which increases the real value of the money supply and in turn produces an expansion-inducing fall in the rate of interest – the so-called *Keynes effect*. Thus in the neo–classical model, real wage adjustments ensure a full-employment level of aggregate supply while a combination of interest rate and price adjustments ensure sufficient aggregate demand. Again the money wage plays a crucial role. There is a unique money wage that renders consistent the supply-determined real wage and the demand-determined price level.

Having reintroduced the labour market, Modigliani found, not surprisingly, that, except for a limiting case, involuntary unemployment (i.e. a level of unemployment above the natural rate) is caused by 'rigid [money] wages' – the traditional classical argument of supply-side imperfection leading to real wage maladjustment. The limiting case to which Modigliani referred is the situation in which the natural rate of interest is too low to be attainable. This can happen either because of the existence of a liquidity trap or because investment is so interest-inelastic that the natural rate of interest is negative. Hence the limiting case is that of interest rate maladjustment leading to a below full employment level of aggregate demand. The causes of involuntary unemployment are essentially the same as those provided by the classical theorists prior to Keynes. The only Keynesian innovation is to alter the analysis of interest rate maladjustment on the demand-side through the introduction of liquidity preference.

Modigliani laid the foundations for the emergence of the *neo-classical synthesis* in which orthodox theorists believed that they had integrated Keynes within the classical tradition. The neo-classical synthesis combines the market-theoretic theory with the Keynesian macro 'style' of analysis. The basic vision is that the economy is a generalized market system in which demand-and-supply analysis is the starting-point for understanding the operation of individual markets. The macro-style of analysis comes into its own when the focus of attention moves from partial equilibrium to general equilibrium. Macro-economics provides a means of 'getting a handle on' the important interrelationships between markets, the multiplier effect being the most prominent. The Keynesian Revolution became regarded as a revolution only in style in which the basic vision of the economic system remained unaltered.

If a market-theoretic approach is adopted, it follows that, in general, the perfect flexibility of all prices (including wages and interest rates) ensures a continual tendency towards a position of generalized market-clearing and, in particular, a full employment equilibrium. This is a basic truth accepted by all who work within the neo-classical synthesis. This implies that if there is a prolonged period of involuntary unemployment, it must be caused by the existence of imperfections that are blocking the free operation of competitive forces on the supply-side and/or the demand-side. The market-theoretic approach necessarily leads to *imperfectionist* theories of involuntary unemployment. The crucial issue becomes the evalution of the degree of imperfection present in the market economy.

The Keynesian–neo-classical debate

The Keynesian–neo-classical debate was a debate *within* the neo-classical synthesis. Both schools accepted the market-theoretic approach and adopted imperfectionist theories of unemployment. They agreed over the fundamentals but differed over the extent and persistence of imperfections in the market economy and whether or not other automatic mechanisms existed which could overcome the effects of these imperfections. The Keynesians were characterized by their belief in the significance of imperfections and in the lack of automatic adjustment mechanisms that would be effective within a short-run time-scale. The neo-classicals, on the other hand, argued for the efficacy of the price mechanism. The Keynesian–neo-classical debate focused on four specific issues.

The form of the aggregate behavioural functions

The consumption function In the Keynesian consumption function, it is the level of current income which determines the level of current consumption. This is the most crucial relationship in Keynesian theory since it is responsible for generating the multiplier process. An increase in the current flow of income leads to an increase in the flow of consumption which, in turn, leads to a further increase in income and so on. Neo-classical theorists, on the other hand, have tended to play down the role of current income, stressing instead the importance of wealth (both current and expected) as well as the rate of interest, as the determinants of consumption. Friedman's permanent income hypothesis and Ando and Modigliani's life-cycle hypothesis are examples of the neo-classical consumption function in which current consumption is partly stock-determined as well as flow-determined (Friedman, 1957; Ando and Modigliani, 1963). The less flow-determined is consumption, the more stable is the economic system, since, in the event of a fall in current income, agents can liquidate some of their stocks of wealth in order to maintain a constant level of consumption.

The investment function Neo-classical theorists see the rate of interest as the most significant determinant of the level of investment, Jorgenson's 'cost of-capital' theory being a more sophisticated development of this traditional supply-side theory of investment

(Jorgenson, 1967). Keynesians, on the other hand, have stressed demand-side factors, usually presented in terms of an *accelerator* mechanism in which the level of investment is determined by changes in the income flow (Chenery, 1952). The accelerator mechanism reinforces the instability effect of the multiplier process.

The demand-for-money function   Neoclassical theorists remained firmly wedded to the quantity theory tradition with a relatively interest-inelastic demand-for-money function, the rate of interest being considered essentially a non-monetary phenomenon. Keynesians took a diametrically opposed view, seeing the rate of interest as a significant factor in the money market rather than the goods market. The Keynesians have argued for an interest-elastic demand-for-money function, the liquidity trap being an extreme case. One important development from the Keynesian viewpoint was Baumol's demonstration that the transactions demand would also be sensitive to the rate of interest (Baumol, 1952).

Overall, in the debate over the aggregate behavioural functions, the neo-classicals have argued for the level of aggregate demand to be the outcome of a stock allocation process in which the rate of interest plays a key equilibrating role. This implies that the economic system is reasonably stable around a full employment equilibrium. Keynesians, however, have tended to highlight the potential instability of the system. This instability is created by the level of aggregate demand being primarily determined by the income flow, stock adjustments and the rate of interest having only a minimal impact in the goods market.

Growth

The Keynesian–neo-classical debate over the *short-run* stability of a market economy had its *long-run* counterpart in the debates between the Keynesian Harrod–Domar growth model and Solow's neoclassical growth model (Harrod, 1939; Solow, 1956). The Harrod–Domar model merged the multiplier and accelerator mechanisms to model the long-run growth path of an economy. The result was the famous knife-edge solution in which it is shown that there is no automatic mechanism to ensure that an economy grows at a rate sufficient to ensure full employment over time. The neo-classical response was to argue that factor-price adjustments provided just such a mechanism. The emergence of long-run involuntary unemployment would tend to lower labour costs relative to capital costs, thereby inducing a transfer towards more labour-intensive production techniques. Thus even in the long run the price mechanism is sufficiently effective to ensure a Golden Age growth path in which full employment is maintained over time as the labour force grows.

The wealth effect

The wealth effect is the overall impact on the level of aggregate demand caused by a change in the real value of the stock of wealth following a change in the aggregate price level. Keynesians argued that the wealth effect operated *indirectly* via the Keynes effect. A price deflation could increase aggregate demand by inducing an investment-stimulating fall in the rate of interest as agents engage in a portfolio readjustment process to remove their excess real cash balances by buying bonds. Keynesians believed that the expansionary effect of a price deflation would be small, there being no effect at all if the economy is in a liquidity trap or if investment is interest-inelastic. Both these situations would render the Keynes effect inoperative.

Neo-classicals countered by arguing that the Keynesians had a very restricted view of the wealth effect. Not only did the wealth effect operate indirectly via the rate of interest, it also had a *direct* impact on the level of aggregate demand via the 'Pigou effect' (Patinkin, 1959). This direct wealth effect follows necessarily from the various neo-classical consumption functions which all include some form of asset variable as a primary determinant of current consumption. The existence of a direct wealth effect ensures that the price mechanism will overcome automatically any involuntary unemployment caused by demand-side maladjustment. Through the Pigou effect, a fall in the aggregate price level will compensate for any inadequacy in the interest rate adjustment mechanism (i.e. the Keynes effect) caused by the existence of a liquidity trap or by investment being interest-inelastic. Thus the Pigou effect overcomes Modigliani's limiting case of demand-side maladjustment, implying that an involuntary unemployment equilibrium occurs if and only if there is supply-side maladjustment. In other words, in the neo-classical view of the world, the ultimate cause of an involuntary unemployment equilibrium is the presence of wage rigidity in the labour market.

Policy implications

Since they believed that involuntary unemployment is due to a lack of aggregate demand, Keynesians advocated government intervention to increase aggregate demand. Furthermore, Keynesians tended to adopt a *fiscalist* stance – a belief that fiscal policy is more effective than monetary policy. Fiscalism is a necessary consequence of the Keynesian belief that the Keynes effect is of relatively minor importance. In such circumstances, fiscal policy becomes all-powerful since there is no crowding-out effect to reduce its impact. On the other hand, monetary policy becomes completely ineffective since the causal chain linking the money and goods markets is broken if there is a liquidity trap or if investment is interest-inelastic.

Neo-classicals argued against an expansionary fiscal policy on two grounds: (1) the crowding-out effect of any fiscal expansion would be very significant: and (2) anyway the problem lay on the supply-side not the demand-side since the price mechanism would be sufficient to overcome any demand-side maladjustment.

Keynesianism phase II

Patinkin's disequilibrium analysis
The link between phases I and II in the development of Keynesian economics is provided by Patinkin in his book *Money, Interest and Prices* (1956). Once the direct component of the wealth effect is considered, movements in the aggregate price level overcome any interest rate maladjustment on the demand side of the economy. Hence, if the economy is in equilibrium at below full employment there must be supply-side maladjustment – i.e. wage rigidity. Patinkin expressed this conclusion in terms of what he called his 'coexistence theorem': the coexistence of money wage flexibility and equilibrium precludes involuntary unemployment. Keynesian economics becomes just the macro-analysis of the effects of wage rigidity – a classical diagnosis of the causes of unemployment.

Patinkin concluded that if Keynes was saying something new, the *General Theory* had to involve a change in the *method* of analysis. Keynesianism Phase I had reached classical conclusions because it retained the classical method that treated involuntary unemployment as a *static equilibrium* phenomenon. Wage rigidity necessarily follows as the cause of this unemployment with the implication that a return to full employment requires a reduction in the real wage rate. An alternative that, according to Patinkin, was adopted at least implicitly by Keynes, is to see involuntary unemployment as a *dynamic disequilibrium* phenomenon. It is this change in approach that marks the beginning of Keynesianism Phase II.

The change in method from a static equilibrium analysis to a dynamic disequilibrium analysis meant that involuntary unemployment was no longer seen in terms of rigidities that prevented any adjustment, but rather in terms of slow *speeds of adjustment*. Involuntary unemployment is caused by the inevitable time-lags involved in the dynamic process of adjustment towards equilibrium. On this view the Keynesian–neo-classical debate is not about the degree of flexibility of prices (including wages and interest rates). Rather it concerns the speed of adjustment of the market mechanism, the neo-classicals believing the market mechanism to be relatively quick whereas the Keynesians believe it to be relatively slow, thereby leading to significant levels of involuntary unemployment during any period of disequilibrium.

Patinkin explained the difference between neo-classical and Keynesian analyses by comparing their respective analyses of the effects of a fall in aggregate demand. In the neo-classical analysis, the fall in aggregate demand automatically triggers market forces which tend to offset it quickly. In particular, the fall in the aggregate price level generates a rise in aggregate demand via the wealth effect. Given the temporary nature of the fall in aggregate demand, firms do not reduce their output and employment levels. Thus no involuntary unemployment occurs under the neo-classical analysis.

In the Keynesian analysis, aggregate demand recovers relatively slowly so that the adjustment process becomes prolonged. Firms eventually have to reduce their output and employment levels to bring them into line with current sales, thus creating involuntary unemployment. In effect, the demand constraint faced by firms in the goods market forces them to move to positions *off* their output supply and labour demand curves. Given the existing set of market prices and wages, firms would like to sell more output and employ more labour but are prevented from realizing these wishes by the lack of aggregate demand. The involuntary unemployment that occurs in the Keynesian analysis is a disequilibrium phenomenon since there are forces at work, albeit slow-working, which will move the economy away from this position. The excess supply of labour will tend to push down the money wage rate while the non-realization of desired output supply will tend to lead firms to reduce their price levels. The combination of price and wage deflation will eventually ensure that there is sufficient aggregate demand for a return to full employment.

Thus, under Patinkin's analysis, involuntary unemployment can exist in a system in which all markets are perfectly competitive and prices and wages are flexible. Money wage rigidity is no longer a necessary condition for the existence of involuntary unemployment. Rather, involuntary unemployment arises from the slowness of adjustment following an exogenous disturbance that reduces aggregate demand. The persistence of insufficient demand eventually forces firms to reduce their output and employment levels. The involuntary unemployment that results is a disequilibrium phenomenon since a slow-working adjustment process exists which will eventually return the economy to a full-employment equilibrium.

Hence involuntary unemployment is necessarily dynamic in nature, involving movements off the demand and supply schedules of agents.

This disequilibrium analysis has two important policy implications. First, it justifies government intervention to stimulate aggregate demand in the event of involuntary unemployment emerging when the speed of the self-adjusting mechanisms within the economy is too slow to ensure a return to full employment within an 'acceptable' time-period. The justification for government intervention is not based on *a priori* principles but is a matter of empirical investigation on the speed of adjustment and political judgement over what constitutes an acceptable period of disequilibrium. Secondly, the view of involuntary unemployment as a dynamic disequilibrium phenomenon implies that a fall in real wages is neither a necessary nor a sufficient condition for the rapid re-establishment of a full-employment equilibrium. If an economy is at full employment and a exogenous shock reduces the level of demand, involuntary unemployment occurs even though the real wage is at the market-clearing level. The return to full employment does not, therefore require a fall in the real wage. The notion that a real wage is necessary for a return to full employment arises from the use of static equilibrium analysis in which involuntary unemployment is ultimately seen to be due to wage rigidities.

Clower and the dual decision hypothesis

In his 1965 paper 'The Keynesian Counter-Revolution: A Theoretical Appraisal', Clower (1979) produced a disequilibrium analysis that complemented Patinkin's contribution. Whereas Patinkin had been concerned with the effects on the labour market of excess supply in the goods market, Clower was concerned with the effects on the goods market of excess supply in the labour market. Clower dealt with the 'other side of the coin' as regards the implications of the price mechanism having a slow speed of adjustment.

Clower proposed the *dual decision hypothesis*. Given the existing price vector, households plan their notional consumption demand on the basis of some notional level of income to be obtained from the sale of their labour services. If the household sells its notional supply it will have sufficient income with which to achieve its notional level of consumption. However, if the household fails to sell its notional labour supply, actual income is less than notional income. The failure to realize notional income necessitates a second round of decisions by the household in which actual consumption demand is reduced. This actual consumption demand based on realized income is what Clower called *effective* demand – demand that can be effected in the market.

Notional consumption demand equates to effective consumption demand at the aggregate level if and only if full employment pertains since, by definition, this is the only circumstance in which all workers realize their notional labour supply. Thus, if involuntary unemployment emerges in the labour market, via the dual decision hypothesis, this will have a spillover effect on the goods market – excess supply in the labour market will generate excess supply in the goods market.

Generalized disequilibrium analysis and the neo-Walrasian interpretation of Keynes
The analyses provided by Patinkin and Clower are complementary. Patinkin showed the process whereby the emergence of excess supply in the goods market would generate excess supply in the labour market while Clower showed the process whereby excess supply in the labour market would generate excess supply in the goods market. These two processes obviously interact in a mutually reinforcing manner. From Patinkin's analysis a fall in aggregate demand leads to involuntary unemployment which, in turn, from Clower's analysis, leads to a further fall in aggregate demand, and so on. There is, in other words, a *multiplier effect* by which an initial disturbance is transmitted through the economy and thereby perpetuated. The integration of the separate analyses of Patinkin and Clower was achieved by Barro and Grossman in their 1971 paper 'A General Disequilibrium Model of Income and Employment' (Barro and Grossman, 1971; 1976).

Barro and Grossman show that, in the absence of price adjustments, the emergence of excess supply in the goods market sets in motion a multiplier process which continues until the economy reaches the quasi-equilibrium in which firms have adjusted their output and employment levels in line with the level of effective demand in the goods market. At this quasi-equilibrium, all agents are optimizing, given the constraints placed on their decisions by the persistence of generalized excess notional supply. The consistency of these constrained behaviour patterns means that the economy may suffer a period of prolonged involuntary unemployment. But such a position is still a disequilibrium one since eventually the pressure of excess notional supply in the goods and labour markets will bring about a fall in prices and money wages. The fall in the price level will induce a positive wealth effect which will stimulate aggregate demand and thereby begin a multiplier process in an expansionary direction, resulting in a return to a full-employment general equilibrium.

Generalized excess supply is the disequilibrium position generated by an adverse movement on the demand-side. Barro and Grossman recognized that this is only one type of disequilibrium. They also considered the case of generalized excess demand caused by an increase in aggregate demand in the goods market which firms are unable to match by increased output and employment levels. Equilibrium is eventually restored when the aggregate price level rises, inducing a fall in demand by lowering the real value of wealth-holdings.

Generalized excess supply and generalized excess demand are not the only types of disequilibrium. In his 1976 Yrjö Jahnsson lectures Malinvaud (1977) extended generalized disequilibrium analysis to cover three cases:

Case I: *Keynesian unemployment* – excess supply in both the goods and the labour markets.
Case II: *Repressed inflation* – excess demand in both the goods and the labour markets.

These are the two cases analysed by Barro and Grossman, both cases being generated by demand-side movements and, therefore, amenable to correction by Keynesian demand-management policies.

Case III: *Classical unemployment* – excess supply in the labour market combined with excess demand in the goods market.

Malinvaud's case of classical unemployment is a supply-side-generated position of disequilibrium. A rise in the real wage leads firms to reduce their output and employment levels, thus creating unemployment in the labour market even though there is no lack of aggregate demand in the goods market. Clearly, Keynesian demand-management policies are ineffective in dealing with classical unemployment since such unemployment is due solely to the real wage being too high. Malinvaud's dichotomy between Keynesian unemployment caused by lack of demand and classical unemployment caused by too high real wages is a significant advance on Phase I Keynesianism where ultimately lack of demand was seen to be caused by too high real wages.

The disequilibrium approach was set within the Walrasian framework by Clower (1979) and Leijonhufvud (1968; 1971; 1979). Walras had suggested that a market economy would tend towards a position of general equilibrium as if there is an *auctioneer* determining prices in all markets simultaneously on the basis of the quantities demanded and supplied by individual agents. Walras postulated a process of *tatonnement* in which the auctioneer would continue to adjust prices in response to excess demands and supplies until all markets cleared, a position of Walrasian equilibrium. Then and only then would trading take place between individual agents. In other words, in the Walrasian model there is no *false trading*, i.e. trading at non-market-clearing prices. It follows that, in a Walrasian equilibrium, all agents are able to effect their notional demands and supplies.

The neo-Walrasian interpretation of Keynes developed by Clower and Leijonhufvud sees the General Theory as the first attempt to deal with the removal of the auctioneer and the *tatonnement* adjustment process from the Walrasian model. The neo-Walrasians make the fundamental assumption that price adjustment is sluggish relative to quantity adjustment. Hence without an auctioneer prices may get stuck at a level that does not imply generalized market-clearing, creating the possibility of false trading in which agents are unable fully to realize their notional demands and supplies. The disequilibrium theories deal with the implications of false trading, showing how, in the absence of efficient price adjustment, agents will adjust the quantities they actually buy and sell. The self-reinforcing nature of the quantity adjustment process creates a multiplier effect which carries the economy towards a quasi-equilibrium in which agents are optimizing given the quantity constraints generated by the departure from Walrasian equilibrium.

Neo-Walrasian analysis has followed two main lines of development:

The non-tatonnement approach This approach, adopted by the French school, has been concerned with the implications of replacing the *tatonnement* process by different quantity adjustment processes in which prices remain fixed. Attention has focused on how the agents form their demands in the face of constraints and on the effects of different rationing schemes. Various rationing schemes have been used: deterministic and stochastic, manipulable and non-manipulable (i.e. whether or not the ration depends on the effective demand expressed by the agent; see Drazen (1980), pp. 287–90).

The imperfect information approach The Walrasian assumption of an auctioneer-plus-*tatonnement* is an 'as if' representation of an economy in which agents have sufficient information to ensure that general equilibrium is achieved. Neo-Walrasian analysis, by dropping *tatonnement*, is trying to deal with a world in which agents possess only imperfect information and foresight. It is informational imperfections which create the possibility that the economy may not reach a full employment equilibrium quickly. This approach forms the essence of Leijonhufvud's interpretation of Keynes, the *General Theory* being seen as an attempt to generalize orthodox theory beyond its self-imposed straitjacket of perfect knowledge and perfect foresight.

To summarize: phase II Keynesianism sees involutary unemployment as a dynamic disequilibrium phenomenon created by the relative slowness of price adjustment. In the absence of an efficient price mechanism, quantity adjustments initially predominate so that in the short-run a fall in aggregate demand generates a downward adjustment of output and employment on the supply-side. The short-run inefficiency of the price mechanism is caused by informational imperfections. However, although phase II Keynesianism provides a sophisticated analysis of the *implications* of quantity adjustment processes when prices fail to respond, there is no explanation of why prices fail to respond. The slowness of price adjustment is assumed as the starting-point and, although there is an attempt to justify this assumption on the grounds of imperfect information, there is no explanation as to why agents with imperfect information do not lower price in the face of demand deficiencies.

Keynesianism phase III

Both phase I and phase II Keynesianism derived the existence of involuntary unemployment on the assumption of exogenously-determined price and wage rigidities. However they did differ in the nature of justifications given for the rigidity assumption. Whereas phase I Keynesianism ultimately came to focus on *imperfect competition* in the labour market, phase II Keynesianism focused on the problems of *imperfect information*. Phase III Keynesianism, which covers the most recent Keynesian writing dating from the mid-1970s, can be seen as an attempt fully to incorporate competitive and informational imperfections (albeit in separate models) within choice-theoretic models, with the aim of deriving the existence of an unemployment equilibrium on the basis of optimizing behaviour by agents without any imposed restriction on the flexibility of wages and prices. Phase III Keynesianism, therefore, offers an end to the search for the micro-foundations of Keynesian macroeconomics.

Imperfect competition

This approach starts from the premise that if an economy is *structurally perfect* – that is, all markets are perfectly competitive – it will tend towards full-employment equilibrium. It follows, therefore, that the emergence of an unemployment equilibrium must be due to the existence of structural imperfection. If there is monopoly power on the supply-side of a market, optimizing behaviour on the part of the monopolist results in supply being lower and price higher than the perfectly competitive outcome. The quantity-restricting effect of monopoly power makes the theories of imperfect competition, particularly Chamberlin's monopolistic competition, an obvious source for the provision of the microfoundations of involuntary unemployment.

The imperfect competition approach has been adopted by several Keynesian theorists in recent years such as Grandmont and Laroque (1976), Benassy (1976), Hart (1982) and Snower (1983). Hart, for example, considers the case where groups of workers have monopoly power in only one particular labour market and firms have monopoly power in only one particular product market, there being no bilateral monopolies. All optimize knowing the *objective* (i.e. actual) demand curves that they face, the position of the demand curves depending on per capita income which is determined endogenously. Hart finds that the resulting imperfectly competitive equilibrium (ICE) will generally be at below full employment, provided that the labour markets are not all perfectly competitive:

> ... the crucial assumption has been the existence of imperfect competition in labour market – it is this that is responsible for the existence of under-employment in our basic model. (Hart, 1982, p. 133)

The existence of monopoly power in the labour market is a necessary and sufficient condition for an underemployment ICE in Hart's model. An under-employment ICE does not require firms to possess monopoly power in the product market.

The imperfect competition approach to involuntary unemployment has been taken a step further by Weitzman (1982) who argues that imperfect competition is itself a symptom of an even more fundamental problem, that of increasing returns to scale. In a world of constant returns to scale there can be no monopoly power in the product market since there are no barriers to entry. Furthermore, there can be no involuntary unemployment since the existence of constant returns to scale implies that the involuntary unemployed are able to become self-employed, producing to fulfil their own demands. Constant returns to scale would mean an economy in which agents are self-sufficient. There is no necessity for units of organized production (i.e. firms) since costs are independent of the scale of production:

> Once granted the powerful assumptions of strict constant returns to scale and perfect competition, the essential logic of an adjustment mechanism seems inescapable. Unemployment equilibrium is impossible in a constant returns world. To have a genuine theory of involuntary unemployment requires a genuine theory of the firm, – i.e. an explanation of the organisation or process from which the unemployed are excluded. (Weitzman, 1982, p. 791)

It is this idealistic world of self-sufficiency which Weitzman argues that the classical theorists believed to be a valid 'as if' parable about the behaviour of actual economies. This classical belief was enshrined, according to Weitzman, in 'Say's Law of Markets':

> 'Say's Law of Markets', the doctrine that supply creates its own demand, is . . . a label for the kind of story being told about a quantity adjustment mechanism which increases output when there is slack capacity. The parable describes how an economy can automatically produce itself out of unemployment by a balanced kind of bootstraps operation . . . Say's Law means that an exact scale replication, by the unemployed, of the production pattern of the employed economy will take place in a linearly homogeneous production system and that it is self-supporting because it generates an equiproportionate increase in demand . . .
>
> The role of Say's Law as an adjustment parable is crucial to the classical belief that underlying forces to restore the economy away from 'temporary derangements' back toward full employment equilibrium. (Ibid., pp. 792–3)

It follows that in order to create the possibility of an unemployment equilibrium it is necessary to introduce increasing returns to scale. Such technological conditions provide the *raison d'être* for the existence of firms and explain why the involuntarily unemployed cannot haul themselves out of unemployment by their own bootstraps by becoming self-employed. They cannot do so because increasing returns to scale necessarily creates barriers to entry since new small-scale entry will face substantial cost disadvantages. Thus increasing returns to scale leads to an imperfectly competitive structure at the micro level and the possibility of involuntary unemployment at the macro level. Imperfect competition is, according to Weitzman, 'the natural habitat of effective demand macroeconomics':

> . . . if you want to build from first principles a broad based microeconomic foundation to a general equilibrium theory that will explain involuntary unemployment, you must start from increasing returns and go the route of imperfect competition. Otherwise, you will forever be struggling one way or another to evade the basic truth of Say's Law under strict constant returns to scale. Modelling the failure of coordination implicit in an 'inability to communicate effective demand' requires increasing returns and product diversity. (Ibid., p. 794)

Imperfect information

Whereas the imperfect competition approach deals with the implications of structural imperfection on the assumption that agents have perfect information about the demand curves they face, the imperfect information approach deals with the implications of relaxing the perfect information assumption but in circumstances of structural perfection (i.e. universal perfect competition).

The problem of imperfect information is being approached in at least two distinct ways. First, there is the *conjectural equilibrium* approach in which agents, without perfect knowledge of the demand conditions they face, make their supply decisions on the basis of the conjectures they hold about the demand conditions. An alternative is the *transactions cost* approach in which agents find it costly to identify, contact and negotiate with a suitable trading partner. These two approaches can be seen as complementary, the existence of transactions costs being the *cause* of the informational imperfections and the use of conjectures the necessary *consequence*.

The conjectural equilibrium approach   The starting-point for the conjectural equilibrium approach is Arrow's discussion of disequilibrium in a perfectly competitive market (Arrow, 1959). Arrow pointed out that the assumption that a perfectly competitive firm is a price-taker is valid only at the market-clearing price. If a perfectly competitive market does not clear, all firms are not able to sell their desired level of output at the market price. In these conditions, firms will no longer continue to be automatic price-takers. Instead, they will become price-makers with the possibility of increasing their sales by lowering price.

Negishi (1979) and Hahn (1978) have used Arrow's insight as the basis of an explanation for why prices may be rigid at non-market-clearing levels. If a perfectly competitive product market does not clear, firms become quantity-constrained, forcing each to make a conjecture about the demand curve it faces. At the existing market price, each firm can sell any level of output up to its quantity constraint. In order to sell any more output the firm will have to lower its price. Thus beyond the quantity constraint the firm faces a downward-sloping demand curve whereas up to the quantity constraint its demand curve is horizontal. This creates a kinked conjectured demand curve with an associated discontinuous marginal revenue curve. The situation is very similar to Sweezy's kinked demand curve analysis of oligopoly, the kink in that case being created by the conjectured asymmetry in rival firms' reactions to the direction of the price adjustment of an individual firm. The kinked conjectured demand curve gives two very important results:

1   Given the firm's conjectures, price rigidity emerges as the profit-maximizing response to a situation of non-market-clearing.
2   It may be profit-maximizing to maintain price in the face of moderate reductions in cost.

Thus the conjectural equilibrium approach can explain why profit-maximizing firms with the power to adjust price may choose to keep prices constant in the face of excess supply in the product market.

Price rigidity becomes an endogenously-generated outcome of optimizing behaviour by agents who have imperfect information about their demand curves. Optimizing behaviour in such circumstances may not be able to overcome quantity constraints created by a lack of aggregate demand. This opens up the possibility that Keynesian demand-management policies may have a role to play. Furthermore, the conjectural equilibrium approach throws doubts on the ability of wage cuts to provide a supply-side stimulus since it is likely that prices in the product market would not respond.

Negishi has extended the conjectural equilibrium approach to the labour market to show how wage rigidity can emerge even if the labour market is perfectly competitive (Negishi, 1979). Suppose that the money wage is above the level necessary for full employment. In a world of imperfect information individual workers conjecture that they can increase their probability of gaining employment by lowering their wage aspirations. However the higher probability of employment is gained at the cost of a lower wage and, therefore, a lower derived utility from employment. Wage aspirations will be reduced until the marginal benefits (via a higher probability of employment) from a lower wage equal the marginal costs (via a lower derived utility from employment). At this point, the money wage becomes rigid and this may occur at a wage above the market-clearing level.

In the conjectural equilibrium approach, therefore, wage and price rigidities can appear at non-market-clearing levels as the result of optimising behaviour with imperfect information. Wage and price rigidities are no longer an exogenously imposed assumption. It should be noted that the conjectural equilibrium approach admits of a Walrasian full-employment equilibrium as a possible outcome unlike the imperfect competition approach which denies the possibility of a Walrasian equilibrium if there is sufficient structural imperfection. This implies that, if the ultimate cause of involuntary unemployment is the existence of monopoly power, a return to full employment requires structural change.

The transactions cost approach   Whereas the conjectural equilibrium approach deals with the implications of using conjectures in the absence of perfect information, the transactions cost approach focuses directly on the cause of imperfect information, namely, the existence of costs of information acquisition. This approach has been developed by Howitt (1985) who starts from the assumption that transactions costs are higher the thinner the market so that as the level of activity increases in a market the average cost of transacting per unit sold falls. Howitt finds that an economy can get stuck at an unemployment equilibrium with a low level of activity where transactions costs are so high as to outweigh the gains from any attempt by firms to sell more output and by workers to sell more labour. Once an economy falls into a low-activity trap in which the low level of trade and the high level of transactions costs are mutually reinforcing, only an exogenous stimulus to the level of activity from, for example, a fiscal or monetary expansion can set in train a multiplier-type process in which the increase in activity lowers transactions costs, thereby giving a further boost to the level of activity, and so on.

Howitt identifies the problem of the collective good nature of transactions costs. If individual agents each expand their level of activity, they each generate a positive externality in the form of lower transactions costs which collectively may be sufficient to support profitably the expanded level of activity. But in the absence of some agency to coordinate an overall expansion of activity, no individual agent will find it profitable to set the ball rolling by expanding its own activities. Hence, rational economic agents, acting from their individual point of view, perpetuate unavoidably a sub-optimal outcome. It is a Prisoner's Dilemma-type situation in which no individual has sufficient information to provide any basis for believing that everyone will act in the common good. Without such information, the resulting unemployment equilibrium is inevitable and creates a clear case for some form of collective intervention.

Mainstream Keynesianism: an evaluation

This survey of developments in mainstream Keynesianism has sought to portray the enterprise as a coherent research programme initiated by Keynes' *General Theory*, with each new phase flowing from the perceived deficiencies of the previous phase. But what has this research programme achieved? The following assessment considers three dimensions of mainstream Keynesianism: its theoretical contribution, its method and its policy prescriptions.

Keynesian theory

Classical theory adopted the market-theoretic approach to understanding the economic system. Its fundamental premise is that if the economy has a universal perfectly competitive market structure in which all agents optimize, the price mechanism ensures that there is sufficient aggregate demand to promote a full-employment equilibrium. This is the essential truth of Say's Law as applied to a generalized market economy. Perfect structure plus perfect behaviour leads to perfect outcome. The macro-outcome of full employment necessarily follows from the twin micro-foundations of a universal perfectly competitive market structure and the rationality of economic agents who possess perfect information, this informational requirement being enshrined in the Walrasian notion of a fictional auctioneer.

The market-theoretic approach implies an imperfectionist theory of unemployment. If the economy settles at an unemployment equilibrium, the ultimate cause must either be structural imperfections such as monopolistic competition in the product markets and trade unions in the labour markets, or informational imperfections that prevent the price mechanism from fully operating.

The principle claim advanced by Keynes in the *General Theory* is the possibility that, due to a lack of demand, an economy could be at a macro-equilibrium with involuntary unemployment. Mainstream Keynesianism has been a continued attempt to substantiate Keynes' claim. The IS–LM model was the frst step since it provided a clear presentation of Keynes' macro-analysis, showing how the key aggregate demand-side behavioural patterns in the *General Theory* – i.e. the consumption, investment and demand-for-money functions – interacted to produce an unemployment equilibrium. But, because mainstream Keynesianism remained firmly wedded to the orthodox market-theoretic approach, the question naturally arose as to how Keynes' macro-analysis could be reconciled with market-theoretic micro-foundations. The search was on for the micro-foundations of Keynesian macroeconomics. From the market-theoretic perspective, a lack of aggregate demand necessarily implies that the price mechanism is not fully operating. Ultimately, this must be caused by the existence of imperfections, either structural or informational, which prevent market forces from ensuring the achievement of general equilibrium. The principal contribution of Keynesian theory has been to elaborate on, in ever greater detail, the various imperfectionist theories of unemployment.

Phase I Keynesianism highlighted two sources of imperfection that could render the price mechanism ineffective: money wage rigidity on the supply-side and degenerate behavioural patterns on the demand-side, such as a liquidity trap or interest-inelastic investment. These demand-side imperfections are all extreme cases and, anyway, are open to the neo-classical counter that the law of supply and demand would only exert itself at the macro-level by another route (e.g. the Pigou effect). Thus, in the absence of such extreme cases, phase I Keynesianism ultimately reduced to a money wage rigidity explanation of unemployment, rationalized in terms of the structural imperfection of the labour market.

Phase II Keynesianism provided a sophisticated analysis of how sluggish price adjustment could result in involuntary unemployment. The neo-Walrasians justified the assumption of short-run price rigidity in terms of informational imperfections, symbolized by the removal of the auctioneer and the no false trading restriction from the Walrasian system. But this neo-Walrasian analysis failed to give any clear explanation as to why imperfect information would lead optimizing agents to prefer quantity adjustment to price adjustment in the short run.

Phase III Keynesianism has sought to 'tie up the loose ends' by clarifying how the two types of imperfection, structural and informational, can lead to involuntary unemployment. The imperfect competition approach has dealt with the effects of structural imperfection, especially in the labour market, while the implications of imperfect information have been pursued by the conjectural equilibrium and transactions cost approaches. The conjectural equilibrium approach has been particularly important since it has provided an explanation of why imperfect information can lead to price rigidity at non-market-clearing levels. Phase III Keynesianism is the culmination of the earlier phases, a final explicit formulation of the inevitable imperfectionist causes of unemployment that follow from the market-theoretic approach.

Overall Keynesian theory must be regarded as having provided a valuable extension of classical theory by developing a greater understanding of the effects of imperfections in the system. There is no fundamental conflict between the mainstream Keynesians and the Classicists since they share a common perspective, that of rational economic agents operating in a generalised market context. The debate has been essentially an empirical one over the degree of imperfection present in actual economies, a debate within a single paradigm rather than between two fundamentally separate paradigms.

Keynesian method
Garegnani (1976) has distinguished two fundamental dimensions of economic analysis, the dimension of *method* and the dimension of *theory*. By method is meant the underlying vision, the abstract conception of the world which provides the criteria for selecting what it is intended to explain. The actual attempts at explanation form the theory, the hypotheses about the causal relationships between the selected variables. Applying this distinction to mainstream Keynesianism, one must conclude that since Keynesian theory has developed within the market-theoretic approach, it has necessarily interpreted Keynes as having remained firmly wedded to the orthodox method of economic analysis. Keynesian theory has sought to explain, in terms of optimizing behaviour by individual

agents, how an unemployment equilibrium could occur within a generalized market economy, the inevitable conclusion being that structural and/or informational imperfections are responsible. It is natural to ask whether or not in reaching this conclusion Keynesian economics has finally uncovered the ultimate meaning of Keynes' *General Theory*. As Grossman (1972) so aptly put it, was Keynes a 'Keynesian'?

Grossman's question can never be answered definitively since the ultimate meaning of Keynes is but a mythical Holy Grail, much sought after but never quite found. The reason for this lies in the nature of method itself. Method constitutes what Polanyi (1973) termed the tacit dimension of knowledge, the formless bounds within which the process of theoretical formulation takes place. 'We always know more than we can tell.' Keynes' own method of analysis in the *General Theory* is tacit and therefore unknowable in any definite objective manner. What the various interpretations of the *General Theory* represent are attempts to render the *General Theory* consistent from the perspective of some *imposed* frame of reference. These interpretations are not the result of investigation, but are preconceived ideas of order into which the *General Theory* is perceived to fit. Likewise this survey of mainstream Keynesianism is an attempt to impose a particular frame of reference that shows the consistency between many diverse theoretical contributions.

From this view, mainstream Keynesianism must be seen as the attempt to interpret the *General Theory* in terms of the orthodox market-theoretic method. This has been by far the most common approach but it is not the only possible approach. Indeed there is much in Keynes' writings which could be interpreted as a rejection of the orthodox method:

> For a hundred years or longer English Political Economy has been dominated by an orthodoxy. That is not to say that an unchanging doctrine has prevailed. On the contrary. There has been a progressive evolution of the doctrine. But its presuppositions, its atmosphere, its method have remained suprisingly the same, and a remarkable continuity has been observable through all the changes. In that orthodoxy, in that continuous transition, I was brought up ... But I myself in writing [the General Theory], and in other recent work which has led up to it, have felt myself to be breaking away from this orthodoxy, to be in strong reaction against it, to be escaping from something, to be gaining an emancipation. (Keynes CW, Vol. VII, p. xxxi)

To interpret Keynes in terms of the orthodox market-theoretic approach is necessarily to deny that Keynes broke away from the method of classical theory. This leads to bounded vision of the highest order, preventing the development of alternative interpretations that give more credence to Keynes' own stated views on the contribution of the *General Theory*. It is for this reason that the interpretations of Keynes proposed, most prominently, by Shackle (1967) and Joan Robinson (1964), which Coddington (1976) has termed *Fundamentalist*, have always remained on the margins of the debate over what Keynes really meant.

Keynes claimed to have developed a more general theory of unemployment that went beyond classical theory which dealt exclusively with frictional and voluntary forms of unemployment, the only possible forms of unemployment that could be conceived of within classical theory. Involuntary unemployment could not exist in the market-theoretic view of the world. A theory of involuntary unemployment necessarily required a change in method. By remaining within the bounds of orthodox method, mainstream Keynesian theory has been unable to view involuntary unemployment as anything other than unemployment caused by structural and/or informational imperfections, precisely those types of unemployment that Keynes defined as voluntary and frictional, respectively. Thus one, as yet not fully developed, answer to Grossman's question, would be that Keynes was much more than just a 'Keynesian'. In what respects Keynes moved beyond the traditional market-theoretic approach is as much in need of debate today as it was when the *General Theory* was first published some fifty years ago.

Keynesian policy

The early phase I Keynesian focus on the demand-side at the macro-level gave a clear justification for Keynesian demand-management policies in stark contrast to the primarily *laissez-faire* stance implied by classical theory. Involuntary unemployment was due to a deficiency of aggregate demand, a deficiency which could be overcome by direct government intervention in the goods market through a fiscal expansion. This, however, has proved to be the high point in Keynesian policy prescription. Ever since there has been a progressive lessening of the theoretical justification for Keynesian demand-management policies as a cure for unemployment.

The main 'nail in the coffin' for Keynesian policies from the theoretical perspective was the switch in theoretical emphasis from macro-demand-side analysis to micro-supply-side analysis. This began with Modigliani and the ensuing neo-classical synthesis which viewed money wage rigidity as the ultimate cause of involuntary unemployment. From this perspective Keynesian policies are dealing with the symptoms, namely demand deficiency, rather than with the fundamental problem of too high a level of real wages due to the structural imperfection in the labour market. Keynesian policies would only work if they created sufficient price inflation to lower the real wage to its market-clearing level. The necessary condition for this to happen is that labour does not use its monopoly power to pursue a real wage resistance objective. This requires either labour to suffer from money illusion or some form of agreed incomes policy in which labour accepts cuts in its living standards in return for higher levels of employment. Otherwise a fiscal expansion would result only in wage-price spiral with little or no effect on output and employment levels.

If the fundamental problem is structural imperfection in the labour market there is no reason to suppose that increasing demand in the goods market will provide a means of returning to full employment that avoids the necessity of structural change in the labour market. This point has been reiterated recently by the imperfect competition approach in phase III Keynesianism, in which structural imperfection in the labour market precludes the attainment of a Walrasian (full-employment) equilibrium.

The other strand of development in Keynesian theory that is concerned with the problems of informational imperfection has also become less clear in its policy implications. Initially, the assumption that imperfect information would result in quantity constraints, did provide a rationale for Keynesian demand-management policies to overcome the quantity constraints. However, once attention moves away from quantity constraints as the supposed symptoms of imperfect information and turns instead to the specific form of the imperfections in the information sets of individual agents, it is no longer clear that traditional Keynesian policies have any role. Although the conjectural equilibrium and transactions cost approaches have both resulted in models in which demand-management can be effective, it is possible that alternative forms of informational imperfection may render such policies ineffective. Thus the efficacy of government macro-intervention remains an open question, depending on the precise nature of the informational problems. These concerns have led Barro (1979) and Grossman (1979), individually, to have 'second thoughts' on the policy implications derived from their earlier work on non-market-clearing disequilibria. Barro, for example, in 1979 wrote:

> ... by mechanically leaving opportunities for mutually desirable trades, the non-market-clearing approach makes government policy activism much too easy to justify. When the arbitrariness of supply unequal to demand is replaced by a serious explanation, such as imperfect information about exchange opportunities, for the failure of private markets to achieve some standard of efficiency, the case for government intervention becomes much less obvious. (Barro, 1979, p. 56)

Overall the message is clear. In turning more and more towards the analysis of structural and informational imperfections in the micro-environment as the ultimate cause of macro-coordination failures, Keynesian theory has, inevitably, become much more ambiguous in its policy prescriptions since it just does not follow that an economy plagued by imperfections in its micro-foundations will necessary respond to intervention at the macro-level.

Keynesian economics: the road to nowhere?

Keynesian economics began with Keynes' claim to have produced a theory that explained involuntary unemployment. For Keynes, involuntary unemployment resulted from a lack of aggregate demand caused ultimately by too low a level of investment. The solution according to Keynes was the 'socialization of investment' which, in practice, came to mean government demand-management, primarily by the use of fiscal policy instruments.

However, since those seemingly revolutionary early days of Keynesianism, mainstream developments have really been a retreat back inside the othodox citadel, the citadel which Keynes claimed to have left behind (Keynes, CW, Vol. XIII, pp 488–9). On the theoretical side, Keynesian economics has sought to rationalize demand deficiency within the orthodox market-theoretic approach, the inevitable conclusions being that demand deficiency at the macrolevel is a symptom of either structural or informational imperfections at the micro-level, the traditional explanations of unemployment. Mainstream Keynesian theory has elaborated on the effects of introducing imperfections into classical theory. In so doing, many theoretical innovations have been made within classical theory in the name of Keynes. This in itself is an important contribution to the development of economic theory not to be dismissed lightly. But the Keynesian adherence to the orthodox method leaves Keynesian theory open to the criticism that it does not warrant the name 'Keynesian', denying as it does Keynes' claim to have escaped from the old ideas. Furthermore, on the policy side, the corollary of the theoretical developments has been the removal of any clear justification of Keynesian demand-management policies. Keynesian economics in its mainstream form has been a road to nowhere new.

Acknowledgements

I would like to thank the following people for their helpful comments in the writing of this paper: John Brothwell, Mike Collins, John Goddard, John Hillard, Will Hutton, Kathy O'Donnell and the participants at the Leeds University – Leeds Polytechnic economic seminar on whom my ideas were first tried out. Many thanks are also due to Elsie Merrick for typing the manuscript.

8   Keynes and the policy of practical protectionism[1]
Hugo Radice

1. Introduction

In fifty years of debate over the nature and significance of Keynes' *General Theory*, discussion of international economic relations have never been important. At first sight, this is hardly surprising, since until Chapter 23, Keynes makes only a few passing references to international matters. On the other hand, it is clear that such issues were very much at the centre to Keynes *practical* work as an economic policy-maker, from the Indian currency question right through to Bretton Woods. If we are to follow Meltzer's (1981) very sensible approach, of drawing on Keynes' practical work in order to gain a better understanding of his theoretical contribution, some exploration of this apparent paradox is surely necessary.

At the same time, the continuing interest in reappraising Keynes is not simply an exercise in the history of economic thought: it is also undertaken to illuminate our present economic condition. The core of the Keynesian heritage has surely been the concept of macroeconomic management itself: that governments could direct the movement of economic aggregates within the national economy, through the manipulation of fiscal and monetary instruments, but without systematic interference in particular markets or in property rights. The validity of this heritage has clearly been challenged, not only by theorists but by politicians, in the years since the end of the postwar boom in the world economy. Most of the *theoretical* criticism has been aimed at Keynesian views about the behaviour of particular economic agents in a capitalist economy. The *practical* difficulties of Keynesianism, however, have equally arisen from the growing exposure of national economies to international economic forces beyond the control of individual governments. The growth in trade as a proportion of national income, the internationalization of industrial and banking capital, the disorder in the world economy since the demise of the Bretton Woods system, have all undermined the efficacy of the conventional Keynesian policy tools.

In this essay, I shall argue that, in the context of the period,

Keynes' theoretical assumption of a closed economy was consistent with a policy practice based on what I call 'practical protectionism'. By this term, I understand whatever practical measures may be required, in order to pursue effectively the primary objective of securing full employment in the national (British) economy. In present-day conditions such practical measures require a much more radical departure from the liberal norms of economic policy, *if* the same objective is to be pursued.

Section 2 looks at the clearest example of Keynes' practical protectionism, his 1933 article, 'National Self-Sufficiency' (CW,Vol.XXI, pp. 233–46).[2] Section 3 examines the *General Theory*, in particular chs 23 and 24, and argues that his views there are very similar. Section 4 looks at three major policy debates in which Keynes played a central role – the return to gold in 1925, the tariff question in 1930, and Bretton Woods – and seeks to show that all three demonstrate the consistent application of the principles of practical protectionism. Finally, section 5 suggests some implications arising from the very different conditions facing British policy-makers today.

2. 'National self-sufficiency'[3]

Keynes begins by recalling that he used to share the orthodox belief in free trade, and says that now 'the orientation of my mind is changed, and I share this change with many others' (p. 234). The belief in free trade now seems part of the 'mental habits of the pre-war nineteenth-century world' (ibid.). His intention is 'to attempt ... a diagnosis to discover in what this change of mind essentially consists' (ibid.), and whether it is entirely justified.

The nineteenth-century free-traders, he says, believed first, that only they were clearsighted and sensible, while any interference with free trade was based on ignorance and self-interest; secondly, that free trade solved poverty by putting the world's resources to best use; and thirdly, that it secured peace, justice and the diffusion of progress. Keynes argues that there are two things wrong with this. First, international peace does not now seem to be assured by maximizing international economic relations, since this involves the protection by each country of its foreign interests, competition for new markets, and 'the progress of economic imperialism' (p. 236). Furthermore, 'advisable domestic policies might often be easier to compass if, for example, the phenomenon known as "the flight of capital" could be ruled out' (ibid.). While it is bad enough to have ownership and management separated on a national basis, 'internationally it is, in times of stress, intolerable' (ibid.), promoting mutual irresponsibility. Hence,

I sympathise, therefore, with those who would minimise, rather than with those who would maximise, economic entanglement between nations ... let goods be homespun whenever it is reasonably and conveniently possible; and, above all, let finance be primarily national ... a greater measure of national self-sufficiency and economic isolation between countries than existed in 1914 may tend to serve the cause of peace, rather than otherwise. (pp. 236–7)

Secondly, on more purely economic grounds, free trade was advantageous in the nineteenth century, partly because migrations required complementary flows of goods and capital, and partly because there were big differences in levels of industrialization. Today, the system of international capital flows has come to serve purely financial interests, while the need for international specialization (apart from that based on climate, natural resources, etc.) has declined:

... over an increasingly wide range of industrial products, and perhaps of agricultural products also, I have become doubtful whether the economic cost of national self-sufficiency is great enough to outweigh the other advantages of gradually bringing the producer and the consumer within the ambit of the same national economic and financial organization. (p. 238)

In addition, with rising living standards, non-traded goods (housing, services) play a larger part in the national economy, so that any cost of increased self-sufficiency in traded goods weighs less heavily upon living standards.

If free trade is no longer so clearly advantageous, are there *positive* reasons for wanting more self-sufficiency? Here, Keynes turns directly to matters of political economy. Since 'international but individualistic capitalism ... is not a success', various experiments are under way which break with the uniform nineteenth-century framework of private competitive capitalism and free trade. New 'modes of political economy' are emerging in Russia and elsewhere, and even Britain and the US are 'striving, under the surface, after a new economic plan' (p.239). This requires as much freedom as possible to pursue one's experiments without interference from outside, so that increased national self-sufficiency may not be an ideal in itself, but a necessary environment for pursuing one's ideals. It is worth quoting at length a passage which directly foreshadows arguments to be found in the *General Theory*:

In matters of economic detail, as distinct from the central controls, I am in favour of retaining as much private judgement and initiative and enterprise as possible. But I have become convinced that the retention of the structure of private enterprise is incompatible with that degree of material well-being to which our technical advancement entitles us, unless the rate of interest falls to a much lower figure than is likely to come about by natural forces operating on the old lines ... but under a system by which the rate of interest finds, under the operation of normal financial forces, a uniform level throughout the world, after allowing for risk and the like, this is most unlikely to occur ... economic internationalism embracing the free movement of capital and of loanable funds as well as of traded goods may condemn this country for a generation to come to a much lower degree of material prosperity than could be attained under a different system. (pp. 240–1)

Thus, with no prospect of a uniform system across the world, and the pressing need to be free from outside pressures, a move to greater national self-sufficiency would 'make our task easier, in so far as it can be accomplished without excessive economic cost' (p. 241).

Lastly, Keynes argues in broader vein that the nineteenth century overemphasized financial criteria and results. Even today, he says, 'we have to remain poor, because it does not "pay" to be rich' (p. 242). Dole money should be spent on urban improvement; agriculture should be maintained, not destroyed to get 'a loaf of bread thereby a tenth of a penny cheaper' (ibid.). If we disobey the accountant's test of profit, we have 'begun to change our civilization' (ibid.). In particular, the state needs to change its criteria: 'It is the conception of the Chancellor of the Exchequer as the chairman of a sort of joint-stock company which has to be discarded' (ibid.). With a broader role for the state, the choice of whether to produce at home or exchange abroad should be 'high among the objects of policy' (ibid.).

Keynes concludes the article by urging moderation. Foolish things are being done where the advocates of national self-sufficiency are in power. Protectionism is not *per se* good: if the approaching Economic Conference (held in June–July 1933) can succeed in reducing tariffs all round, this would be admirable. The dangers of doctrinaire 'silliness', of forcing the pace of change, and of intolerance of criticism, must all be avoided – with Stalin's Russia held up as the prime example of these dangers.

I have outlined Keynes' argument in this article at some length, because it represents the most thorough direct analysis anywhere in his writings of the general relation between national economic policy and the international regime. To those accustomed to the orthodox postwar Keynesian advocacy of free trade and currency convertibility, it undoubtedly appears a protectionist aberration, as it did to Harrod (1951) and more recently to Meltzer (1983). But the main points of the article are clearly argued as applicable to the post-1914 world *in general*, and not just the dire circumstances of 1933. First, the overall economic and political benefits of free trade have been reduced by the industrial maturation of Britain's nineteenth-century trading partners; secondly, the conscious pursuit of economic well-being through government policy requires that the constraints imposed by economic internationalism, notably on interest rates, be broken; and thirdly, the desired increase in national self-sufficiency is to be achieved by practical and moderate measures, and not by classical protectionism as such. It is these three points which I propose to summarize as a policy of 'practical protectionism',[4] whose objective is to facilitate measures to increase national economic well-being.

3. The 'General Theory' and the national economy

In what sense is the *General Theory* a theory of the national economy? Or more directly, to what extent does it support or complement the practical arguments of the 1933 article?

In the first place, the central arguments concerning the determination of aggregate employment, the rate of interest and money are constructed on the assumption of a closed economy. The 'classical system' outlined in Chapter 2 is explicitly set out on this assumption in section 2. After Chapter 2, there are only four passing references to an open economy until Chapter 23. In each case, Keynes notes modifications which would be required to his analysis if there were foreign economic relations, but these modifications are not accorded any theoretical significance.[5]

Secondly, the economic aggregates and functional relationships which form the constituent parts of the theory are defined and measured over a given community or society. Keynes endows this community with a collective psychology in his theories of consumption and investment; and the measure of aggregate output by a quantity of employment (1936, pp. 40–1) endows it also with a physical character, as a set of productive activities within the community. The role of money wages, as opposed to real wages, implies also a given currency. All in all, Keynes' commonsense approach to aggregation seems to point clearly to an economic theory of the *national* economy, in which his abstract propositions are formulated in terms of a consistent set of economic aggregates, defined over a given geographical-political space.

Thirdly, and above all, the whole thrust of the *General Theory* is towards its public policy conclusions, and public policy necessarily implies state, government and national sovereignty. Although the book does not explicitly discuss policy until the closing chapters, there is no question that his intention in attacking the 'classical theory' was to destroy its pernicious influence on economic policy (1936, ch. 1). In Chapter 24, Keynes finally sets out the 'social philosophy' which matches his economic theory in proposing an

extended role for the state in the modern capitalist economy: this is
for him '... the only practicable means of avoiding the destruction
of existing economic forms in their entirety and ... the condition of
the successful functioning of individual initiative' (1936, p.380).
This enlargement of state functions can in normal circumstances
only extend over the state's sovereign territory.

Direct arguments concerning international economic relations
can be found in Chapters 23 and 24. The discussion of mercantilism
in Chapter 23 reflects very closely the arguments in 'National Self-
Sufficiency'. Keynes begins by referring again to his own earlier
belief in the free trade case, and then outlines the 'scientific truth'
he now perceives in mercantilist doctrine. In conditions of *laissez-
faire*, economic growth depends upon the inducements to invest.
Domestic investment opportunities are governed in the long run by
the domestic rate of interest; and foreign investment, by the size
of the trade balance; these are therefore the proper concerns of
government. Given that the wage unit, liquidity preference and
banking conventions are stable, the trade balance will determine
changes in the quantity of precious metals forming the monetary
base, and these in turn will determine the rate of interest. Because
of the limited role and powers of the state at the time, the trade
balance was the *only* available policy instrument through which the
state could, along this chain of cause and effect, influence national
prosperity (1936, pp. 335–6).

There were limitations to this policy approach (pp.336–7), and
furthermore it does not necessarily imply import restrictions, since
free trade may maximize the favourable balance, as in nineteenth-
century Britain (p.338). To aim for an excessive balance, furthermore, may spark off 'senseless international competition' (ibid.).
However, the nub of the argument is *at this point* theoretical:
'against the notion that the rate of interest and the volume of
investment are self-adjusting at the optimum level, so that pre-
occupation with the balance of trade is a waste of time' (p. 339).
From this theory, the City of London unfortunately developed a
practice – bank rate management plus rigid exchange parities –
which had dire consequences:

> ... the objective of maintaining a domestic rate of interest consistent
> with full employment was wholly ruled out. Since, in practice, it is
> impossible to neglect the balance of payments, a means of controlling it
> was evolved which, instead of protecting the domestic rate of interest,
> sacrificed it to the operation of blind forces. (ibid.)

Against this the 'practical wisdom' of the mercantilists is greatly to
be preferred.

Delving into the theories underlying mercantilist thought, Keynes draws out elements close to his own views. First, the rate of interest will not adjust automatically to an appropriate level, and should not be too high. Secondly, 'selling cheap' in order to win export markets tends to reduce the terms of trade. Thirdly, scarcity of money and the 'fear of goods' can cause unemployment. Lastly, the mercantilist aim of directly fostering national economic welfare involved a realism 'much preferable to the confused thinking of contemporary advocates of an international fixed gold standard and *laissez-faire* in international lending' (p. 348). The conclusion of his brief examination bears most directly on policy choices, not only in 1936 but also today:

> It is the policy of an autonomous rate of interest, unimpeded by international preoccupations, and of a national investment programme directed to an optimum level of domestic employment, which is twice blessed in the sense that it helps ourselves and our neighbours at the same time. And it is the simultaneous pursuit of these policies by all countries together which is capable of restoring economic health and strength internationally, whether we measure it by the level of domestic employment or by the volume of international trade. (p.349)

These arguments recur in section 4 of Chapter 24, which includes Keynes' more famous calls for the euthanasia of the *rentier* and a 'somewhat comprehensive socialization of investment' (in sections 2 and 3, respectively). The only possible conclusion is that the Keynes of the *General Theory* held the same views on the national economy and the international regime as the Keynes of 'National Self-Sufficiency': that the world of *laissez-faire* is dead, and that the pursuit of domestic expansion must take priority over the determination of interest rates by international financial markets. The main discernible change is that the policy objective is now explicitly a higher level of domestic employment, rather than simply 'material prosperity'. Peripheral though it may be to the main concerns of the *General Theory*, Keynes' practical protectionism is clearly visible.

4. Three policy cases
This consistency in views between 1933 and 1936 could, however, still be regarded as a passing phase in Keynes' thought: a response to the catastrophic decline in world trade since 1929, the end of the Gold Standard in 1931, and the 'new experiments' in Russia, Germany and the USA. In this section, I shall argue that Keynes' practical protectionism is evident long before and long after this period (1924–25 and 1940–46), and in the subtleties of his position on tariffs in 1929–31.

The return to gold in 1925
Keynes' opposition to the return to the Gold Standard contained several distinct layers of argument. Once the decision to return

became inevitable, his opposition focused directly on the over-valuation of sterling at the $4.86 rate. Thus, in 'The Economic Consequences of Mr. Churchill', he argues that at this exchange rate, money wages and prices are about 10 per cent above internationally competitive levels. Given the inflexibility of wages and prices, the necessary reductions can only come about through the pressure of unemployment, strikes and lockouts, deliberately intensified by deflationary monetary policy (CW, Vol. IX, esp. pp. 214–15). Although some breathing space might be bought by the embargo on foreign loans and by the use of American credits, eventually the maintenance of the $4.86 rate will require a reduction in the ratio of UK to US export prices in order to improve the trade balance. With little prospect of a general rise in prices in the US deflation would be unavoidable (ibid.).

Before the decision to return, however, the scope of Keynes' opposition was much wider. Throughout 1924, Keynes was advocating monetary reform – a 'managed currency' – as an alternative to the Gold Standard *as such*. If both the USA and Britain could so manage their currencies as to stabilize prices, the exchange rates would be stabilized not only between the two countries but more generally, without a return to gold, or even a 'binding agreement' between the two countries or more broadly (RES Annual Meeting, 14 April 1924; CW, Vol. XIX (1), pp. 206–14). The really great advantage of such a managed currency is that it allows the government to attack unemployment by means of appropriate monetary policies and public investments (*Nation & Athenaeum*, 24 May 1924, CW, Vol. XIX (1), pp. 219–23). Over the summer of 1924, Keynes also developed a sustained attack against investment abroad: if the flight of capital continued, it would eventually require an increase in exports or a fall in imports, hence a depreciation of sterling, and a painful adjustment process which would probably raise unemployment (ibid., 7 June 1924; CW, Vol. XIX (1), pp. 227–8). He also argued that foreign investment was being artificially stimulated by the Trustee Acts (ibid., 9 August 1924; CW, Vol. XIX (1), pp. 279–84). The sensible solution to this was to stimulate domestic investment through public initiative (ibid., 7 June 1924; CW, Vol. XIX (1), p. 229).

Both Keynes' theoretical understanding, and the circumstances of the British economy as they appeared to him at the time, were of course still a long way from 1933 or 1936. In the 1923 articles on free trade, which he dismissed so scathingly ten years later, it was not only his analysis of international trade that was orthodox: on unemployment, his list of influences emphasized, apart from purely contingent factors, cycles in trade and credit, and population growth

(*Nation & Athenaeum*, 24 November and 1 December 1923; CW, Vol. XIX (1), pp. 147–56). Within days of these articles, further-more, he embarked on a series of talks and writings, following the publication of the *Tract on Monetary Reform*, in which he clearly located the primary cause of *avoidable* unemployment in *monetary* factors. His advocacy at this time of public investments and of cheap money were plainly presented as temporary or counter-cyclical. The theory of effective demand had to await both the theoretical break-throughs of the *General Theory*, and the realization, as the depres-sion dragged on, that unemployment could no longer be regarded as merely cyclical or contingent.

None the less, when Keynes brought his broader arguments together in a final plea against the return to gold, before the Com-mercial Committee of the House of Commons in March 1925, the analysis of later years is plainly breaking through the orthodoxies:

> The essence of a gold standard, in modern conditions, has very little to do with gold itself regarded as a commodity of intrinsic value. Its main object is to establish a uniform standard of currency, which shall be independent of national politics. Unfortunately, these advantages can-not be obtained without the penalty of having to regulate our credit system, with all the far-reaching effects which this exercises over our industry and trade, with reference, not solely or even mainly to our own internal requirements, but to the conditions of credit in the world at large and more particularly in the United States. The main object of monetary reformers, on the other hand, is to evolve a standard of currency regulated primarily by reference to the requirements of the credit system at home and to the stability of internal prices, even when this is only possible at the expense of fluctuations in terms of the standards of other countries, for example, the mark or the dollar. (*Nation & Athenaeum*, 21 March 1925; CW, Vol. XIX (1), p. 338)

Keynes thus gives priority to domestic policy objectives, specified as 'the mitigation of the curses of unemployment and trade instability' (ibid., p. 342), in almost exactly the terms used in 1933. A year later, in 'The End of Laissez-Faire' (CW, Vol. IX, pp. 272–94) he began the search for 'a new set of convictions' (ibid., p. 294) that was to lead to the *General Theory*; the *practical* departure from orthodoxy had already begun.

Unemployment and protection, 1929–31
Between 1925 and 1933, the main elements of Keynes' mature views fell into place, including the main policy weapon now regarded as Keynesian – deficit financing.[6] Within the framework of practical protectionism, and alongside the development in particular of his monetary theory, Keynes continued to press for policies that would deal effectively with unemployment. Although he was realistic

enough to accept that for the time being the Gold Standard would remain, he continued to attack it by implication, and sometimes openly (as in his memorandum to Lloyd George of 31 January 1928; CW, Vol. XIX (2), pp. 729–31). His main proposal up to the 1929 election was usually a programme of expansion based on government financing of development projects, and to this end his critique concentrated on the 'orthodox Treasury dogma'[7] that state borrowing and expenditure could not create extra employment.

With the Wall Street crash and the steep slide into world-wide depression that followed, the worsening situation in Britain forced Keynes into a more far-ranging search for alternatives to orthodoxy.[8] The Labour government, especially the Chancellor, Philip Snowden, proved even more attached to the Treasury view than the Conservatives. However, with powerful dissenters like Oswald Mosley in their ranks, and rising protectionist sentiment, they established the Macmillan Committee in November 1929 with extremely broad terms of reference. This, together with the formation of the Economic Advisory Council in February 1930, gave Keynes the platform he required.

Keynes' own evidence to the Macmillan Committee (CW, Vol. XX, pp. 38–157) began with an exposition of how bank rate operates to regulate the balance of payments under the Gold Standard. It regulates the current account via its effects on the domestic price level, and the capital account via interest rates, with the two effects working in the same direction. However, since the underlying objective is to ensure a sufficient current account surplus to finance investments abroad, rather than relying on short-term capital inflows, it is the effect on the price level which is critical in the long run. Given that wages and prices are sticky downwards, further deflationary pressure by raising the Bank rate merely leads to a fall in domestic investment, increasing unemployment, and excess savings which seek an outlet abroad. This further exacerbates the payments problem and requires a further rise in bank rate. In short, 'a bank rate which is high enough to prevent us lending too much abroad is too high to enable us to have the right amount of enterprise at home' (ibid., p.94).

Keynes then offered seven remedies to this problem. The first is to leave the Gold Standard, but 'there is no likelihood of such a remedy being adopted in present circumstances' (p. 100). Secondly, there could be an agreed general reduction in money incomes: this would be the ideal remedy, but it too is 'chimerical' (p. 106). The third remedy is to give subsidies to some or all industries, thus helping to restore profits without cutting wages, but there are practical difficulties in this. The fourth is to improve productive efficiency through schemes of rationalization, but this is a slow remedy, and it involves an increase in unemployment in the meantime.

All these remedies, said Keynes, are designed to lower the gold costs of production, and restore equilibrium by increasing output and exports. The next two remedies are of greater interest for this paper (the seventh being international cooperation among central banks to raise prices): the fifth remedy of protection, and the sixth, of increasing domestic investment.

Keynes made his case for protection by arguing first that a free trade policy, such as removal of the McKenna duties, must lead to higher unemployment, since the aim is to stop producing goods such as cars, which are more efficiently produced elsewhere. In the long run, this unemployment will be absorbed by expansion elsewhere, but only in a 'fluid system' in which money wages fall. Thus, 'the free trade argument is very similar to the Bank rate policy argument' (p. 114), and must be rejected for the same practical reason, that the system is *not* fluid: 'we get jammed at the point of unemployment' (ibid.). However, he is less sure about the impact of imposing new duties, rather than removing old ones: it depends on 'what alternative remedies there are and how long the present situation is to last' (p. 115). At the next session of the Committee six days later, he re-emphasized this point:

> I am frightfully afraid of protection as a long-run policy; I am sure that it is radically unsound, if you take a long enough view, but we cannot afford always to take long views, and I am almost equally clear that there are certain short-term advantages in protection. (p. 120)

A further qualification of Keynes' proposal was evident in his strong preference for the sixth remedy. Protection, like the first four, aims at restoring economic equilibrium by allowing an increase in foreign investment to absorb excessive domestic savings: so why not increase domestic investment instead? Within the familiar arguments for expansionary policies (e.g. an attack on the Treasury view) a new suggestion emerged: to separate by some means the markets for home and foreign lending, for example by a special tax on foreign bond issues (pp. 139–40). Clearly this was more than just a technical matter, for at the end of that session he argued more broadly that '*laissez-faire* in foreign lending is utterly incompatible with our existing wages policy' (p. 147), since it inevitably implies that our wages will be equalized downwards to the level prevailing elsewhere; although the same may not be true of the United States, because 'they approximate very closely to a closed system, and are therefore able to go in for all kinds of things that we are absolutely cut off from' (p. 148). Keynes presented similar arguments in the sessions in November and December on measures to strengthen the Bank of England's powers; he suggested that the unofficial embargoes on foreign issues, operated from time to time since the war, proved the necessity of such measures (p. 232), and possible tax systems are discussed.

Harrod's view is that Keynes' advocacy of tariffs was 'momentous' (1951, p. 424). It certainly appeared as a betrayal of free trade to Harrod at the time (ibid., p. 427), and to Robbins in the deliberations of the Committee of Economists of the Economic Advisory Council in the autumn of 1930 (CW, Vol. XX, ch.4, esp. 'A Proposal for Tariffs plus Bounties', pp. 416–19; Howson and Winch, 1977, pp. 6–72, esp. p.57). Moreover, when Keynes finally went public in March 1931 with the 'Proposals for a Revenue Tariff' (*New Statesman & Nation*, 7 March 1931; CW, Vol. IX, pp. 231–8; see also CW, Vol. XX, pp. 489–515), he came under fierce attack from Beveridge and other free-traders (Beveridge *et al.*, 1931). The Macmillan Committee does not seem to have been shocked by the original proposal made to them, because of Keynes' careful qualifications noted above; but as time went by, and especially as the Labour government continued to do nothing, the tariff solution appealed more and more to Keynes. His advocacy also became stronger because, despite his best efforts, he could not arouse enthusiasm for controls on foreign investment (as he noted in his EAC proposal; CW, Vol. XX, p. 416).

Drawing on all the presentations which he made in 1930–31, the logic of his tariff proposal is clear. Devaluation was ruled out; free trade could not work in present circumstances because of unemployment and wage rigidity; other solutions were impractical or too slow; a general revenue tariff could be removed once it was no longer needed; and the revenue itself would help the government to avoid further budget cuts. The real difficulty was the *political* one of distinguishing a practical proposal for a tariff, hedged around with conditions and qualifications, from the 'full protectionist programme' which Baldwin was ready to offer (CW, Vol. IX, p. 238). In the event, after Britain was forced off the Gold Standard, Keynes followed the strict logic of his argument by withdrawing the tariff proposal, but by then full protectionism, rather than Keynes' practical variety, was firmly in the saddle.

From the Clearing Union to the IMF, 1940–46
By the time Keynes began to consider the possible shape of the postwar international order late in 1940, Britain had had nearly ten years of experience of a managed currency, cheap money, trade preferences, bilateral settlements, and so on. Tentative international

initiatives in the late 1930s towards a more open regime had been set aside with the onset of war. Furthermore, both institutions and beliefs had adapted to the point where support for traditional free trade policies was very limited indeed, outside the ranks of economists.

As his proposals for an International Clearing Union took shape over 1941–43, Keynes found himself caught between those who advocated a firm continuation of bilateralism and Imperial preference after the war was over, and those who advocated a swift restoration of multilateralism and free trade. To the bilateralists, Keynes insisted that Britain could not isolate itself from the United States and the rest of the world outside the Empire. This view was enshrined, even against Keynes' better judgement, in Article VII of the Mutual Aid Agreement (Lend-Lease) in February 1942, in which Britain agreed to 'move away from discriminatory policy, so far as governing economic conditions allowed', as Harrod put it (1951, p. 517). To the free-traders, on the other hand, Keynes insisted that a return to multilateralism must be tempered by the fact that domestic policy was to be given absolute priority. This position emerges clearly in all the Clearing Union drafts, and in the 1943 White Paper.

To begin with, it was hoped that the expansionist bias of the Clearing Union proposals (with sanctions against creditors as well as debtors), and the adoption of full-employment policies in the main trading nations, would eliminate the need for bilateral restrictions, once the unavoidable difficulties of the transition to peacetime were resolved. In any case, the CU proposals allowed 'deficiency' countries to use restrictive measures. Secondly, the proposals envisaged that the Union, far from interfering in the domestic policy choices of member governments, would be 'passive' in granting overdraft facilities up to a substantial amount; more generally, in the words of the 1943 White Paper's preface, 'the technique of the plan must be capable of application, irrespective of the type and principle of government and economic policy existing in the prospective member states' (CW, Vol. XXV, p. 234)

However, the main protection for domestic policy would be central control over capital movements, which Keynes repeatedly advocated as a permanent feature of the system. From the draft of November 1941 (ibid., pp. 53–4) through to the White Paper (ibid., pp. 185–7), the object of capital controls is

> to have a means of distinguishing – (a) between movements of floating funds and genuine new investment for developing the world's resources; and (b) between movements, which will help to maintain equilibrium, from surplus countries to deficiency countries, and speculative

movements or flights out of deficiency countries or from one surplus country to another (pp. 53, 186–7).

Foreign investments must not be allowed beyond the limits set by a favourable trade balance, and speculative flows in particular had to be prevented: this would require stringent exchange controls. However, the *underlying* objective was given by Keynes in his speech to the House of Lords in May 1943, where he argued that 'we cannot hope to control rates of interest at home if movements of capital moneys out of the country are unrestricted' (ibid., p. 275).[9]

These important features of the Clearing Union, and especially that of capital controls, show that Keynes was still advocating practical protectionism as defined earlier. As the Clearing Union gradually gave way to White's Stabilization Fund in the US/UK negotiations of 1943–44, and then as the final composition of the International Monetary Fund came increasingly to be decided by the Americans alone from Bretton Woods to the Savannah meeting of March 1946, it was over these features that Keynes fought his fiercest rearguard actions. For example, he criticized a July 1943 version of the Stabilization Fund, because it would tie currencies too rigidly to gold 'with complete surrender of sovereignty', and because the Fund would have full discretion to deal in particular currencies or not; but he was willing to concede on the limitation of liability, on the 'subscription principle' (as opposed to the credit-creation or banking principle of the CU), on the US formula for quota and voting powers, and indeed on 'the general shape of the SF' (ibid., pp. 316–20). By the time of the Joint Statement of April 1944, Keynes had accepted also the abandonment of a new international currency; and the sharp reduction in the total amount of funds initially available, given that relief and reconstruction were to be financed by other means. On the other hand, currency convertibility was still to be limited to current account transactions, excluding capital transfers and accumulated balances (these being the Sterling balances, which were to be dealt with separately), and this implied the maintenance of exchange controls. In addition, the Fund's resources could not be used to finance capital outflows (ibid., pp. 437–42; see also Joint Statement, ibid., p. 474).

Keynes' interpretation of the broader implications too remained the same. To the House of Lords on 23 May 1944, he argued that there would be three central objectives of British post-war economic policy:

> [First,].... in future, the external value of sterling shall conform to its internal value as set by our own domestic policies, and not the other way round. Secondly, we intend to retain control of our domestic rate of interest, so that we can keep it as low as suits our own purposes, without

interference from the ebb and flow of international capital movements or flights of hot money. Thirdly, whilst we intend to prevent inflation at home, we will not accept deflation at the dictate of influences from outside. (CW, Vol. XXVI, p. 16)

He insisted that the Fund proposals safeguarded these aims, because they gave the explicit right to control capital movements, and because the role of gold in the new system was merely as 'a convenient common denominator', while Britain retained the right to fix the sterling price of gold. Indeed,

> it provides that its [sterling's] external value should be altered if necessary so as to conform to whatever *de facto* internal value results from domestic policies, which themselves shall be immune from criticism by the Fund. (ibid., p. 18)

In the run-up to Bretton Woods, Keynes was well aware that differences remained between the British and American views of the Fund. He outlined these to the Commonwealth delegates as follows. First, the US placed much more emphasis on stability of exchange rates, while the UK wanted more flexibility. Secondly, the US stressed the rights of the Fund *vis-à-vis* member countries, while the UK stressed the opposite. Thirdly, the UK wanted a larger fund, and fourthly, they wanted also a longer transitional period to the full implementation of the scheme (CW, Vol. XXVI, p. 56). The first three points were plainly in line with Keynes' desire to safeguard the autonomy of the UK government in domestic matters. The main substantive argument over flexibility and autonomy (points one and two) concerned exchange rate adjustment, and on this, IMF Article IV, with the famous phrase 'fundamental disequilibrium', appeared to end up close to Keynes' position, much to the satisfaction of the Chancellor of the Exchequer (ibid., pp. 93–4). The transitional period was, as the UK delegation urged, in the end left unspecified in duration. Thus, although he had had to give way on the size of quotas, Keynes could reasonably feel at the end of Bretton Woods that Britain's interests were not threatened.

In the following months, following an initial query from D.H. Robertson (ibid., pp. 114–17), a major dispute rose – chiefly within the British camp – over the interpretation of convertibility under Article VIII of the Agreement. Keynes maintained that *rights* of convertibility related solely to the balances of central banks, and not to individuals; hence, exchange controls, and indeed trade controls of whatever kind, were consistent with IMF rules. For Keynes, the right to restrict private convertibility if conditions required it was a crucial defence against a run on the reserves (ibid., e.g. pp. 150, 157). This particular argument seems to have petered out, following an eventual American response which supported Keynes' interpretation (ibid., pp. 183–4).[10]

Keynes also welcomed the news that the US representatives to the Fund and the Bank would be responsible to a National Advisory Council consisting of members of the Administration, rather than to Congress, since it was the latter that seemed more likely to seek to use the new institutions to further American foreign economic policies at the expense of common international interest (ibid., p. 197). He was, however, concerned that Congress was pushing a much narrower objective for the Fund than appeared to be set out in Article I: in essence, restricting the use of the Fund's resources to dealing with cyclical fluctuations. Such an amendment, wrote Keynes,

> runs the risk of losing the last vestige of the central idea of the Clearing Union and also of destroying the unqualified accessibility of the Fund to members, to which in previous negotiations we have attached fundamental importance. (ibid., p. 202)

Keynes' fears have proved entirely justified.

The concessions that Keynes, finally, had to make at the Savannah meeting in March 1946 on the location and management of the Fund and the Bank, and his misgivings about their prospects, are well known (Harrod, 1951, pp. 625–37; Crotty, 1983, p. 65, note 9). Much the same retreat and misgivings occurred in the loan negotiations in Washington in 1945, which Keynes finally sold to a reluctant Labour government when the only alternative was seen as an unbearable degree of austerity. Despite some temporary setbacks, international *laissez-faire* was eventually established, under US hegemony, to a degree well beyond anything Keynes could have imagined. However, it seems clear that between 1940 and 1946 Keynes mapped out, and consistently followed, a pragmatic path between 'Schachtian' bilateralism and protectionism on the one hand, and a return to international *laissez-faire* on the other. Although this path turned out to be a tightrope that soon after vanished into thin air, it was in essence the same programme of practical protectionism that he had followed since 1924.

5. Conclusions: a practical protectionism for the 1980s

Was Keynes' practical protectionism only relevant to the period surveyed, or is there a feasible 1980s version? In some obvious respects, the last fifteen years have been similar to the interwar period, notably in the return of mass unemployment, and the absence of an international 'economic order'. As regards the latter, external considerations have certainly dominated exchange-rate and interest rate policies, at the expense of the needs of domestic policy – exactly the problem to which Keynes' practical protectionism was a response. Keynes had warned of the consequences of extreme international capital mobility in 1941:

> Social changes affecting the position of the wealth-owning class are likely to occur or ... to be threatened in many countries. The where-abouts of 'the better 'ole' will shift with the speed of the magic carpet. Loose funds may sweep round the world disorganising all steady business. (CW, Vol. XXV, p. 31)

Today, it is nothing as alarming as 'social changes', but merely speculative expectations about exchange rate and interest rate changes, that lead to movements of short-term capital. The end result is that a government's ability to maintain exchange rates that bear some relation to conditions in the production of traded goods and services, and interest rates that meet domestic investment requirements, depends entirely on how international capital markets judge the 'soundness' of its economic policies.

The uncontrolled expansion of international private money markets took place in the 1970s because of the failure of major governments and international institutions to rebuild a *public* international order after the breakdown of the Bretton Woods system. In the absence of an effective public system, it was left almost entirely to private banks to organize the recycling of oil revenues, and to mobilize savings during world recession. The Keynesian solution to this problem is surely to restore public control over international liquidity, so that national governments can in turn regain control over their own domestic monetary systems. Furthermore, some of the factors underlying international monetary disorder, such as violent fluctuations in commodity prices and the mushrooming of Third World debts, might well not have arisen in the first place if the post war order had included *other* elements that Keynes regarded as essential. Among these elements were a commodity control system based on buffer stocks, and a genuine world bank for long-term public loans that would *replace*, rather than support or merely complement, private capital flows. Indeed, at first sight it seems clear that a Keynesian answer to the international problems of the 1980s should include all the 'inefficient arrangements' and 'sub-optimal policies' so scathingly dismissed by Meltzer (1983, p. 78). In the British case, at national level, the Keynesian approach would then include controls on capital exports, a major public investment programme, and, at least temporarily, trade restrictions as well.

Two important qualifications, however, must be made. First, both Keynes and his present-day followers almost wholly neglect the organization of industry in their analyses. Although Keynes himself was involved in rationalization proposals (notably of the Lancashire cotton industry from 1926 on; see CW, Vol. XIX(2), ch.7), the *General Theory* assumes competitive markets, and later Keynesians have never really succeeded in linking their macroeconomic theory to a more realistic view of industrial organization. For the present discussion, the most important feature of industry today is its multinational character: it is dominated by firms whose operations abroad are so significant that, regardless of their ownership, their business strategies are global, rather than national. The impact of this development runs deep into the fabric of the industrial economy of Britain, since its individual productive units are guided to a large extent by international market forces, or by administrative decisions taken abroad. Such an economy cannot be expected to respond predictably and coherently to national economic policy measures, and in the extreme it may scarcely respond at all. Given the parallel, and often linked internationalization of British banking, the potential for control over the supposedly national monetary and financial system is also greatly reduced. A *national* approach to policy, pursuing domestic objectives such as full employment free from the constraints of international financial opinion or of economic conditions elsewhere, would today require a very drastic reorganization of industry and finance to be effective. The socialization of investment would have to be more than *somewhat* comprehensive, to recall Keynes' phrase.

Secondly, Keynes could never really accept that policy conflicts might reflect truly irreconcilable conflicts of interest. As a good Liberal and a rationalist, he always justified and defended his own policy prescriptions as the *only* appropriate ones, which would in the end benefit even those who appeared to lose out. He assumed that *his* sort of expansionist, interventionist internationalism had been universally accepted by 1945, because everyone seemed to agree that the basic common objective was full employment. He would have been astonished at the speed with which the old, externally-oriented City interests came once again to dominate British economic policy, enforcing deflation to maintain the value of sterling, whatever the cost in unemployment and slow growth.

His successors, likewise, seem unwilling to accept that mass unemployment in Britain today is not just a matter of ignorance and stupidity on the part of politicians and financiers, but rather part of a deliberate policy to deal with the 'labour problem'. Keynes' words to Professor F.D. Graham in 1943 seem prophetic indeed:

> How much otherwise unavoidable unemployment do you propose to bring about in order to keep the Trade Unions in order? Do you think it

will be politically possible when they understand what you are up to? (CW, Vol. XXVI, p. 36)

If today's Keynesians still wish to pursue what was Keynes' own primary objective, full employment in the United Kingdom, they must now fight the vested interests of internationalized private capital, and help everyone to understand 'what they are up to'. If today's Keynesians do *not* want to pursue the objective of full employment, then they should give the *General Theory* and the rest of Keynes's works a decent burial, and go about their business.

Notes

1. This essay develops an argument put forward in a more general paper on internationalization and the British economy (Radice, 1984). Two recent papers which have helped me to develop my views are Willoughby (1982) and Crotty (1983). Williamson (1983) surveys more broadly Keynes views on the international economic order; Thirlwall (ed.) (1976) provides valuable historical perspectives, notably in papers by Kahn and Balogh.
2. CW citations are to the *Collected Writings* of Keynes.
3. This article has been frequently cited recently: see Block (1977), Brett, Pople and Gilliatt (1982), Willoughby (1982), Williamson (1983) and especially Crotty (1983). Harrod (1951) rightly calls it 'a further reaction from Free Trade', but sees this reaction as a temporary departure from more liberal views. More specifically, he attributes the paper in part to 'revulsion from the futilities of the World Economic Conference' (p. 446). This cannot be the case, since the paper was first presented by Keynes in Dublin in April 1933, two months before the Conference opened. An interesting echo to the paper came from Keynes' friend Walter Lippmann in the US (Lippmann, 1934).
4. With the emphasis on 'practical', for as Keynes had earlier remarked: 'the theoretical arguments which free traders and protectionists have each used are, many of them, as I think, invalid or misapplied. Each, on the other hand, has got hold of an important practical maxim' (*The Listener*, 30 November 1932; CW, Vol. XXI, p. 204).
5. The four references are in ch. 10 (1936, p. 120), ch. 19 (pp. 262–3, 270) and ch.21 (pp. 301–2).
6. Pollard (1970, p. 157) notes that also in 1933 Keynesian arguments were explicitly used in the collection by Oxford economists, Cole (ed.) (1933).
7. The phrase was Churchill's, quoted by Keynes in a typical piece, 'A Cure for Unemployment', *Evening Standard*, 19 April 1929 (CW, Vol. XIX (2), pp. 808–12).
8. His *immediate* response to the crash was optimistic: it would lead to cheap money, and after a 'bad winter of unemployment' this would in turn lead to recovery (*New York Evening Post*, 25 Feb. 1929; CW, Vol. XX, pp. 1–3).
9. He made the same point still more strongly to Harrod, who favoured the abolition of capital controls (CW, Vol. XXV, pp. 148–9; Harrod, 1951, pp. 567–8).
10. However, as Williamson points out (1983, p. 90), the IMF has in fact always taken Robertson's interpretation, in pressing for the liberalization of *all* exchange transactions.

9   Keynes, Hayek and the monetary economy

Michael Hudson

Introduction

To pair the names of Keynes and Hayek in the title of an essay is likely to suggest that the long-enduring and often sharp scientific disagreement between the two economists is to be worked through once again. After all, the dispute between them in the early and later 1930s is well enough known. On the one hand, there is Keynes' view that one of Hayek's main works, *Prices and Production*, 'is an extraordinary example of how, starting with a mistake, a remorseless logician can end up in Bedlam' (Keynes, 1931, p. 394); while on the other hand, Hayek's attitude to the *General Theory* was that '[Keynes'] whole analysis [was] based on a crucial error' (Hayek, 1983). Similarly, there was the antagonism between the LSE and the Cambridge Schools (see Coats, 1982), an antagonism perhaps best summed up in the letter to *The Times* by Hayek, Robbins *et al.* of LSE,

> We are of the opinion that many of the troubles of the world at present are due to improvident borrowing and spending on the part of public authorities ... If the government wish to help revival, the right way is ... not to revert to their old habits of lavish expenditure ... (quoted in Hutchinson, 1978, p. 185)

Less well known, but equally sharp, was Hayek's attack on the proposal of Keynes and others during the 1920s to stabilize the price-level by variations in the quantity of money (McCloughry (ed.), 1984, p. 17).

It is not the intention of this essay, however, to traverse once again what is very likely such well-known ground. Rather, the aim is a more limited one: to point to the fact that both Keynes and Hayek, in attempting to develop theories of fluctuations in the level of economic activity, sought to grapple with precisely that feature of received economic theory which made it so difficult (even, both would say, logically impossible) to do so: the equilibrium habit of theorising which can be summed up by the phrase 'adherence to Say's Law'. We shall see that to both Keynes and Hayek the means of overcoming this problem lay in the introduction of money as an essential feature of the analysis. It was money, or more generally the nature of a monetary economy, that enabled what might be called the 'equilibrium vice' to be overcome.

The aim of the essay is thus to show how a perceived logical inadequacy in the body of general economic theory led both Keynes and Hayek to fix upon money as the means by which that inadequacy could be transcended. It is *not* a full-scale review of the way, or more correctly the basic differences in the way, in which their respective analyses embodied this insight, though some reference will be made to this in what follows. Nor is it an attempt to assess the validity/invalidity of the two approaches, but rather a survey of the two approaches themselves. Nor, finally, is it yet another attempt to elicit Keynes' 'ultimate meaning', for it may reasonably be argued that such a search has become increasingly in danger of concentrating upon an issue whose significance for the further development of economic thought is at best secondary.

Keynes

If, in general terms, the purpose of the analytical apparatus deployed by Keynes in the *General Theory* is to demonstrate that Say's Law is invalid, some of the instruments he developed to do so seem less appropriate than others. Both Keynes and later commentators have emphasized the significance of the consumption function for macroeconomic theory: that a rise in disposable income will not be reinjected by its recipients in its totality into the circular flow of income, but a greater or lesser proportion of it (depending upon the magnitude of the marginal propensity to consume) will 'leak' into savings (see Keynes, CW, Vol. VII, p. 96; Ackley, 1961, p. viii). In this way, the volume of output cannot find a market which wholly absorbs it, unless the leakage into savings is precisely offset (in magnitude) by an 'injection' from the side of investment, and the outcome is a decline in aggregate income. Add to this the assumption that those who save and those who invest are different 'people' (Stewart, 1967, p. 92), and that they perform their respective activities for different and non-congruent reasons; draw the conclusion that, therefore, the volume of purchasing power which 'households' plan to abstract from the circular flow and that which 'businesses' are planning to inject into it are likely to be the same only fortuitously; and the crucial role of the consumption function seems to have been demonstrated.

In fact, this goes nowhere near to providing an adequate demonstration that a situation of 'general overproduction' can, and is highly likely to, arise and that as a result Say's Law has been shown to be invalid. That most classical economists accepted the validity of Say's Law seems indisputable; but it is equally indisputable that their adherence to it was not dependent upon a denial of the proposition that not all of any rise in income would be immediately re-expended but that part of it would be saved. It was not the act of saving in itself that was of significance, but what was done with the funds saved. The problem in interpreting classical economics in this context has always been due to imprecision in defining just what it was that those economists understood by the phrase 'Say's Law'. If this is clarified, then it can be shown that the postulate of a marginal propensity to consume of less than unity is neither a sufficient nor necessary condition for demonstrating the invalidity of Say's Law. In turn, if this is so, it follows that we must look elsewhere in Keynes' 'toolbox' for the implement which is of key significance in this regard. And it will be found not in the consumption function but in the particular characteristics of money, that is, in the nature of a monetary economy. It is here that the decisive locus of Keynes' attack upon Say's Law is to be found.

Of the many meanings that can be attributed to 'Say's Law' (see Baumol, 1977), two are relevant for the present analysis. The first is probably that which springs to the mind of most economists when they see that phrase: 'Supply creates its own demand', that is, that every act of sale is at once, not simultaneously but by its very nature, an act of purchase. Hence no deficiency of *aggregate* demand is possible, though 'partial gluts' may emerge. In this form, Say's Law appears to be indisputably true only in a barter economy: the act of saving, which breaks the link between sale and purchase, lacks any form other than that of commodities in which to embody itself. Accumulation could take place only in the form of material commodities, which are subject to storage costs and are liable to deteriorate in quality, ultimately to perish, if they *are* stored. Even in a barter economy, however, it is always possible for producers to mis-estimate the demand for their products: 'too much' of some things, 'too little' of others may be produced. Yet the impossibility of accumulating stocks of goods means that shifts in relative exchange values will rapidly take place, markets will be cleared, and the equality of aggregate demand and aggregate supply will be restored.

It seems difficult to accept that it was this form of Say's Law to which classical economists adhered: from Smith onwards, they had depicted the advantages of money, and in particular the benefits to be gained from substituting a paper money whose cheapness of production economized upon the loss of productive resources otherwise involved in making a gold currency the means of circulation (see Smith, 1958, pp. 285, 289; Ricardo, in Sraffa (ed.), 1952, p. 42). Hence the Say's Law on which their macro-analysis was based could not have been that which applied *only* to a barter economy. We shall take up below the proposition that they argued that a monetary economy could be sensibly visualized as if it were simply a barter economy with money added, and show the way in which this approach was linked to the length of the time period to which their analysis applied. But at this point, we must move to a second formulation of Say's Law: that there is no net hoarding. Thus James Mill argued that

> of the two parts of the annual produce, that which is destined for reproduction and that which is destined for consumption, the one is as completely expended as the other ... (Winch, 1966, p. 132)

And equally forcefully J.S. Mill:

> The person who saves his income is no less a consumer than he who spends it: he consumes it in a different way; it supplies food and clothing to be consumed, tools and material to be used, by productive labourers. (Mill, 1844, p. 48)

What are the implications of this postulate which are of significance here? Most importantly, it shows the essential irrelevance of the consumption function *as such*, and the analysis derived from it that has been outlined above, for the validity or otherwise of Say's Law. In a monetary economy, saving can be performed, and the link between sale and purchase can be (at least temporarily) broken; savers and investors can be two different sets of 'people', undertaking their respective activities on the basis of different motivations; and yet, provided that no net hoarding takes place, Say's Law in this form remains valid. It is not the *presence* of money that is of significance; rather, it is the *nature* of the money, the primary function which it serves, and hence its implications for the behaviour of those who do not consume all of any increase in their income, that is the aspect upon which to concentrate.

A way of advancing the discussion a step further and to tie it directly into Keynes' approach is to briefly consider the dispute between Malthus and Ricardo as to whether a 'general glut' could occur, i.e. a condition logically excluded by Say's Law. Malthus argued that Ricardo was quite wrong to insist that 'consumption and accumulation equally promote demand', and that it is in fact quite possible to conceive of situations in which what might be termed the power to accumulate outran the power to demand, a deficiency of effective demand thereby arose, and there was a decline in the level of income (Malthus, 1820, Introduction and ch. VII, section III). Underlying this proposition is a chain of reasoning which appears to rest upon a theory of value peculiar to Malthus himself, and a related more general doctrine of 'proportions' or 'balance' which Malthus was wont to employ. On the former, Malthus argued that the existence of an unproductive class in the economy was necessary to ensure that total output could find a market at prices which returned a normal rate of profit to the capitalist. What he seems to have had in mind is some idea of a declining 'marginal efficiency of capital'. An increase in 'accumulation' (that is, saving) by capitalists would expand output, certainly, but, by reducing the relative proportion of unproductive labourers in the overall workforce, that output could only be sold at lower prices (if at all) and hence the capitalists' profit rate would decline (Malthus, 1820, ch. VII, section XIII). Malthus then links this with the proposition of the necessity of an appropriate balance between production and consumption if the 'motive to accumulate and produce' is not to diminish. Again, Malthus argued, while there could be 'too little' saving, there could also be, on the basis of the above argument, 'too much' (Pullen, 1982, p. 274).

It was on the basis of such considerations as these that Keynes enrolled Malthus among the ranks of his scientific predecessors. Yet his doing so exhibits the perils often associated with quests of this type. Even leaving aside the confused nature of Malthus's model of the possibilities of general gluts, it was accompanied by an explicit acceptance on his part of the central propositions of that form of Say's Law under discussion here: in Malthus's own words, 'no political economist of the present day can by saving mean mere hoarding.' The outcome of the preceding analysis is, therefore, that neither saving as such nor the introduction of money were in themselves sufficient to shake the adherence of the classical economists to Say's Law. In particular, they saw money as a helpful piece of machinery, raising the economy's productivity by making possible a more extensive division of labour and economising on resources in the way mentioned above. But its presence made no basic difference to the operation of the economy: in effect, a monetary economy was but a barter economy with money added. Another implication is equally clear: the view of money thus held focused entirely upon only one of its 'functions', its role as a transactions medium, something not capable of being desired for its own sake but merely a stopping-place in the circulation of purchasing power to and from the sphere of production (though an important qualification to this will be noted below).

Yet, given the actual frequency of 'financial panics' during the period in which classical economists were writing, this attitude seems at first sight startling. The first half of the nineteenth century in Britain was punctuated by a number of business collapses which, whatever their origins, issued in a panic flight to liquidity on the part of those participating in economic activity (see Gayer, Rostow and Schwartz, 1953), and the economists of the time clearly realized that this was what was happening (see Fetter, 1965). But if so, surely the implication was that money possessed some characteristic other than its medium of exchange role which could cause it to be demanded in some circumstances for its own sake, that is, for its liquidity. This implication was in fact realized, but its consequences for Say's Law could be turned aside in one of two ways:

First, it could be argued, as J.S. Mill did, that Say's Law needed only to be appropriately postulated to be able to take full account of the apparent difficulties. Simply, define 'money' as merely one commodity, the nth commodity, alongside the other $n-1$ commodities. In a general equilibrium system of n markets, then, excess demand for money could exist (in the nth market) alongside excess supply of all other commodities (in $n-1$ markets), and there could be no *general* oversupply of commodities. This, however, offered no satisfactory solution to the underlying problem, but merely evaded it by recourse to a type of Walrasian equation-counting. In particular, the existence of money was not regarded as making any significant difference to the way in which the economy operated: an economy with money was basically a barter economy with money simply added to it, to $n-1$ commodities had been added an nth. Moreover, that n^{th} commodity had initially been added solely for its function as numeraire, not because it possessed any of the characteristics of money which created difficulties for Say's Law.

Second, the procedure more normally adopted and persisting until Keynes, was to face up to the difficulties, develop a more or less elaborate theory of demand for money which was framed in terms of what was later to be termed 'liquidity preference', but to confine its application to the short-run, 'abnormal', *disequilibrium* state of the economy (see Fisher, 1930, p. 216). Thus James Mill himself referred to periods of uncertainty in which

> there is a general disposition to hoard: a considerable portion, therefore, of the medium of exchange is withdrawn from circulation, and the evils of scarcity of money are immediately felt ... and calamity is widely diffused (quoted in Skinner, 1967, p. 163)

... but clearly abstracted from this possibility in the rest of his analysis. Marx's comment on this type of procedure is to the point: at times of market crisis:

> the sole form of wealth for which people clamour at such times is money, hard cash ... This sudden transformation of the credit system into a

monetary system adds theoretical dismay to the actually existing panic
... (Marx, 1971, p. 147)

That is, classical economics proceeded as if money could be handled
by the type of Walrasian equation-counting discussed above. At
least normally: yet crises constituted occasions in which such a
procedure would no longer do, and the resulting attempts to theorize
this situation did not fit smoothly (if, even, at all) into the general
theoretical framework employed by classical economists.

In one sense, therefore, the classical economists' procedure represented *ad hoc* theorizing: real situations recurred for which an
explanation had to be found. But in a more basic sense it was
disintegrated theorizing. The emphasis upon the long-run equilibrium state of the economy reflected the belief that this was the
more important phenomenon to be studied, the period during which
economic developments could be regarded as wholly explicable in
terms of developments in the real economic factors of technical
progress, population growth, and so on. It was, in short, the framework of analysis wonderfully well captured by Keynes in his remark
that

> ... this *long run* is a misleading guide to current affairs. In *the long run*
> we are all dead. Economists set themselves too easy, too useless a task if
> in tempestuous seasons they can only tell us that when the storm is past
> the ocean is flat again. (Keynes, CW, Vol. IV, p. 65)

Once emphasis is shifted to the short run, however, the defence
of Say's Law by penning all factors which might threaten its validity
into the category of 'abnormalities' will no longer do, and this is
especially true of money. Not merely must the theory of demand for
money be given the attention which the significance of money demands. That theory must also be integrated into the overall theory
which seeks to explain the operation of the macroeconomy. An
economy with money, a monetary economy, is then not simply a
barter economy with money added; in terms of the preceding discussion, money is not merely the nth commodity. Rather, it is an
economy whose behaviour can and will display fundamentally different characteristics from that of a barter economy. It is, above all,
an economy in which a general overproduction, or in more modern
terms, a deficiency of effective demand is not merely possible but
probable. Say's Law no longer holds.

The basic elements of Keynes' theory of the demand for money
are too well known to need rehearsing here (see Morgan, 1978). For
the present purpose, emphasis need only be given to the crucial
significance conferred upon money by the uncertainty pervading all
economic activity. Money provides a means of hedging against that

uncertainty: it is perfectly liquid, in the sense of being instantaneously realisable without loss, and it is an asset whose 'liquidity-premium is always in excess of its carrying costs' (CW, Vol. VIII, p. 239). Or, in an earlier formulation, '[the] expenses [of] storage, risk and deterioration . . . are reduced to a minimum approaching zero in the case of money' (CW, Vol. XXIX, p. 86). Similarly, while in Chapter 13 of the *General Theory* the speculative demand for money is seen partly in terms of speculation in the narrow sense, 'the object of deriving profit from knowing better than the market what the future will bring forth' (CW, Vol. VII, pp. 169, 170), in Chapter 15 it becomes dominantly determined by the demand for money due to uncertainty regarding the future. Finally, it is the characteristic of money as a means of postponing decision, and thus of effecting hoarding, which Keynes uses to answer his own question: 'Why should anyone outside a lunatic asylum want to hold money as a store of wealth?'

Hayek

In the 1920s the economics profession in Germany had turned itself to the study of 'business cycles' with an intensity that was hitherto unknown (see Loewe, 1925). As only one example of the concern, the behaviour of the leading professional body, the Verein für Sozialpolitik (VfS), may be instanced: even before the outbreak of the depression, one of its annual meetings had been specifically concerned with the explanation of business cycles, that in Zurich in 1928 (Diehl, 1928). It had also issued a special volume of essays on the problem. Moreover, an increasingly central issue in these discussions was the role of money in business fluctuations, in its particular form of the 'monetary theory of the business cycle', although there was little agreement as to precisely what was meant by that phrase. In this, the discussions taking place in Germany ran parallel to and reacted to what was happening in Britain and the USA, where Hawtrey, Keynes, Bellerby and Fisher (to name only a few) were caught up in a debate as to whether the price level could be stabilized by monetary policy, and thus business cycles be eliminated or at least reduced in severity (see Hudson, 1977). As Hayek later remarked, with respect to the general problem of financial instability, and its implications for overall economic stability, 'we all held similar ideas in the 1920s' (quoted in Friedman, 1969, p. 88).

The general proximate cause of such concern was, of course, the enormous fluctuations in prices and the money supply characteristic of the war and postwar experience of most European countries and the successor states of Central and Eastern Europe. But in Germany these experiences had assumed dimensions which few living at the time could have imagined possible. The Great Inflation of 1923/24 need only be named to conjure up an image of the most frightful inflation and subsequent monetary collapse. But even after the stabilization of the mark had been achieved, the German economy remained subject to short, sharp fluctuations in the level of its activity throughout the rest of the 1920s (see Borchardt, 1976). The problems raised in attempting to explain these fluctuations within the inherited general corpus of economic theory must therefore have been particularly evident to German economists. For, in a framework of theory which was built upon market-clearing and a self-equilibrating economic system, how could such fluctuations be theorized? If, in terms of that model, 'general overproduction' was logically impossible, how could it be that general overproduction did in fact quite obviously arise at successive intervals? Or, as one participant in the debate put it: if Say's Law precludes the possibility of general over-production, how can this be fitted in to a general theory of business cycles and crises? (Miksch, 1929, p. 84).

On an 'internalist' view (see Stigler, 1960) of the development of German economic thought in this connection during this period, it is difficult to overemphasize the contribution of Adolf Loewe. It was his 1926 article, 'How Can a Theory of Business Fluctuations be Derived from the Current Corpus of Economic Theory?', which summed up the dissatisfaction with inherited theory, Loewe argued that the system of thinking dominant in economics was based upon a concept of equilibrium which made it difficult for business fluctuations to be due to anything but disturbances extraneous, alien, to the economy itself, and hence outside the sphere of strictly economic explanation:

> Either the problem of the cycle falls outside the framework of economic theory, and belongs to that large number of facts which, like earthquakes or war, certainly have great economic effects but which can be at most a *datum* for theory, never a factor which it must *explain*. (1926, p. 170)

Or, Loewe continues,

> it is possible in *principle* to solve the problem but only in *opposition* to the logical conditions of the more general economic system (i.e.) a theory of the cycle can be constructed only by assuming that that system behaves with a logic other than that currently recognised.

In short,

> an economic system that works with the concept of equilibrium must necessarily be a closed, inter-dependent system, and therefore a static system. (ibid., p. 173)

Loewe thus stated the problem clearly: if theory is satisfactorily to explain the business cycle, it cannot do so simply by imposing upon an otherwise static economy an exogenous, literally unexplainable, disturbance and tracing out its effects upon the data of the system. Rather, it must seek for some causal factor which is immanent to the system itself, and whose origin and effects are capable of being theorised. What is needed, in other words, is some factor immanent to the system which can wrench apart the set of equilibrium inter-relationships which otherwise ensures its overall stability. Loewe himself regarded the system-immanent disturbing factors as stemming from the goods side, with money playing at best an inter-mediate causal role (Loewe, in Diehl, 1928, p. 366). But to some German economists, and above all Hayek, the most promising line appeared to lie in the direction of money.

While Hayek's views on economic fluctuations first became well known to English-speaking readers through his *Prices and Production*, he had already in 1928 extensively set forth his views in the volume of essays published by the VfS and in the Zurich meeting of the same group. He, like Loewe, begins with the fundamental difficulty faced by traditional theory in explaining fluctuations in the general level of economic activity: it must use the logic of its under-lying approach, equilibrium theory. Yet this logic, he continues, can do no more than to show that the economic system will always respond to external disturbances of equilibrium by the formation of a new equilibrium. The basic problem is that, within the framework of this general attitude, there is no reason why a 'general discrepancy between supply and demand should arise'. If, as it assumes, supply and demand are automatically equilibrated via the price mechanism, no shift *within* the system can give rise to that general discrepancy; the disturbing factor must therefore be something purely exogenous.

Hayek than asks: how can this mechanism of static theory handle such problems? And answers that it cannot, unless it can be extended in such a way as to explain the occurrence of divergencies between supply and demand. And 'the obvious and only possible way out of the dilemma' is to take account of the consequences of the introduction of money into the system. Here he points out that the economy with which we are dealing is not a barter but an 'indirect exchange' economy, that is, goods are not exchanged directly for goods but for money, which will then be laid out on the purchase of the goods required by the sellers. But,

> money being a commodity which, unlike all others, *is incapable of finally satisfying demand*, its introduction does away with the rigid inter-dependence and self-sufficiency of the 'closed' system of equilibrium. (Hayek, 1933, p. 16)

The phrase emphasized in the quotation above immediately implies that, if Hayek has resorted to money as the factor whose introduction has sprung the equilibrium system and made endogenous fluctuations both possible and necessary, he has done so for reasons which are ultimately far removed from those of Keynes. All theories of the business cycle must be, in Hayek's terms, 'monetary' theories: 'every explanation of business cycles must take as its starting-point the influences arising from money' (Hayek, in Diehl, 1928, p. 282). Or again: 'the starting-point for an explanation of crises has to be formed by the change in the money supply automatically occurring in the normal course of events, and not evoked by any forcible interventions' (ibid., p. 286). But while 'it is *monetary causes* which *start* cyclical fluctuations, those fluctuations are *constituted* by the successive changes in the real structure of production' (Hayek, 1933, p. 17).

It is not necessary for our present purposes to outline Hayek's theory of business fluctuations in any detail; reference need only be made to *Prices and Production* in that regard. It suffices here to say that it is the banking system which plays a key role in setting in train fluctuations through its lending activity, and the subsequent effects of that upon the relationship between the natural and the money rates of interest. A credit expansion may not be set off by the banking system lowering the money rate, but rather by its meeting at an unchanged money rate an increase in the demand for credit evoked by a rise in profitable investment opportunities, e.g. technical innovations or a surge in entrepreneurial expectations, and hence a rise in the natural rate (Hayek, 1931, p. 95). In effect, the credit expansion enables the economy to devote, or to attempt to devote, a higher proportion of its current income to investment than its volume of savings is making available for that purpose. Two points are worth emphasizing here: first, the upswing is not called forth but *enabled* to occur by an expansion of bank lending. In the case of a rise in business optimism, for example, the new investment that fuels the upswing is not at least initiated on the basis of the re-injection of funds into the circular flow that had previously been held idle. Moreover, while 'forced saving' plays a part in the upswing in channelling command over resources from certain categories of consumers to investors, the continuance of the upswing is primarily dependent upon the continued willingness of the banks to expand their loans.

Second, the banking system and *its* motivations occupy centre stage in explaining the start of an upswing, and, in the same conditioning way, the subsequent downswing.

It might be objected that a theory thus based proximately on the behaviour of the banking system is fully as open to the charge of exogeneity of the triggering disturbance which was levelled by Hayek at the non-monetary theories. But Hayek does not believe so. It is inherent in the nature of a modern economic system, he argues, that it possesses an 'elastic currency': if the banks are facing an increased demand for credit because of, for example, a wave of optimism among businessmen, they are able to accede to it because the ratio of their reserves to their deposits is not constant but variable. To put more credit into circulation, therefore, they do not have to arbitrarily cut the market rate to below the natural rate. They have only to maintain their money rate constant, and utilize the margin given to them by the variability of their reserve:deposit ratio to meet the increased demand for loans. This is a situation which, Hayek concludes, must always recur under the existing organisation of credit; it is an inherent tendency in our economy (1931, pp. 170-4).

The only exogenous factor which Hayek regards himself as drawing upon is what may be described as entrepreneurial expectations (which are likely to be shared by the banks). It is on the basis of those expectations that entrepreneurs utilize the monetary institution, and the dominant source of the money supply, the banking system, to undertake their creative functions. If, as Hicks suggests, 'expectations do appear in the General Theory, but (in the main) ... as *data*, as autonomous influences that come in from outside' (Hicks, 1969, p. 313), in Hayek they appear in no more but also in no less the same way.

Conclusion

Neither to those who seek to explain the development of economic analysis in purely 'externalist' terms, nor to those whose preference is for purely 'internalist' explanations, should the implications of the above analysis be welcome. On the one hand, externalists can point to the unprecedently sharp fluctuations in the price level and the volume of economic activity in the post-1918 period to account for the fact that economists' attention became focused upon these matters in a much more concentrated way than probably ever before. On the other hand, internalists can point out that it was a perceived logical problem in the general body of economic theory that led both Keynes and Hayek to see a monetary economy as possessed of possibilities/necessities of fluctuation which prevailing theory was logically unable to account for, even if it assumed *ad hoc*, exogenous disturbances. Hayek was especially clear on the rule of pure theory in this respect: while the statistics being accumulated especially in America were helpful in prognostication and (to a certain extent) prediction, they could provide at best a '*symptomatology* of the course of the cycle'. But they were of little help when 'what is at issue is ... the cause of cyclical fluctuations in general'; then recourse would have to be had to the explanations offered by 'abstract' theories (McCloughry (ed.), 1984, p.7).

What Keynes and Hayek had in common, therefore, was the insight of the fundamentally different character of a monetary economy. In the present context, the difference in the respective ways they embodied it in their analysis is of secondary importance. 'In the present context' must be emphasized: the limited purpose of the present essay is not meant to justify a neglect of the wider issues involved. It still remains incumbent upon us to arrive at a judgement of how successfully the two economists informed their analysis by their insight, and how adequate were the theories of fluctuations in economic activity which they developed.

10   Value and protection in the *General Theory*
John Weeks

Introduction

Above all others, two theorists stand out, their influence if not the mechanics of their theories surviving the ravages of time: Karl Marx, the greatest intellectual influence on economics of his century, and John Maynard Keynes, the greatest of this century. The influence of the former upon the latter was probably slight,[1] but both shared a vision of the capitalist economy which sets them in common category. Both Marx and Keynes operated from the premise of intuition that capitalist economies are by their nature unstable and prone to fluctuations.[2] This vision or intuition is in sharp contrast to modern, neo-classical analysis that models the capitalist economy on the presumption of inherent stability, epitomized in general equilibrium analogs.[3]

A basic goal of Keynes in the *General Theory*, he tells us, was to provide an integration of the theory of money and the theory of value, a task which he felt previous economists had either attempted and failed or prided themselves in rejecting.[4] Marx also sought to integrate the theory of value and the theory of money, though in the context of capital accumulation rather than short-run employment and output determination. This common vision of the theoretical task of political economy is in contrast to the marginalists-neoclassicals with their tendency to analyze conditions of optimal allocation with money 'neutral'.

The pursuance of the task of integrating value theory and money involves a fundamental conceptual difficulty: how does one specify the relationship between the monetary value generated by a capitalist economy, on the one hand, and the material production arising from the labour process, on the other? Since the onset of the marginalist revolution, mainstream economics had treated this issue as one of 'aggregation', with its difficulties subsumed under the rubric of 'index number' problems. This is, however, a trivialization of a profound conceptual building-block of economic theory. It is not too much to say that the manner in which the reconciliation between money value and material production is made is the core of economic theory, determining basic method and subsequent analytical detail.

On this basic issue, Keynes stands out from the marginalists who preceded him and the neo-classicals to follow, even from the post-Keynesians of the Robinson–Kaldor School and most assuredly from the Clower–Leijonhufvud 'reappraisal' approach. Keynes' introduction of the concept of the 'labour unit' early in the *General Theory* is his analytical vehicle to relate money value to material production, and represents his most revolutionary break with the theory of his contemporaries, for it implies the abandonment of the marginalist theory of value. While the labour unit is a far cry from the concepts of value developed either by Ricardo or Marx, the logical consequences of its introduction displaces Keynes' method from the world of the marginalists–neo-classicals into the classical tradition.[5]

But as Brothwell shows elsewhere in this volume,[6] Keynes chose not to break with the marginal productivity theory of production and distribution; on the contrary, he explicitly endorsed the concept of the marginal physical product of labour (the 'first classical postulate'). Thus, his use of the labour unit appears as an idiosyncratic moment of eclecticism, contradicted by what went before (acceptance of the 'first classical postulate') and what follows. Not surprisingly, the labour unit and its associated concepts such as 'user cost' disappeared from view almost at once, becoming at most a curiosity known only to students of the history of economic thought. Anyone dredging up these ideas after fifty years renders himself or herself equally curious.[7]

In what follows below, I argue that Keynes' introduction of the labour unit was profoundly important, and his own ambivalence about it disastrous for the subsequent development of macro-economics. It helped pave the way for the counter-revolution of the neo-classicals, in which the composite commodity aggregate production function devastates the theoretical insights of the *General Theory*. As a result of Keynes' endorsement of the 'first classical postulate', the integration of the theory of value and the theory of money becomes an unlikely prospect in the *General Theory*. The basis of the real monetary dichotomy remains unchallenged, only complicated in situations of disequilibrium. As a consequence, a second marginalist–neo-classical assumption that Keynes did not seriously challenge – the 'autonomous' money supply – provides the *coup de tête* for the project of theoretical integration of money and value.

The purpose of this paper is not to offer yet another interpretation of the *General Theory*, but rather an essay on method, exploring the implications of Keynes' treatment of aggregates at certain points in his theory of employment. It shall be argued that Keynes' treatment of aggregates is in sharp contrast to neo-classical theory. But reviving his discussion of aggregation cannot be the basis of a general interpretation of the *General Theory*, for Keynes himself did not pursue the more radical implications of his own analysis. In a sense the neo-classical synthesis school was quite right in discarding Keynes' novel approach to aggregates and constructing its macro-economic theory upon marginalist foundations. Analogies between social sciences and the physical sciences are suspect, but Keynes' role in economics can be compared to that of Copernicus in astronomy, who replaced a geocentric model with a heliocentric one, but did not challenge the Ptolemaic system of celestial mechanics. Like Copernicus, Keynes replaced the full-employment model with one having effective demand at its centre, but did not challenge marginal productivity theory. The debate over Keynes' contribution almost entirely involves his Copernican contribution – the role of effective demand with marginalist mechanics. This orientation is faithful to the general context of the argument in the *General Theory*. In what follows, our interest is in the *General Theory* as a shot fired (and it was perhaps little more than that) in a Newtonian revolution in economics, in which the entire basis of marginalist theory is challenged, as the general laws of gravitation challenged the Ptolemaic view of the harmony of spheres and perfect symmetry of the heavens.

My method of argument reverses the chronological development of economic theory. First considered is the macroeconomic model of the post-Keynesian synthesis. The purpose here is to demonstrate the internal inconsistencies arising from use of the marginal productivity theory of production and distribution. These problems are well known, though of little consequence in the actual practice of neo-classical modelling. The argument is that these inconsistencies derive from the particular manner in which the relation between money value and material production is treated. Here, I briefly consider the critique of the Clower–Leijonhufvud school and the 'capital controversy'. With these familiar controversies in mind, I then turn to Keynes, to argue that the labour unit provided the *General Theory* with the vehicle to avoid these inconsistencies. The concept of the labour unit itself has much in common with Ricardo's value theory, notwithstanding Keynes' critique of Ricardo for his attacks on Malthus' under-consumptionism.[8] However, use of the labour unit in the analysis of a money-exchange (capitalist) economy requires that it be monetized (which Ricardo failed to do). The particular way Keynes achieved this monetizing of the labour unit, converting it into the 'wage unit', resulted in a concept of extremely limited use. This, perhaps as much as Keynes's own ambivalence about abandoning marginal productivity theory, explains the still-birth of the labour unit as a concept of analysis. Finally, I present Marx's solution to the relation between money values and material production, and argue that it provides a way forward in macro-economic analysis.

The neo-classical synthesis

While on virtually every issue in economics, theoretical or empirical, there is disagreement and controversy, one finds general assent as to what constitutes the 'neo-classical' macroeconomic model. It is a model incorporating mathematical functions to explain personal and business expenditure, money demand and supply, and labour demand and supply. It is a general equilibrium mode, since in the absence of arbitrary limits (e.g. 'rigid money wages'), the values of all variables are determined simultaneously, and given the 'parameters' of the model the solution is unique. The unrealistic general equilibrium solution necessarily implies full employment of resources. In this model there can be no involuntary unemployment as such,[9] a powerful ideological conclusion that places the blame for unemployment upon the working class itself (or, at least, its leaders), and pre-empts all serious criticism of a capitalist economy. Indeed, taken to its logical conclusion in the hands of the 'Rational Expectation' school, we learn from the neo-classical general equilibrium model that the Great Depression which prompted Keynes' *General Theory* never, in fact, occurred.[10]

So we are at all times clear about the exact part of the model under scrutiny, it is useful to summarize it in a table. This is done in Table 10.1, where salient characteristics are briefly elaborated. As can be seen, the functions involve variables which conveniently and purposefully divide themselves into the 'real' and the 'monetary'. The real variables are consumption, investment, output and employment, as well as the capital stock which appears implicitly. The precise sense in which these variables are real is a subject of some controversy, as we shall see. The system apparently has three price variables (the price level, the money wage and the interest rate), but whether all three function as prices in the model is also subject to question. Finally, there is the 'money supply'.[11] Though it is by definition a monetary variable, it has a real form, represented by M*/P, the purchasing power of money.

In anticipation of the critique of this model, we now consider its analytical progression. Presume the system initially to be

Table 10. 1 : The neo-classical macroeconomic general equilibrium model

Functional relation	Arguments	Comment
1. Investment=savings relationship (the IS curve)	$y = c(y,r)$ $+ j(y,r)$	y, c, i in physical units, 2 commodities on expenditure side
2. Money demand= money supply (the LM curve)	$M^*/P = L(y,r)$	money supply given, bonds also appear as financial asset
3. Production function	$y = f(N)$	capital stock given, only one commodity in production
4. Labour demand	$W/P = f'(N)$	wage rate denominated in units of the only commodity produced
5. Labour supply	$N = g(W/P)$	supply price of labour denominated as in no. 4, above.

Guide: y   = real output
       c   = real consumption
       i   = real investment
       N   = employment
       r   = interest rate
       P   = price index of real output
       W   = wage rate in monetary units
       M*   = money supply

characterised by 'perfectly flexible wages and prices', and that in any non-equilibrium state, the response of sellers and buyers is to adjust prices not quantities. Since the system is a general equilibrium one, a starting-point is arbitrary; but it is convenient to begin with the labour market, since the general equilibrium solution will necessarily require $N^d = N^s$. If labour demand by firms is less than the supply offered by potential workers, then the sellers of labour services respond by offering those services at a lower price. The lower price reduces costs of production and induces capitalists to expand output and hire more workers. An increased output requires more money to circulate it, since the transactions velocity of money is constant (but not the average velocity, considering all uses of money).

However, the supply of money is given, so more output cannot be circulated unless there is an endogenous adjustment. This endogenous adjustment occurs through two mechanisms: (1) since money wages fall, unit costs fall, resulting in greater than normal profits, and competition erodes these supra-normal profits by reducing prices; and (2) the excess transactions demand for money pushes up the interest rate, which lowers bond prices, inducing wealth-holders to shift from money to bonds thus releasing money for transactions purposes. Thus, the increased output is circulated by virtue of lower unit prices and a shift of money from idle balances to active circulation. It now only remains to determine the distribution of expenditure between consumption and investment, and this is dictated by the interest rate.

The analysis is not significantly changed if one introduces arbitrary limits to variables; the result is to generate an 'unemployment equilibrium'. If, for example, the money wage rate is fixed and above its full employment level, then the money wage implies a price level inconsistent (too high) for full employment, given the exogenous money supply. Each solution is unique, however, in the sense that if any one variable is arbitrarily set, unique values for all the others are implied.

There is hardly an aspect of this model which has not come under devastating attack from within the orthodox analytical framework of the economics profession. Indeed, what is amazing is that not only does the model survive robustly, but is presented to students and used in policy-making as if these criticisms were trivial and peripheral.

Now over thirty years old, the 'capital critique' (or 'capital controversy') undermines the entire supply side of the model. What this critique demonstrates is that the 'capital stock' cannot be taken as given except in the case of a one-commodity system. Note that this has nothing to do with the question of whether or not the system is in equilibrium. The often given defence of marginal productivity theory, that it 'holds in general equilibrium', refers only to the uniqueness of a particular solution, and not the comparison of general equilibrium states. Consider two systems in general equilibrium which differ from each other in that in one the real wage is higher and the profit (interest) rate lower than in the other. It is not possible to say in which system the capital:labour ratio will be higher.[12] Therefore, it is not possible in a multi-commodity system to presume that workers offering their labour services at a lower money wage (implying a lower real wage with prices momentarily constant) will result in the rational capitalist selecting a lower capital:labour ratio. On the contrary, it may be the case that the lower real wage results in a higher capital:labour ratio for a given level of output. Thus, the neo-classical model is *necessarily* a one-commodity model on the production side. I return to this point below.

With regard to its analysis of monetary phenomena, the model suffers from another serious and potentially devastating difficulty. The entire monetary analysis turns on the concept of an exogenous money supply. In H.G. Johnson's words; 'if the supply of money is not determined by factors independent of the demand for money, we have no basis for analysis.'[13] The reason for this is easily seen: since money is valueless, the price level in the system is determined by the relationship between money in circulation and 'real output' (given the transactions velocity of money). If the money supply is endogenous then the price level is indeterminant within the model, as are money wages. Since equilibrium values of the 'real' variables require the adjustment of monetary variables, the entire system becomes indeterminant except explicitly as a barter economy.

The assumption of a 'given' money supply is neither empirically justifiable nor consistent with the theory of money itself. Textbooks in monetary economics tell us that anything can serve as money as long as it is consistently accepted by the parties to exchanges. If this is the case, how can the authorities fix the money supply? Indeed, does the term 'money supply' have any meaning when money has no value and can be created in private transactions (at least in principle)? Of course, the assumption of a given money supply is a theoretical simplification (abstraction) which no one seriously argues corresponds to reality. However, the central issue remains: is this a theoretically valid abstraction? The justification of the view that the 'authorities' control the money supply is based upon a particular theory of bank behaviour, which has been questioned by a number of neo-classical economists.[14] Further, considerable doubt has been cast upon the idea of an exogenous money supply on institutional and empirical grounds with the Radcliffe Report being the best-known presentation of the view that the supply of money adjusts endogenously to the level of transactions.[15]

A new generation of theoretical criticism has called other aspects of the model into question, criticisms associated with the 'post-Keynesian' school. The general import of these criticisms is that the neo-classical model is constructed in such a way that the monetary aspect of a capitalist economy is trivialized. One aspect of this, stressed by Leijonhufvud and Chick, is that the use of the aggregate production function (even if one suspends disbelief and ignores the capital controversy critique) renders the system one in which relative prices play no role.[16] Since there is only one commodity, there can be only one commodity price, and it is open to question what 'price' means in such a context. In effect, 'the price of output' in this context serves only as a deflator allowing us to revert to barter analysis.

Working within a one-commodity system has a number of important theoretical implications, not the least of which is the begging of the aggregation question. Independently of the problem of specifying the aggregate production function, the concept of 'aggregate output' is theoretically valid only if the relative prices of the commodities which make up the aggregate are invariant as the endogenous variables in the system change. This implies that the price of consumer commodities relative to investment commodities must be unaffected by movements in the rate of interest (or rate of profit), a rather strange result indeed. This invariance with respect to the interest rate has prompted critics to point out that in the model the rate of interest is not a price at all, but merely the rate of transformation of present into future consumption.[17] In any case, there would seem to be something basically amiss in a model in which expenditure behaviour is specified separately for consumption and investment, and in the same breath the relative price of the two types of commodities is assumed invariant. Consider the impact of an exogenous upward shift in investment when the system is in full employment equilibrium. One consequence of this must be a change in the composition of output, with investment commodities increasing their share of 'real output'. But somehow the new excess demand for investment commodities must be signalled to producers and then eliminated by increased production, all in the context of no relative price change before, during or after.

The necessity of using the one-commodity assumption is inherent in the neo-classical macro-model, and the comments so far do not exhaust its implications. It is closely related to another common aspect of the model, that there is no 'money illusion' and the demand for commodities is 'homogeneous of degree zero in prices and income'. This implies that a proportionate increase in prices and incomes leaves the consumer at the same point on his/her indifference map. While simplistic examples can be imagined to lend credibility to such an assumption,[18] it is based, in fact, on the presumption of a single commodity. The real importance of the 'homogeneity postulate' presents itself in labour market analysis. In a one-commodity economy, workers consume the same product which they produce, so that there is no difference between the cost of labour services from the point of view of capitalists and the standard of living; one is merely the reciprocal of the other. As a consequence, deflation (W/P and P/W) is not merely a 'real calculation' on the part of economic agents, but the implicit treatment of the capital–labour exchange as barter.[19] In consequence, the 'behavioural' assumption that workers are not victims of 'money illusion' is merely the restatement of the equilibrium condition for the labour market in the guise of an adjustment response to disequilibrium.

The neo-classical macroeconomic model is not basically an analysis based on simplifying assumptions; simplification is unobjectionable and necessary in all theorizing about social phenomena. Rather, the model is an analysis upon *prima facie* absurd premises which quickly manifest their logical inadequacies.[20] These become modes of thought whose contradictions fade through repeated use and familiarity. These assumptions are well characterized by Leijonhufvud as tribal myths,[21] whose acceptance comes through constant repetition and the ostracism of dissenters.

However, there is a theoretical aspect of the one commodity system which has been insufficiently stressed by critics. Its essential role in the neo-classical macro-model is to resolve the relationship between money value and material production, a central problem of political economy which we stressed in the introduction, and which is the theme around which the remainder of the discussion revolves.

Value and production

The neo-classical composite commodity
Some habits of thought are so engrained in the thinking of economists that not only do they go unquestioned, but those who raise doubts are judged to be poorly trained, mentally deficient, or some mixture of both. One of these habits of thought is the concept of 'output', and its index number-haunted familiar, 'real output'. If the common man or woman were asked, 'What is the output of the coal industry', the humble informant no doubt would answer, 'coal'; and if particularly well-informed, he or she would quote a certain tonnage of coal referring to some discrete time-period. The same informant would, of course, be surprised to discover from the neo-classical economist that the coal industry does not for purposes of economic theory produce coal, but value added; and the fact that something that goes on in the coal industry results in a product which can be burned in a grate to generate heat is of no theoretical importance (except as a source of utility to the consumer).

Any first-year student of economics knows well how to model the activity of a coal-producing firm (or any other). Output is obtained by combining capital and labour, the former fixed in the short run and the latter subject to diminishing returns. If coal firms are cost-minimizers, then these two factors are used according to the rule that their prices equal their contributions to output at the margin. Further, assuming no other factors of production and no depreciation, the 'output' of the coal firm is equal to wages plus profits (or, more euphemistically, labour income plus capital income), W + P = pQ.

A moment's reflection results in the nagging doubt that we may have a tautology here. The 'Q' in the equation, purporting to be a certain amount of coal, is not in fact the amount of coal which either exits from the pit or appears on the market during a discrete time-period. Rather, it is the amount of coal which is equal to wages plus profits. It is to be noted that this problem of relating a portion of the output to the value added generated (and to do so in a way which is not tautological) has nothing to do with the famous 'index number problem'. It arises even in the case of a homogeneous material output such as coal. Keynes was considerably disturbed by the tautological definition of 'output', which represented the conventional wisdom even in his time. The habit of thought in which 'output' equals value added has such a powerful grip upon the profession that the chapter in which he expresses his concern is probably the least read of the *General Theory*.[22]

The problem of relating money value to material product in this manner (W + P = Y) is in no way reduced by moving from the level of the firm to the economy as a whole, but only obscured by incantating warnings against the sin of 'double counting'. At the level of the economy as a whole, the familiar aggregate production function tells us that the production of 'final goods' arises from the combination of labour and capital, and that this 'real output' resolves itself into factor incomes (wages plus profits in the simplest case). Yet clearly the collection of machinery available to society in any moment, combined with the workers to operate that machinery, does not in fact produce only 'final goods', but also produces intermediate commodities. Thus, the neo-classical 'output' which is the result of labour using machines is not the actual commodities emerging from production processes, but the income generated in these processes. The well-known aggregate function $Y = f(K,L)$ is not a *production* function, but a *value-added function*.

The question then arises, in what units is this value-added function to be measured? This is the point at which the index number problem arises. Monetary units will not serve, for this would render the function a complete tautology, making $Y = W + P$ a function of wL and rK (wages times the number employed plus the rate of return times the capital stock). Measurement must be in terms of some commodity or commodities. If the system produces more than one 'final good', then measurement is possible only if (1) the various commodities are always produced in the same proportion, or (2) their proportions change, but they are combined by an unchanging weighting system. The first solution is tantamount to assuming a single commodity, as many writers have pointed out. The second solution is the index number problem in its pure form, since the set of weights neo-classicals have in mind are commodity prices of some base period.

The need for neo-classical production theory to restrict itself to a one-commodity world thus arises prior to the phenomenon of re-switching which has dominated the theoretical debate over the value-added function. Sraffa offered a solution to the problem of how to relate the income generated in production to the quantity of commodities produced, but this solution is itself a critique of marginal productivity theory and implies its invalidity.[23]

The basic problem with neo-classical aggregate production theory is that its solution to relating the value of output to material output is on the one hand trivial and on the other fraught with internal contradictions. In as far as the solution is based upon an aggregate production function in a one commodity world the solution is trivial. Under these conditions, value production is material production, and the 'aggregate supply of final commodities' identically equal to income generated. The identity stands because there is no inter-mediate production in the system. When expanded to include more than one commodity, the theory takes on characteristics similar to that of the Ptolemaic system of celestial motion, with addition assumptions and restrictions complicating the model in the manner of epicycles. The function of these is not to bring the analysis closer to the concrete, but to render it increasingly abstract in order to provide logical support for established modes of thought.

Keynes on aggregation

Among the least noted parts of the *General Theory* are its passages treating the problem of aggregation. These are largely ignored even by those taking issue with neo-classical aggregation procedure with their critique apparently inspired by Keynes.[24] The lack of attention given to them is in contrast to Keynes' statement that proper choice of units of measurement and the definition of income were two of the 'three perplexities which most impeded my progress'.[25] At an early stage in the *General Theory*, Keynes takes issue with his contemporaries' treatment of aggregation:

> The National Dividend, as defined by Marshall and Professor Pigou, measures the volume of current output or real income, and not the value of output or money income. ... But it is à grave objection to this definition for such a purpose [formulating economic models] that the

> community's output of goods and services is a non-homogeneous complex which cannot be measured, strictly speaking, except in certain special cases, as for example when all the items of one output are included in the same proportions in another output.[26]

It would appear from the last part of this quotation that Keynes' concern is over the problem of weighting, the index number problem as such. However, it quickly becomes clear that his disquiet is not with the relatively banal (though unsolvable) difficulty that index numbers ignore substitution effects. This we see in his famous reflection upon the content of comparing the relative happiness and statecraft of Queens Elizabeth and Victoria.[27] Indeed, he explicitly accepts price and quantity deflators as valid tools for calculating historical comparisons of income and welfare. His objection is not to statistical measures, but rather to conceptual devices employed in abstract modelling; namely, the 'general price level' and 'real income'. These 'vague concepts' that are 'avowedly imprecise and approximate', whose use should be limited to cases 'when we are attempting historical comparison'.[28]

His particular objection is to the concept 'real income', whose 'precise definition is an impossible task.'[29] With this conclusion in hand, Keynes abandons the concept of 'real income' altogether for purposes of theorizing, and in doing so, abandons also the marginalist camp. For if real income cannot be defined precisely, the aggregate output which is the result of combining capital and labour is a will-o'-the-wisp, having the role in economics played by the unicorn in zoology. His analysis, he tells us, will use other categories,

> In dealing with the theory of employment I propose ... to make use of only two fundamental units of quantity, namely quantities of money-value and quantities of employment. ...
>   It is my belief that much unnecessary perplexity can be avoided if we limit ourselves strictly to the two units, money and labour, when we are dealing with the behaviour of the economic system as a whole.[30]

If we do 'limit ourselves strictly' to money and labour, then we necessarily must reject the entire neo-classical macroeconomic model, since all of its equations are calculated in units of 'real income/output' or employ the 'imprecise and approximate' measure identified as the general level of prices (see Table 10.1). Here in Chapter 4 of the *General Theory* Keynes makes a fundamental break with his fellow economists (and subsequent ones). What is involved is much more profound than merely a selection of appropriate units. Indeed, it is unfortunate that he called Chapter 4 'The Choice of Units', for it would be better described as 'Choice of Method'.

The choice of money and labour as theoretical quantities indicates a particular method of abstraction. These are not concepts created by the mind of the theorist, but categories the theorist confronts in the concrete ('real world'). While neither is a simple category – many things can serve as money and labour comes in many varieties – for all of their complexities they are categories which cannot be refuted, discredited through logic. One can argue that they are not the appropriate categories upon which to construct a theory of employment, but one cannot question their validity. In other words, here Keynes has not created abstractions, but drawn his abstractions out of the confusing complexity of reality. At this point, at least, his basic method of abstraction is similar to that employed by Marx, who selected the category 'commodity' from the concrete in order to construct his theory.[31]

Neo-classical categories are by contrast creations of the theory in many cases. 'Utility' is an obvious example, which imposes a certain interpretation upon consumption, income and leisure, when other interpretations are possible.[32] The concept of 'real income/output' is also a mental construct, with no direct analog in the economic process. While obviously people's material circumstances improve and deteriorate, and countries at different times produce more and less wealth, these do not in the concrete take the form of a homogeneous or composite commodity, much less one which can be continuously differentiated with respect to labour and capital. Real output, the general price level, and the stock of capital are all concepts whose relation to reality is not obvious, which accounts for their 'imprecise and approximate' character.

Whether or not Keynes was aware of the basic methodological distinction between ideal abstractions (creations of the mind) and abstractions drawn from reality is difficult to judge, for one finds little explicit treatment of methodology in his writings.[33] However, there is considerable circumstantial evidence in the *General Theory* to suggest that at the very least he had a strong intuition that reality should inspire theory. This orientation manifests itself frequently, particularly in his discussion of expectations, where his abstract analysis continuously interacts with his concrete experience of the financial world of his time.[34] His open contempt for mathematic models is another example.[35] Even more striking by its contrast to neo-classical theory is his lengthy discussion of the basis of the macro-economic variables income, consumption, investment and saving, all of which are defined with reference to the categories of the capitalist enterprise, prior to employing them in an abstract model.

For one used to neo-classical parables such as 'capital arises in the abstinence from current consumption', Keynes' method of definition is extraordinary. His definitions are all derived from the cash-flow or net worth position of capitalist firms. Income, for example, is defined as the sales of the capitalist firm, minus purchases from other firms, with a complicated adjustment for the change in the value of equipment.[36] Here he has been faithful to his pledge to adhere strictly to money values, as well as defining categories so they are directly quantifiable. More important theoretically, and little noted, his treatment of income involves no tautological identity with aggregate supply. Income in the *General Theory* is *not* the value added generated by the production of final goods and services (as in the neo-classical production function), but business receipts from sale of all commodities, minus intermediate costs (user cost).

Further, because this conceptualization of income is empirically based, it is necessarily dynamic, while the neo-classical concept, real income = aggregate supply, is static. Neo-classical theory income determination is static because of its comparative static, general equilibrium context. But methodological causality runs the other way, too: the measure of income itself is static, based upon 'normal economic motives in a world in which our views concerning the future are fixed and reliable in all respects'.[37] Neo-classical real output is that income which accrues to the factors of production when all firms use the same technique, with technology unchanging, and capital values given.

Keynes' money income is defined and measured net of anticipated and unanticipated changes in the value of equipment and inventories due to the interaction of technical change and competition.[38] In the concrete operation of a money economy, capitalist firms continuously suffer capital losses or enjoy capital gains as a result of price changes. These, in turn, affect the distribution of cash flow between factor incomes and non-factor costs. If technical change results in a fall in the value of the firm's equipment, then the full value of the equipment at time of purchase cannot be recaptured in product sales. This fact of business life, which is independent of the issue of whether expectations are fulfilled or not,[39] shows why it is necessary to define income independently of the production of final commodities (aggregate supply).[40] Because of changes in the valuation of equipment and stocks, money income may be less, the same, or more than the money value of consumption commodities plus investment commodities.

Thus, in Keynes' theory there are three aggregates, defined independently of each other (though not functionally independent):

1. total factor income, equal to sales minus intermediate cost, with adjustment for accumulation of equipment and changes in the value of stocks and equipment due to price changes;
2. aggregate supply of final commodities, the consumption and investment commodities which capitalists place on the market; and
3. aggregate demand, the expenditure by workers and capitalists on consumption commodities, and the expenditure of capitalists on investment commodities.

In neo-classical theory there are only two aggregates for the first two above are the same by definition. To my knowledge, Keynes and Marx are the only important theorists to distinguish clearly these three aggregates, though Marx did so on a quite different basis.[41] With only two aggregates, macroeconomics is the analysis of the matching of expenditure and income (value added), so we do indeed have an 'income–expenditure' model in the strictest sense. With three aggregates, the analysis is inherently dynamic, which partly explains how Keynes could consider dynamic processes while employing what appears to be comparative statics, an apparent contraction commented upon by numerous authors.[42]

Before turning to Keynes' specification of aggregate supply and the labour unit, it is important to bring out a further characteristic of his treatment of income in Chapter 6. It is to be noted that income is defined with reference to the *total value* of entrepreneurial sales and stock accumulation.[43] In this procedure, it is the total money value of commodities which is taken as the independent variable. That is, Keynes agrees with the person in the street that the value of coal is equal to the price one pays for it, not the wages paid out by coal firms plus the profits they obtain.

Treating the value of commodities as their true value – intermediate cost plus factor income – brings Keynes close to a full break with marginalist value theory. On this basis, he could move on to relate the money value of commodities to their material production and completely break the income–output tautology. Indeed, in his appendix to Chapter 6, he seems on the verge of this step. After defining 'user cost', whose largest component is in general materials cost, he says that user cost 'has, I think, an importance for the classical [marginalist] theory of value which has been overlooked'; and that,

> The concept of user cost enables us, moreover, to give a clearer defini-
> tion than usually adopted of the short period supply price of a unit of a
> firms' saleable output. For the short period supply price is the sum of the
> marginal factor [labour] cost and the marginal user cost.[44]

The reason for this clearer definition arises from the nature of commodity prices themselves, as he goes on to say.

> Whereas it may be occasionally convenient in dealing with *output as a whole* to deduct user cost, this procedure deprives our analysis of all reality if it is habitually (and tacitly) applied to the output of a single industry or firm, since it divorces the 'supply price' of an article from any ordinary sense of its price . . .[45]

If one continues down this road, the labour theory of value awaits the traveller, or at the least, the Sraffian standard commodity. With explicit consideration of intermediate costs, a part of the value of a commodity (however measured) is not created in production but represents the passed-on value of other commodities. Since a machine also passes on its value through depreciation in use – what Keynes calls the 'sacrifice' of equipment[46] – it is not at all clear why equipment should be singled out among non-labour inputs for the distinction of creating value. Keynes was well aware of this line of logic, and explicitly endorsed it in a strikingly nineteenth-century classical passage in his chapter on capital.

> It is much preferable to speak of capital as having a yield over the course of its life in excess of its original cost, than as being *productive* . . .
>
> I sympathise, therefore, with the pre-classical doctrine that everything is *produced by labour*, aided by what used to be called art and is now called technique, by natural resources which are free or cost a rent according to their scarcity or abundance, and by the results of past labour, embodied in assets, which also command a price according to their scarcity or abundance. It is preferable to regard labour . . . as the sole factor of production, operating in a given environment of technique, natural resources, capital equipment and effective demand. *This partly explains why we have been able to take the unit of labour as the sole physical unit which we require in our economic system, apart from units of money and time.*[47]

Thus, we find a consistent thread of argument from the definition of income via user cost to some labour-based value theory. The labour-based value theory would then provide the link between material production and money aggregates, the first measured in homogeneous labour units and related to the second via a theory of the purchasing power of money. When these passages are extracted from context and strung together, it appears that Keynes was on the verge of a Newtonian revolution in economics. One possible theoretical line coming out of these passages is the mark-up theory of pricing claimed by some post-Keynesians as the true microeconomics of aggregate analysis.[48] However, Keynes' explicit endorsement of a labour-based value theory would provide a considerable improvement upon the current mark-up literature.[49] A major empty box in mark-up models is the theory of total profit, for while the degree of monopoly might be a plausible explanation of differential mark-ups, it cannot explain the average mark-up for the economy as a whole.[50] A labour-based value theory resolves this problem, since wages plus profits equal the current labour input, and the division between the two can be determined in a number of ways.[51]

However, these quotations from Keynes are passages taken out of a basically marginalist context and can by no stretch of the imagination nor textual interpretation be said to characterize the *General Theory*. After in one place carefully defining the concept of user cost and warning the reader that industry supply curves should not be constructed on the basis of marginal labour cost alone, Keynes proceeds to abandon his own advice and use supply functions net of user cost.[52] Whatever might be the validity of specifying aggregate demand and aggregate supply net of user cost, it is a complete tautology to specify industry demand and supply in this way. Industry supply net of user cost is the value added of the industry. But the expenditure by purchasers on an industry's output minus user cost yields no recognizable economic category; it is purely arbitrary. It is not the industry's value added (though it may equal it if supply equals demand), and it does not equal the final demand for the industry's output. If the industry produces a con-sumer commodity or an investment commodity, its entire output is 'final', and nothing should be netted out, neither from the supply function nor from the effective demand function. If the industry produces an intermediate commodity, then none of its demand is final, net or gross of user cost. Thus, specifying industry supply and demand functions net of user cost is arbitrary, and cannot be the basis for aggregation to economy-wide aggregate supply of 'final goods' on the one hand, and the effective demand for these, on the other. This is what Keynes does, though warning the reader against such an exercise. At the end of Chapter 6, he writes:

> It is easily shown that the conditions of supply ... can be handled in terms of our two chosen units [money and labour] ... without reference to quantities of output, whether we are concerned with a particular firm or industry or with economic activity as a whole.[53]

This is allegedly achieved 'for a given firm (and similarly for a given industry or for industry as a whole)', by the following function,

$$Z_r = \phi r(Nr).$$

Where Nr is employment and Z_r 'the return expectation of which will induce a level of employment Nr'. It is quickly clear that this rather vague and convoluted definition of Z is nothing more than price times quantity. For he then specifies an output function, Or = $\psi_r(N_r)$, and writes,[54]

$$p = \frac{Z_r}{O_r} = \frac{\Phi_r(N)}{\psi_r(Nr)}$$

Once an output function is introduced as the implicit basis of the aggregate supply function, we are back to a neo-classical-style production function which Keynes proclaimed that he wanted to avoid. The close kinship of the Z-function to the familiar Y = f(K, L) is shown in Chapter 20 when Keynes does some mathematical manipulations. Here he is considering the elasticity of employment with respect to changes in aggregate demand, and we are told that in general the first derivative of Z with respect to N is less than unity. In other words, there are diminishing returns to labour. Just as a rose by any other name would smell as sweet, a functional relationship between output and labour in which the addition of labour results in diminishing returns is a neo-classical production function, whatever it may be called.[55] Thus, the neo-classical synthesis model with a one-commodity aggregate production function can find a close cousin, if not a virtual twin, in the *General Theory*.

In summary, one can conclude that Keynes was certainly concerned with the marginalist treatment of the relationship between material production and money values. He was concerned enough to propose some of the elements of an alternative treatment, and to include in passing an endorsement of pre-marginalist value theory. However, he was not concerned enough to abandon marginal productivity theory, preferring to incorporate it into a theory of employment whose innovative features were the stress on effective demand, the dynamics of a money exchange economy, and the role of expectations.

Marx on value and production

In the economics profession Marx is treated as a bizarre eccentric to be ignored or a dangerous dogmatic to be refuted (usually in the form of a straw man). This is unfortunate, but not surprising, for Marx was a bitter critic of the economic system which provides the livelihoods of most economists. Much of the treatment of Marx's contribution directs itself to his value theory. Obsession with Marx's theory of value and exploitation has resulted in little attention being directed to his analysis of capitalism as a money economy, even by Marxists.

It was argued above that a fundamental problem when analysing a money economy is the relationship between the values generated by production and the material output of production. Only when this relationship is specified can one produce a theory of distribution, employment and accumulation. An analysis of distribution pre-supposes a determinant quantity to be distributed; a theory of employment is derivative from a theory of what the employed produce; and accumulation must ultimately be limited by material production over and above current resource use. Neo-classical theory, as we have seen, provides a particular solution to this analytical problem. Output is apparently defined in 'real' terms. The move from quantities to money value is achieved via the quantity theory of money. This formulation of the relationship between physical quantities and money values becomes increasingly complex and intricate due to the contradictory nature of the basic concepts, real output/income and money.[56] While the purpose of elaboration and complexity should be to move theory closer to reality, in the neo-classical synthesis greater complexity makes theory more at variance with reality and increasingly limited even in formal application. The analytic movement is from the abstract to the more abstract,[57] until one reaches the point where the apparently simple parables hold only in general equilibrium states.

Keynes was not content with this theoretical method. In the *General Theory* his attempt is to theorize in a way that moves the analysis from the abstract to the concrete, so that complications reveal rather than obscure the great variety of economic pheno-mena. He did not, however, break with the marginalist solution to the relationship between material quantities and money values. His alternative, with the labour unit playing the role of theoretical mediation, is so fraught with analytical difficulties[58] that it is hardly surprising that subsequent economists retreated to the pre-Keynesian solution.

Considerable literature has been devoted to Marx's theory of the value of commodities. Virtually none has taken up his macro-economics as such, what he called the analysis of the circulation of commodities, though recent work by Foley could be interpreted as doing so.[59] Marx argued:

> [T]he difficulty [in aggregate analysis] does not lie in analysing the value of the social product itself. It arises when the *value* components of the social product are compared with its *material* components.[60]

That is, the problem arises when, as one must, the theorist seeks to relate the money income generated in production to some portion of society's output. To say that income is the money value of 'final goods' is sheer tautology except when there is equilibrium in the goods market. If there is excess demand or excess supply in the goods market, then money income maps on to the production of final goods only because convention defines inventory change as investment.[61] But if we define 'final goods' as those bought by the consumer or by capitalists with the characteristic of being used to produce other goods and having a life longer than the current period, then in general, money income does not represent the quantity of final goods produced. And if one accepts the assertion that economies are never actually in equilibrium, then it follows that money income never corresponds with the production of final goods, measured in real or money units. How, then, is income to be related to production?

Marx sought to resolve this problem with a two-part argument. First, he pointed out that every commodity has two aspects – it has an exchange aspect (its price) and a material aspect. The difference between the two is manifested in any exchange, in which the seller appropriates the money value of the commodity, and the buyer takes possession of its material form. The point is an obvious one. Modern macroeconomics, following a tradition going back to Adam Smith,[62] treats the material character of commodities as being of no analytical importance, focusing solely upon the value added generated by production. This treatment is justified by arguing that to do otherwise would be 'double-counting'. However, the double-counting argument is merely the way one measures value added with logical consistency. It is not a defence of why macroeconomics should address itself to value-added aggregates rather than total commodity value inclusive of intermediate costs. For example, input–output analysis does not make double-counting errors, though it analyses commodity production and circulation in terms of the gross value of those commodities.

In Marx's theory of circulation, the 'price' of a commodity corresponds to what one normally means by that term – what is paid for it. With prices defined in this way, he must necessarily include on the production side all of the inputs that constitute the cost of production, including those consumed in production – intermediate commodities. We should note that 'intermediate' here is defined with respect to each commodity, for the output of any production process may serve as the input to another. Further, for the economy as a whole, the flow of new products over a period includes articles of personal consumption, equipment, and inputs which will be consumed in production in the next or subsequent periods. It is true, of course, that theoretical situations can be constructed in which value added is equal to the money value of consumer commodities and investment commodities, or even where value added equals consumption commodities alone and net investment is zero (Marx called the latter situation 'simple reproduction').

However, even in these two cases the value of intermediate commodities cannot be said to be included within the value of final commodities, nor their demand derivative from the latter. These intermediate commodities will be carried forward and consumed in the production of commodities in the subsequent period. Further, the demand for intermediate commodities produced but not used in the current period is obviously not determined by the demand for final commodities in the current period, but the demand for the latter in subsequent periods. Finally, some intermediate commodities of the current period go to produce intermediate commodities in the next period, in an infinite chain that never involves a final commodity. This implies that a portion of total output is never incorporated into final commodities in any meaningful sense.

For a neo-classical theorist such an argument is like passing from a Euclidian to a non-Euclidian world, in which suddenly one encounters impossible angles and shapes. These non-Euclidian flows never appear in a neo-classical model because it is an equilibrium-based system in which time does not exist; and, more fundamentally, commodities are not produced, but rather it is income that is produced. Because income or value added is by its nature homogeneous, the temptation to employ a one-commodity assumption is irresistible.

The great advantage of the gross product approach to macroeconomics is that it corresponds to the way economies actually function – commodities are in fact produced with intermediate products. This, however, is an argument that would leave most economists cold, notwithstanding how sensible it is. In terms of abstract analytics, considering the gross product lends an inherent dynamism to the theory, with each period organically linked to the next through the current use of past production. Instability can be analysed in terms of the conditions of production (productivity and costs) in one period differing from conditions of exchange (income flows and demand) in the next. Technical change, banished to the 'long run' in neo-classical (and post-Keynesian) analysis serves as the major destabilizing factor. Commodities carry forward stamped with the production conditions of a particular kind, entering circulation with market conditions unsettled by innovations. In this way, one can consider the gains and losses in capital values which Keynes stressed in the *General Theory*. Further, this framework is well suited for incorporating expectations.

However, the gross product framework would seem to suffer from at least one serious difficulty. By considering the material character of commodities, has it not abandoned macro-aggregates altogether and reduced the economy to an infinite number of markets and production processes? At this point, one moves to the second step in Marx's analysis, his method of aggregation. Marx's procedure was to divide all commodities between those intended for consumption by people and those intended for use in the production of other commodities. This division is not to be confused with either the intermediate/final commodity dichotomy nor the consumption/investment commodity distinction. Production commodities ('means of production') include both equipment (fixed capital) and inputs which are completely consumed in the production process.

This division of the total product implies an analysis of aggregate demand quite different from the Keynesian or neo-classical formulation. Production in the current period is initiated by capitalists advancing money in exchange for the means of production and labour services.[63] This exchange, money capital converted to productive capital in Marx's terminology, has some kinship with Keynes' 'finance motive', particularly in recent elaboration of that concept.[64] This advance of money capital determines the aggregate demand for the current period, directly for means of production and indirectly for consumption commodities by the payment of wages. Since the time-period of analysis corresponds to a production period, consumer commodities are produced and sold in the current period, while means of production sold currently were produced in the previous period. This treatment of production and sale, which corresponds to the way that firms operate, links each period with the next, as mentioned above.

This commodities-into-commodities framework captures a fundamental feature of capitalist economies which is largely lost in neo-classical general equilibrium: the impulse to production and exchange comes from the owners of capital, for output is determined by their decision about how much capital to advance. We find the same stress in Keynes' supply functions (for a firm, industry or the economy as a whole). However, in Marx's framework, the central role of 'entrepreneurs' is made much more explicit by dropping the derived demand treatment of inputs and labour, and considering the demand for these as the first step in commodity circulation and production.

This alternative macroeconomic framework, in as far as it is an analysis of markets and money aggregates only, is in no way dependent upon a labour theory of value.[65] The labour theory of value enters to resolve the fundamental relationship between the material aspect of commodities and their exchange or money aspect. Means of production and consumer commodities are each aggregated on the basis of the labour time necessary to produce them, past and current, under prevailing techniques.[66] While aggregating by labour time certainly has its difficulties, these difficulties are probably less theoretically debilitating than those associated with the concept of 'real income'.

Conclusion

It is unfortunate that Keynes felt that Marx's contribution to economic science could be digested in an afternoon. This dismissal, along with his preference for Malthus over Ricardo, the other great value theorist of the pre-marginalist school, resulted in his discarding the foundation for an alternative to marginal productivity theory. Had he not been so taken by the kinship of his effective demand theory to the under-consumptionism he found in Malthus' apologetics for the British landlord class, he might have given Ricardo his due, as Marx certainly did.[67] However, had Keynes pursued the Ricardian and Marxian insights, it is quite possible that he would have been written off by his fellow economists as a hopeless eccentric, for the majority of them found even his innovations within the marginalist framework to be unpalatable. Had Keynes taken the more radical route and made a clear break with his 'classicals', the fiftieth anniversary of the *General Theory* might have gone unheralded by the economics profession.

Notes

1. Here comes to mind Keynes' famous comment that he read Marx in an afternoon.
2. An interesting discussion of Keynes on this issue is found in Fine (1980), pp. 46 ff.
3. Recent neo-classical literature has developed disequilibrium dynamics. This analysis remains in the context of a general equilibrium framework, representing a generalization of the basic neo-classical model of an inherently stable capitalist economy. See Muellbauer and Portes (1978).
4. See Leijonhufvud (1968), pp. 22 ff.; and Keynes (1936, ch. 21).
5. I shall use the term 'classical economics' to refer to the pre-marginalist economists from Smith to the latter Mill, as opposed to Keynes' use of the term.
6. John Brothwell, 'Why aren't we all Keynesians now …'. Chick argues that Keynes did not accept marginal productivity theory as one usually thinks of it, because his demand for labour is the *effective* demand, not the *notional* demand.
7. Chick, for example, to whom we refer below. See Victoria Chick, 'Time and the Wage-Unit in the Method of The *General Theory*: History and Equilibrium', in Lawson and Pesaran, (ed.) (1985).
8. Keynes, 1936, pp. 362–4.
9. For a clear discussion of this, see Harris (1981), pp. 241, 261.
10. On this extraordinary argument and an insight into how logic can subdue reality and lead to Bedlam as Keynes put it, see Sargent (1976) and Darby (1976).
11. Because the money supply is constant, it is not necessary to treat non-uniqueness which results from money being neutral.
12. This is because of 're-switching'. A technique which had been abandoned as too 'capital-intensive' in the high wage system, when (say) wages fell to their

current level in that system, may be the prevailing technique in the low-wage system. Of the many discussions of re-switching, one of the clearest is in Fine (1980), pp. 98–118.

13. Johnson (1972), p. 59.
14. The neo-classical treatment of bank behaviour is critically assessed in Chick (1979), pp. 14 ff.
15. HMSO (1959).
16. Leijonhufvud (1968), pp. 89 ff.; and Chick (1983), ch. 7.
17. Leijonhufvud (1968), pp. 157–85.
18. Branson, for example, seeks to convince one of realism of this assumption by offering the case in which one morning we awake to discover that there has been a currency reform, so, for example, ten 'old pounds' will be replaced by one 'new pound'. The analytical correspondence between this example and an actual process of inflation with time lags between price changes and income changes – not to mention distributional effects – is not clear. Branson (1972), pp. 61–2.
19. See Chick (1983), ch. 7.
20. Other inadequacies we have not mentioned are: the inconsistency of Walras' Law with the Quantity Theory, the stylized treatment of market behaviour, and that Heath Robinson figure, the Walrasian auctioneer. On these, see respectively Harris (1981), pp. 58–60; Coddington (1983), pp. 92–4; Clower, in Hahn and Brechling (eds) (1965).
21. Leijonhufvud (1981), ch. 7.
22. These are Chapters 4 and 6, and appended to the latter, 'Appendix on User Cost'.
23. Sraffa (1960, ch. IV).
24. Leijonhufvud (1968), for example, in his insightful chapter, 'The Aggregate Structure of Alternative Models', makes no reference to Keynes' lengthy discussion of economic aggregates, appearing in Chapters 4, 6 and 7 of *The General Theory*.
25. Keynes (1936), p. 37.
26. Ibid., pp. 37–8.
27. Ibid., p. 40.
28. Ibid., p. 43.
29. Ibid., p. 39.
30. Ibid., p. 43.
31. For a brief discussion of Marx's method, see Weeks (1983), ch. 2 and appendix.
32. Implicit in the concept of utility is a particular ends-means value judgement, postulating that work is the arduous means by which one achieves the pleasurable end of consumption (or non-work). On the arbitrariness of the ends-means dichotomy, see Leijonhufvud (1968), pp. 233–4.
33. Here we refer to methodology in the broadest, epistemological sense.
34. See Keynes (1936), chs 5, 11 and 12.
35. Keynes (1936), p. 280, footnote, for example.
36. Ibid., pp. 53–4. Again, comparisons with Marx present themselves.
    See Marx's reference to empirical categories in the context of his analysis of value and surplus value. Marx (1976), ch. 15.
37. Keynes (1936), p. 294.
38. Ibid., pp. 57–60, where he distinguishes between basic and current supplementary cost.
39. Whether anticipated or unanticipated, smooth or irregular, technical change results in the devaluation of old equipment – unless one believes there is no such thing as inferior technologies.
40. Keynes was quite explicit about this. Referring to his treatment of income, he says

> . . . [W]e are still left with the advantage that we do not require at any stage of the analysis to allocate the factor cost between the goods which are sold and the equipment which is retained. (Keynes, 1936, p. 67)

41. Marx's treatment of aggregates is found in Volume II of *Capital*, where he brings forward from the first volume his distinction among money capital, productive capital, and commodity capital. The first corresponds to aggregate demand, the third to aggregate supply, and the second allows for the analysis of the generation of value added. Marx (1978), chs 1–3.
42. See Chick (1985); and Leijonhufvud (1968), pp. 50 ff.
43. In Keynes' notation, A is total sales, A_1 purchases of commodities from other capitalists, and G and G' the value of equipment and stocks at the beginning and end of the period over which income is measured. Current value accruing to the entrepreneur is thus: $A - A_1 + (G' - G)$. Current income is this money value minus expenditure on maintenance of equipment and stocks (noted as B' by Keynes). For a rare (and not very sympathetic) discussion of Keynes' definition of income, see Tew (1953).
44. Keynes (1936), p. 67.
45. Ibid.
46. Ibid., p. 53.
47. Ibid., pp. 213–14, last emphasis added.
48. Eichner and Kregel (1975), p. 1276.
49. See Coddington (1983), pp. 92 ff.
50. Fine and Murfin (1984).
51. For an exposition of the argument that 'bargaining power' or 'class struggle' determines factor shares, along with a labour-based value theory to justify the argument, see Edward Nell, 'The Fall of the House of Efficiency', in Weintraub (ed.) (1973).
52. Keynes (1936), pp. 23–5.
53. Ibid., p. 44.
54. He defines the price as $p = Z_r/O_r$, which he calls the 'ordinary supply curve'. It is unclear what he means by this, for it certainly is not the Marshallian supply curve, which is $p = MCr$.
55. Chick has a different interpretation of the Z function, arguing, 'variations in output per man due to diminishing returns ... have been removed from the labour unit' (Chick, 1985, p. 205). She has pointed out that only in Chapter 3 of *The General Theory* does Keynes refer to a production function for output as a whole.
56. In particular, the re-switching phenomenon, the inconsistency between Walras' Law and the Quantity Theory, and the inclusion of the Walrasian auctioneer to avoid 'false trading'.
57. Coddington puts it succinctly:

    [I]n order to provide a basis for a manageable analysis of market phenomenon, the [neoclassical] analysis of individual choice has to be of a particularly stereotyped and artificial kind. (Coddington, 1983, pp. 92–3)

58. While sympathetic to Keynes' attempt, Chick judges it 'incomplete and unsatisfactory' (1985, p. 205).
59. Foley (1982). Sraffian analysis is a special case. While it considers material production, it does not have a theory of money values.
60. Marx (1978), p. 506.
61. Part of the accumulation of inventories represents intermediate commodities. Since they have not been incorporated in final commodities, they cannot be eliminated by a double-counting argument.
62. It would be a relatively familiar world to a Sraffian, however, for we are describing 'the production of commodities by means of commodities'.
63. Marx used the term 'labour power' to refer to the commodity that workers sell.
64. Graziani notes the intellectual lineage of the 'finance motive' from the work of Marx. Graziani (1984), p. 13. For an empirical study of the finance motive, see Smith (1979).
65. It is, however, inconsistent with the marginal productivity theory of value, since means of production, currently consumed or long-lived, pass their value

(however defined) on to subsequent periods. That is, they cannot create value as the neo-classical 'capital stock' does.

66.   Much recent debate in non-marginalist value theory is over the validity of aggregating in terms of labour time. See Steedman and Sweezy (eds) (1981); and Weeks (1982), chs I and II.

67.   Marx considered Ricardo to be the best representative of British or continental political economy, and devoted the lion's share of his history of economic thought (*Theories of Surplus Value*), to Ricardo's analysis.

Bibliography

Ackley, G. (1961) *Macroeconomics*, Macmillan, New York.

Aldcroft, D. H. (1970) *The Interwar Economy: Britain, 1919–1939*, Batsford, London.

Ando, A. and Modigliani, F. (1963) 'The "Life-Cycle" hypothesis of saving: aggregate implications and tests', *American Economic Review*, 53, pp. 55–84.

Arrow, K. J. (1959) 'Toward a theory of price adjustment', in M. Abramovitz *et al.*, *The Allocation of Economic Resources*, Stanford University Press, Stanford.

Artis, M. J. (1981) 'Incomes policies: some rationales', in Fallick, J. L. and Elliot, R. F., *Incomes Policies, Inflation and Relative Pay*, George Allan and Unwin, London.

Artis, M. J. (1982) 'Why do forecasts differ', *Panel Paper no. 17*, Economics Division, Bank of England, London.

Artis, M. J. and Lewis, M. K. (1981) *Monetary Control in the UK*, Philip Allan, London.

Balogh, T. (1973) *Fact and Fancy in International Economic Relations*, Pergamon, London.

Balogh, T. (1982) *The Irrelevance of Conventional Economics*, Weidenfeld and Nicolson, London.

Barrett, C. R. and Walters, A. A. (1966) 'The stability of Keynesian and monetary multipliers in the United Kingdom', *Review of Economics and Statistics*, 48, pp. 395–405.

Barro, R. J. (1979) 'Second thoughts on Keynesian economics', *American Economic Review Papers and Proceedings*, 69, pp. 54–9.

Barro, R. J. and Grossman, H. I. (1971) 'A general disequilibrium model of income and employment', *American Economic Review*, 61, pp. 82–93.

Barro, R. J. and Grossman H. I. (1976) *Money Employment and Income*, Cambridge University Press, Cambridge.

Baumol, W. J. (1952) 'The transaction demand for cash: an inventory theoretic approach', *Quarterly Journal of Economics*, 66, pp. 545–56.

Baumol, W. J. (1977) 'Say's (At Least) Eight Laws, or what Say and James Mill may really have meant', *Economica*, n.s., 44, pp. 145–61.

Beenstock, M., Capie, F. H. and Griffiths, B. (1984) 'The UK economic recovery in the 1930s', *Panel Paper no. 23*, Economics Division, Bank of England, London.

Benassy, J. P. (1976) 'The disequilibrium approach to monopolistic price setting and general monopolistic equilibrium', *Review of Economic Studies*, 43, pp. 69–81.

Benham, F. C. G. (1938) *Economics*, Pitman, London.

Benjamin, D. K. and Kochin, L. A. (1979) 'Searching for an explanation of unemployment in inter-war Britain', *Journal of Political Economy*, 87, pp. 441–78.

Beveridge, W. H. (1930) *Unemployment. A Problem of Industry*, 2nd edn, Longmans, Green & Co., London.

Beveridge, W. H. (ed.) (1931) *Tariffs: the Case Examined*, Longmans, London.

Beveridge, W. H. (1936) 'An analysis of unemployment I', *Economica*, n.s., 3, pp. 357–86.

Beveridge, W. H. (1937) 'An analysis of unemployment II', *Economica*, n.s., 4, pp. 1–17.

Beveridge, W. H. (1937) 'An analysis of unemployment III', *Economica*, n.s., 4, pp. 168–83.

Beveridge, W. H. (1944) *Full Employment in a Free Society*, George Allen & Unwin, London.

Block, F. L. (1977) *The Origins of International Economic Disorder*, University of California Press, Berkeley.

Bohm-Bawerk, E. (1930) *The Positive Theory of Capital*, Stechert, New York.

Booth, A. E. and Glynn, S. (1975) 'Unemployment in the inter-war period: a multiple problem', *Journal of Contemporary History*, 10, pp. 611–36.

Booth, A. E. (1983) 'The "Keynesian Revolution" in economic policy making', *Economic History Review*, 2nd ser., 36, pp. 103–23.

Booth, A. E. and Glynn, S. (1983) 'Unemployment in inter-war Britain: A case of re-learning the lessons of the 1930s?', *Economic History Review*, 2nd ser., 36, pp. 329–48.

Booth, A. E. and Glynn, S. (1985) 'Building counterfactual pyramids', *Economic History Review*, 2nd ser., 38, pp. 89–94.

Borchardt, K. (1976) 'Wachstum und Wechsellagen 1914–1970', in Auben, Hermann and Zorn, Wolfgang (eds) *Handbuch der Deutschen Wirtschafts und Sozialgeschichte*, Stuttgart.

Branson, W. H. (1972) *Macroeconomic Theory and Policy*, Harper & Row, New York.

Bretherton, R. A., Burchardt, F. A. and Rutherford, R. (1941) *Public Investment and the Trade Cycle in Great Britain*, Oxford University Press, Oxford.

Brett, E. A., Gilliatt, S. and Pople, A. (1982) 'Planned trade, Labour Party policy and U.S. intervention: the successes and failures of post-war reconstruction', *History Workshop Journal*, 13, Spring, pp. 130–42.

Broadberry, S. N. (1984) 'Fiscal policy in Britain during the 1930s', *Economic History Review*, 2nd ser., 37, pp. 95–102.

Brothwell, J. F. (1975) 'A simple Keynesian's response to Leijonhufvud', *Bulletin of Economic Research*, 27, 1 May, pp. 3–21.

Brothwell, J. F. (1976) 'Rejoinder', *Bulletin of Economic Research*, 28, 2 November, pp. 102–3.

Brothwell, J. F. (1982) 'Monetarism, wages and employment policy in the U.K.', *Journal of Post Keynesian Economics*, 4, 3, Spring, pp. 376–87.

Brown, A. J. (1938) 'The liquidity preference schedules of the London clearing banks', *Oxford Economic Papers*, n.s., 1, pp. 49–82.

Brown, A. J. (1939) 'Interest, prices and the demand schedule for idle money', *Oxford Economic Papers*, n.s., 2, pp. 46–91.

Burchardt, F. A. *et al.* (1944) *Economics of Full Employment*, Basil Blackwell, London.

Butkiewicz, J. L., Koford, K. J. and Miller, J. B. (eds) (1986) *Keynes' Economic Legacy*, Praeger, New York.

Callaghan, Rt Hon. J. (1976) *Report of 74th Annual Conference*, Labour Party.

Cassel, G. (1931) *Theory of Social Economy*, Harcourt Brace, New York.

Chamberlin, E. H. (1933) *The Theory of Monopolistic Competition*, Harvard University Press.

Chenery, H. (1952) 'Overcapacity and the acceleration principle', *Econometrica*, 20, pp. 1–28.

Chick, V. (1979) *The Theory of Monetary Policy*, Basil Blackwell, London.

Chick, V. (1983) *Macroeconomics after Keynes*, Philip Allan, Oxford.

Chick, V. (1985) 'Time and the wage-unit in the method of *The General Theory*: history and equilibrium', in Lawson, T. and Pesaran, H. (eds) *Keynes' Economics: Methodological Issues*, Croom Helm, London & Sydney.

Clower, R. W. (1969) *Monetary Theory*, Penguin, Harmondsworth.

Clower, R. W. (1979) 'The Keynesian counter-revolution: A theoretical appraisal', in Korliras, P. G. and Thorn, R. S. (eds) *Modern Macroeconomics*, Harper and Row, New York.

Coats, A. W. (1982) 'The distinctive LSE ethos in the inter-war years', *Atlantic Economic Journal*, X, March, pp. 18–30.

Coddington, A. (1976) 'Keynesian economics: the search for first principles', *Journal of Economic Literature*, 14, pp. 1258–73.

Coddington, A. (1983) *Keynesian Economics: The Search for Fir̃t Principles*, George Allen & Unwin, London.

Cole, G. D. H. (ed.) (1933) *What Everyone Wants to Know About Money*, Gollancz, London.

Collins, M. (1982) 'Unemployment in interwar Britain: still searching for an explanation', *Journal of Political Economy*, 90, pp. 369–79.

Corry, B. and Laidler, D. E. W. (1967) 'The Phillips relation: a theoretical explanation', *Economica*, n.s., 34, 134, pp. 189–97.

Cowling, K. *et. al.* (1981) *Out of Work: Perspectives of Mass Unemployment*, Department of Economics, University of Warwick.

Cross, R. (1982) 'How much voluntary unemployment in interwar Britain?', *Journal of Political Economy*, 90, pp. 380–5.

Crotty, J. R. (1983) 'On Keynes and capital flight', *Journal of Economic Literature*, 21, March, pp. 59–65.

Dalton, H. (1923) *Principles of Public Finance*, Routledge, London.

Darby, M. R. (1976) 'Three and a half million U.S. employees have been mislaid: or, an explanation of unemployment, 1934–1941', *Journal of Political Economy*, 84, February, pp. 1–16.

Davidson, P. (1972) *Money and the Real World*, Macmillan, London.

Davidson, P. (1977) 'Money and general equilibrium', *Economie Appliquée*, 30, 4, pp. 541–64.

Davidson, P. (1983) 'The marginal product curve is not the demand curve for labour and Lucas's labour supply function is not the supply curve for labour in the real world', *Journal of Post Keynesian Economics*, 6, Fall, pp. 105–17.

Davidson, P. (1984) 'Reviving Keynes's revolution', *Journal of Post Keynsian Economics*, 6, Summer, pp. 561–75.

Davidson, P. *et al.* (1985) 'Symposium: increasing returns and unemployment theory', *Journal of Post Keynesian Economics*, 8, Spring, pp. 350–403.

Diehl, K. (ed.) (1928) *Beiträge zur Wirtschaftstheorie. Zweiter Teil:*

Konjunkturforschung und Konjunkturtheorie, Schriften des VfS, München/ Leipzig.

Dimsdale, N. H. (1984) 'Employment and real wages in the inter-war period', *National Institute Economic Review*, 110, November, pp. 94– 103.

Dow, J. C. R. (1968) *The Management of the British Economy, 1945–60*, Cambridge University Press, Cambridge.

Drazen, A. (1980) 'Recent developments in macroeconomic disequilibrium theory', *Econometrica*, 48, pp. 283–306.

Eatwell, J. (1983) 'The long-period theory of employment', *Cambridge Journal of Economics*, 7, pp. 269–85.

Eatwell, J. and Milgate, M. (eds) (1983) *Keynes's Economics and the Theory of Value and Distribution*, Duckworth, London.

Eichner, A. S. and Kregel, J. A. (1975) 'An essay on post-Keynesian Theory: a new paradigm in economics', *Journal of Economic Literature*, 13, 4, December, pp. 1293–314.

Feinstein, C. H. (1972) *National Income, Expenditure and Output of the United Kingdom, 1855–1965*, Cambridge University Press, Cambridge.

Feinstein, C. H. (ed.) (1983) *The Managed Economy: Essays in British Economic Policy and Performance since 1929*, Oxford University Press, Oxford.

Fender, J. (1981) *Understanding Keynes*, Wheatsheaf Books, Brighton.

Fetter, F. W. (1965) *The Development of British Monetary Orthodoxy 1797–1875*, Harvard University Press, Cambridge, Mass.

Fine, B. (1980) *Economic Theory and Ideology*, Edward Arnold, London.

Fine, B. and Murfin, A. (1984) *Macroeconomics and Monopoly Capitalism*, Wheatsheaf Books, Brighton.

Fisher, I. (1930) *Theory of Interest*, Macmillan, New York.

Foley, D. (1982) 'Realisation and accumulation in a Marxian model of the circuit of capital', *Journal of Economic Theory*, 28, pp. 300–19, December.

Friedman, M. (1953) 'The methodology of positive economics', in *Essays in Positive Economics*, University of Chicago Press, Chicago.

Friedman, M. (1956) 'The quantity theory of money – a restatement', in *Studies in the Quantity Theory of Money*, University of Chicago Press, Chicago.

Friedman, M. (1957) *A Theory of the Consumption Function*, Princeton University Press, Princeton.

Friedman, M. (1968) 'The role of monetary policy', *American Economic Review*, 58, March, pp. 1–17.

Friedman, M. (1969) *The Optimum Quantity of Money and Other Essays*, Macmillan, London.

Garegnani, P. (1976) 'On a change in the notion of equilibrium in recent work on value and distribution', in Brown, M. *et al.* (eds) *Essays in Modern Capital Theory*, North-Holland, Amsterdam pp. 25–45.

Garegnani, P. (1983) 'Notes on consumption, investment and effective demand', in Eatwell and Milgate (eds) (1983).

Garside, W. R. (1980) *The Measurement of Unemployment*, Basil Blackwell, Oxford.

Garside, W. R. and Hatton, T. J. (1985) 'Keynesian policy and British unemployment in the 1930s', *Economic History Review*, 2nd ser., 38, pp. 83–8.

Gayer, A. D., Rostow, W. W. and Schwartz, A. J. (1953) *The Growth and*

Fluctuation of the British Economy 1790–1850, Vol. I, Clarendon Press, Oxford.

Glynn, S. and Howells, P. G. A. (1980) 'Unemployment in the 1930s: the "Keynesian solution" reconsidered', *Australian Economic History Review*, 20. pp. 28–45.

Goodwin, R. (1985) 'A personal perspective on mathematical economics', *Banca Nazionale del Lavoro Quarterly Review*, 38, 152, pp. 31–43.

Grandmont, J. M. and Laroque, G. (1976) 'On temporary Keynesian equilibria', *Review of Economic Studies*, 43, pp. 53–67.

Graziani, A. (1984) 'The debate on Keynes' finance motive', *Economic Notes* (Siena), 13.

Grossman, H. I. (1972) 'Was Keynes a "Keynesian"?: A Review Article', *Journal of Economic Literature*, 10, pp. 26–30.

Grossman, H. I. (1979) 'Why does aggregate employment fluctuate?', *American Economic Review Papers & Proceedings*, 69, pp. 64–9.

Haberler, G. (1937) *Prosperity and Depression*, League of Nations, Geneva.

Hahn, F. H. and Brechling, F. P. R. (eds) (1965) *The Theory of Interest Rates*, St Martin's Press, New York.

Hahn, F. H. (1978) 'On non-Walrasian equilibria', *Review of Economic Studies*, 45, pp. 1–17.

Hansen, B. (1970) *General Equilibrium Systems*, McGraw-Hill, New York.

Harris, L. (1981) *Monetary Theory*, McGraw-Hill, New York.

Harrod, R. F. (1936) *The Trade Cycle*, Clarendon, Oxford.

Harrod, R. F. (1937) 'Mr Keynes and traditional theory', *Econometrica*, 5, pp. 74–86.

Harrod, R. F. (1939) 'An essay in dynamic theory', *Economic Journal*, 49, pp. 14–33.

Harrod, R. F. (1951) *The Life of John Maynard Keynes*, Macmillan, London.

Harrod, R. F. (1972) *The Life of John Maynard Keynes*, Penguin, Harmondsworth.

Hart, O. (1982) 'A model of imperfect competition with Keynesian features', *Quarterly Journal of Economics*, 96, pp. 109–38.

Hatton, T. J. (1984) *Vacancies and Unemployment in the 1920s*, Centre for Economic Research, Discussion Paper no. 10.

von Hayek, F. A. (1931) *Prices and Production*, Routledge, London.

von Hayek, F. A. (1933) *Monetary Theory and the Trade Cycle*, Jonathan Cape, London.

von Hayek, F. A. (1939) *Profits, Interest and Investment*, Routledge, London.

von Hayek, F. A. (1971) 'The use of knowledge in society', in H. Townsend (ed.) *Price Theory*, Penguin, Harmondsworth (first published in *American Economic Review*, 35, 1945, pp. 519–30).

von Hayek, F. A. (1975) *Full Employment At Any Price?*, IEA, London.

von Hayek, F. A. (1978) *New Studies in Philosophy, Politics, Economics and the History of Ideas*, Routledge & Kegan Paul, London.

von Hayek, F. A. (1983) 'The Austrian critique', *The Economist*, 11 June.

Henderson, H. D. (1932) *Supply and Demand*, Nisbet, London.

Henry, S. G. B. and Ormerod, P. A. (1978) 'Incomes policy and wage inflation: empirical evidence for the UK', *National Institute Economic Review*, no. 95.

Henry, S. G. B. (1981) 'Incomes policy and aggregate pay', in Fallick, J. L. and Elliot, R. F., *Incomes Policies, Inflation and Relative Pay*, George Allen & Unwin, London.

HMSO (1940) *Royal Commission on the Distribution of the Industrial Population. Report*, Cmd. 6153, London.

HMSO (1944) *White Paper on Employment Policy*, Cmd. 6527, London.

HMSO (1959) *Committee on the Working of the Monetary System: Report*, Cmd. 827, London.

HMSO (1971) Department of Employment, *British Labour Statistics: Historical Abstract, 1886–1968*, London.

HMSO (1986) Central Statistical Office, *Economic Trends Annual Supplement*, London.

Hession, C. H. (1984) *John Maynard Keynes*, Macmillan, New York.

Hicks, J. R. (1932) *The Theory of Wages*, Macmillan, London.

Hicks, J. R. and Allen, R. G. D. (1934) 'A reconsideration of the theory of value', *Economica*, n.s., 1, pp. 52–76, 196–219.

Hicks, J. R. (1937) 'Mr. Keynes and the "Classics": a suggested interpretation', *Econometrica*, 5, pp. 147–59.

Hicks, J. R. (1939) *Value and Capital*, Clarendon Press, Oxford.

Hicks, J. R. (1969) 'Automalists, Hawtreyans and Keynesians', *Journal of Money, Credit and Banking*, I, 3 (August).

Hicks, J. R. (1973) 'Recollections and documents', *Economica*, n.s., 40, 157, February, pp. 2–11.

Hicks, J. R. (1974) *The Crisis in Keynesian Economics*, Basil Blackwell, Oxford.

Hicks, J. R. (1977) *Economic Perspectives*, Clarendon Press, Oxford.

Hicks, J. R. (1980–81) 'IS–LM: An explanation', *Journal of Post Keynesian Economics*, 3, Winter, pp. 139–54.

Howitt, P. (1985) 'Transaction costs and unemployment', *American Economic Review*, 75, pp. 88–100.

Howson, S. and Winch, D. (1977) *The Economic Advisory Council 1930–1939*, Cambridge University Press, Cambridge.

Hudson, M. A. (1977) *The Quantity Theory, Irving Fisher and the Stability of the Dollar: A Study in Monetary Theory and History*, PhD Thesis, Leeds University.

Hutchinson, T. W. (1978) *On Revolutions and Progress in Economic Knowledge*, Cambridge University Press, Cambridge.

Johnson, H. G. (1972) *Macroeconomics and Monetary Policy*, Aldine Publishing Company, Chicago.

Jorgenson, D. W. (1967) 'The theory of investment behaviour', in Ferber, R. (ed.) *Determinants of Investment Behaviour*, Columbia University Press, New York.

Kaldor, N. (1942) 'Professor Hayek and the concertina effect', *Economica*, n.s., 9, no. 36, pp. 359–82.

Kaldor, N. (1983) 'Keynesian economics after fifty years', in Worswick and Trevithick (eds) (1983).

Keynes, J. M. (1931) 'The pure theory of money: a reply to Dr Hayek', *Economica*, 11 November, pp. 387–97.

Keynes, J. M. (1936) *The General Theory of Employment, Interest and Money*, Macmillan, London.

Keynes, J. M. (1937) 'The general theory of employment', *Quarterly Journal of Economics*, Vol. 51, pp. 209–23.

Keynes, J. M. (1939) 'Relative movements of real wages and output', *Economic Journal*, March.
Keynes, J. M. (1940a) *How to Pay for the War*, Macmillan, London.
Keynes, J. M. (1940b) Letter to *New Statesman and Nation*, 6 April.
The Collected Writings of John Maynard Keynes (edited for the Royal Economic Society by Elizabeth Johnson, Donald Moggridge and Sir Austin Robinson), Macmillan/Cambridge University Press.
I   Indian Currency and Finance (1913).
IV   A Tract on Monetary Reform (1923).
V   A Treatise on Money, 1 The Pure Theory of Money (1930).
VI   A Treatise on Money, 2 The Applied Theory of Money (1930).
VII   The General Theory of Employment, Interest and Money (1936).
IX   Essays in Persuasion (1931) (with additional essays).
X   Essays in Biography (1933) (with additional essays).
XIX   Activities 1922–29: The Return to Gold and Industrial Policy.
XXV   Activities 1940–44: Shaping the Post-War World: The Clearing Union.
XXVI   Activities 1941–46: Shaping the Post-War World: Bretton Woods and Reparations.
XXIX   The General Theory and After (Supplement to Volumes XIII and XIV).
Knight, F. H. (1921) *Risk, Uncertainty and Profit*, Houghton, New York.
Latsis, S. J. (1976) 'A research programme in economics', in Latsis, S. J. (ed.) *Method and Appraisal in Economics*, Cambridge University Press, Cambridge.
Lee, F. S. (1981) 'The Oxford challenge to Marshallian supply and demand: the history of the Oxford Economists' Research Group', *Oxford Economic papers*, n.s., 33, pp. 339–51.
Lehfeldt, R. A. (1926) *Money*, Oxford University Press, London: Milford.
Leijonhufvud, A. (1968) *On Keynesian Economics and the Economics of Keynes*, Oxford University Press, Oxford.
Leijonhufvud, A. (1971) *Keynes and the Classics*, Institute of Economic Affairs, London.
Leijonhufvud, A. (1979) 'Keynes and the Keynesians: a suggested interpretation', in Korliras, P. G. and Thorn, R. S. (eds) *Modern Macroeconomics*, Harper and Row (first published in *American Economic Review*, 57, 1967, pp. 401–10).
Leijonhufvud, A. (1981) *Information and Co-ordination*, Oxford University Press, Oxford.
Leijonhufvud, A. (1983) in Worswick and Trevithick (eds) (1983).
Lippmann, W. (1934) 'Self-sufficiency: some random reflections', *Foreign Affairs*, 1, 12, no. 2, January.
Lipsey, R. G. (1960) 'The relation between unemployment and the rate of change of money wage rates in the United Kingdom 1862–1957: a further analysis', *Economica*, n.s., 27, February, pp. 1–31.
Loewe, A. (1925) 'Der gegenwärtige Stand der Konjunkturforschung in Deutschland', in Bonn, M. J. and Payli, M. (eds) *Die Wirtschaftswissenschaft nach dem Kriege*, München/Leipzig, Zweiter Band, S. 332.
Loewe, A. (1926) 'Wie ist Konjunkturtheorie überhaupt möglich?', *Weltwirtschaftliches Archiv*, 24 Bd., Heft 2, Oktober.
Lowe, A. (1965) *On Economic Knowledge*, Harper and Row, London.
Lucas, R. E. and Sargent, T. J. S. (1981) *Rational Expectations and Econometric Practice*, Allen & Unwin, London.

McCloughry, R. (ed.) (1984) *Money, Capital and Fluctuations: Early Essays* [by] F. A. Hayek, Routledge & Kegan Paul, London.

MacFie, A. E. (1934) *Theories of the Trade Cycle*, Macmillan, London.

MacGregor, D. H. (1949) *Economic Thought and Policy*, Oxford University Press, London.

Machlup, F. (1967) 'Theories of the firm: marginalist, behavioural, managerial', *American Economic Review*, 57, pp. 1–33.

Malinvaud, E. (1977) *The Theory of Unemployment Reconsidered*, Basil Blackwell, Oxford.

Malthus, T. R. (1820) *Principles of Political Economy*, John Murray, London.

Marshall, A. (1920) *Principles of Economics*, 8th edition, Macmillan, London.

Marx, K. (1976) *Capital*, Vol. I, Penguin, Harmondsworth.

Marx, K. (1978) *Capital*, Vol. II, Penguin, Harmondsworth.

Marx, K. (1971) *A Contribution to the Critique of Political Economy*, Lawrence and Wishart, London.

Meade, J. E. (1936) *An Introduction to Economic Analysis and Policy*, Clarendon Press, Oxford.

Meltzer, A. H. (1981), 'Keynes' *General Theory*: a different perspective', *Journal of Economic Literature*, 19, March, pp. 34–64.

Meltzer, A. H. (1983) 'Interpreting Keynes', *Journal of Economic Literature*, 19, March, pp. 66–78.

Metcalf, D., Nickell, S. J. and Floros, N. (1982) 'Still searching for an explanation of unemployment in interwar Britain', *Journal of Political Economy*, 90, pp. 386–99.

Middleton, R. (1985) *Towards the Managed Economy*, Methuen, London.

Middleton, R. (1981) 'The constant employment budget balance and British policy, 1929–39', *Economic History Review*, 2nd ser., 34, pp. 266–86.

Middleton, R. (1982) 'The Treasury in the 1930s: political and administrative constraints to acceptance of the "New" Economics', *Oxford Economic Papers*, n.s., 34, pp, 48–77.

Middleton, R. (1983) 'The Treasury and public investment: a perspective on interwar economic management', *Public Administration*, 61, pp. 351–70.

Middleton, R. (1984) 'The measurement of fiscal influence in Britain in the 1930s', *Economic History Review*, 2nd ser., 37, pp. 103–6.

Miksch, L. (1929) *Gibt es eine allgemeine Überproduktion?* Jena.

Mill, J. S. (1844) *Essays on Some Unsettled Questions in Political Economy*, Parker, London.

Modigliani, F. (1944) 'Liquidity preference and the theory of interest and money', *Econometrica*, 12, pp. 45–88.

Moggridge, D. E. (ed.) (1974) *Keynes: Aspects of the Man and his Work*, Macmillan, London.

Mommsen, W. J. (ed.) (1981) *The Emergence of the Welfare State in Britain and Germany, 1850–1950*, Croom Helm, London.

Morgan, B. (1978) *Monetarists and Keynesians, Their Contribution to Monetary Theory*, Macmillan, London.

National Institute of Economic and Social Research (1984) *National Institute Model 7*, National Institute of Economic and Social Research, London.

Negishi, T. (1979) *Microeconomic Foundations of Keynesian Macroeconomics*, North-Holland, Amsterdam.

Ogilvy, J. (1977) *Many Dimensional Man*, Oxford University Press, New York.

Ohlin, B. (1937) 'Some notes on the Stockholm theory of savings and investment', *Economic Journal*, 47, pp. 53–69, 221–40.

Omerod, P. A. and Worswick, G. D. N. (1982) 'Unemployment in interwar Britain', *Journal of Political Economy*, 90, pp. 400–9.

Patinkin, D. (1958) *Money, Interest and Prices*, 1st edn, Harper and Row, New York.

Patinkin, D. (1959) 'Keynesian economics rehabilitated: a rejoinder to Professor Hicks', *Economic Journal*, 69, pp. 582–7.

Patinkin, D. (1965) *Money, Interest and Prices*, 2nd edn, Harper and Row, New York.

Peden, G. C. (1980) 'Keynes, the Treasury and unemployment in the late nineteen-thirties', *Oxford Economic Papers*, n.s., 32, pp. 1–18.

Peden, G. C. (1983) 'Sir Richard Hopkins and the "Keynesian Revolution" in employment policy, 1929–45', *Economic History Review*, 2nd ser., 36, pp. 167–81.

Peden, G. C. (1984) 'The "Treasury View" on public works and employment in the interwar period', *Economic History Review*, 2nd ser., 37, pp. 167–81.

Phillips, A. W. (1958) 'The relation between unemployment and the rate of change of money wage rates in the United Kingdom, 1861–1957', *Economica*, n.s., 25, 100, November, pp. 283–99.

Phillips, G. A. and Maddock, R. T. (1973) *The Growth of the British Economy, 1918–1968*, George Allen & Unwin, London.

Pigou, A. C. (1928) *A Study in Public Finance*, Macmillan, London.

Pigou, A. C. (1920) *The Economics of Welfare*, Macmillan, London.

Pigou, A. C. (1927) *Industrial Fluctuations*, Macmillan, London.

Pilling, G. (1986) *The Crisis of Keynesian Economics: A Marxist View*, Croom Helm, London.

Piore, M. (1983) 'Labour market segmentation: to what paradigm does it belong?', *American Economic Review*, 73, pp. 249–53.

Polanyi, M. (1973) *Personal Knowledge*, Routledge & Kegan Paul, London.

Pollard, S. (1970) 'Trade union reactions to the economic crisis', in Pollard, S. (ed.) *The Gold Standard and Employment Policies Between the Wars*, Methuen, London.

Pullen, J. (1982) 'Malthus on the doctrine of proportions and the concept of the optimum', *Australian Economic Papers*, 21, December, pp. 270–85.

Radice, E. (1939) *Savings in Great Britain*, Clarendon Press, Oxford.

Radice, H. K. (1984) 'The national economy – a Keynesian myth?', *Capital and Class*, 22, Spring, pp. 111–40.

Reichenbach, H. (1951) *The Rise of Scientific Philosophy*, Berkeley.

Richardson, H. W. (1967) *Economic Recovery in Britain, 1932–9*, Weidenfeld & Nicolson, London.

Robbins, L. (1935) *The Nature and Significance of Economic Science*, Macmillan, London.

Robinson, E. A. G. (1972) 'J. M. Keynes: economist, author, statesman', *Economic Journal*, 82, pp. 531–46.

Robinson, E. A. G. (1986) 'A child of the times', *The Economist*, 20 December.

Robinson, J. (1933) *The Economics of Imperfect Competition*, Macmillan, London.

Robinson, J. (1964) *Economic Philosophy*, Penguin, Harmondsworth.

Robinson, J. (1973) 'What has become of the Keynesian Revolution?', Presidential Address, Section F, British Association 1972. Reprinted in *After Keynes*, Basil Blackwell, Oxford.

Robinson, J. (1977) 'Michael Kalecki', *Oxford Bulletin of Economics and Statistics*, February, pp. 1–17.

Robinson, J., Garegnani, L. L. *et al.* (1966) 'Paradoxes in capital theory: a symposium', in *The Quarterly Journal of Economics*, 80, 4, pp. 503–83.

Robinson, M. E. (1922) *Public Finance*, Cambridge University Press, Cambridge.

Rollings, N. (1985) 'The "Keynesian Revolution" and economic policy-making: a comment', *Economic History Review*, 2nd. ser., 38, pp. 95–100.

Rotheim, R. J. (1981) 'Keynes's monetary theory of value (1933)', *Journal of Post Keynesian Economics*, 3, 4, Summer, pp. 568–85.

Samuelson, P. A. (1939) 'Interactions between the multiplier analysis and the principle of acceleration', *Review of Economics and Statistics*, 21, May, pp. 75–8.

Samuelson, P. A. (1939) 'A synthesis of the principle of acceleration and the multiplier', *Journal of Political Economy*, 47, December, pp. 786–97.

Sargan, J. D. (1964) 'Wages and prices in the UK: a study in econometric methodology', in Hart, P. E., Mills, G. and Whitaker, J. K. *Econometric Analysis for National Economic Planning*, Butterworths, London.

Sargan, J. D. (1980) 'A model of wage-price inflation', *Review of Economic Studies*, 47, January, pp. 97–112.

Sargent, T. J. (1976) 'A classical macro-economic model for the United States', *Journal of Political Economy*, 84, April, pp. 207–37.

Sawyer, M. C. (1982) *Macro-economics in Question*, Wheatsheaf Books, Brighton.

Sayers, R. S. (1938) *Modern Banking*, Oxford University Press, London.

Sayers, R. S. (1940) 'Business men and the terms of borrowing', *Oxford Economic Papers*, n.s., no. 3, pp. 23–31.

Schumpeter, J. A. (1952) *Ten Great Economists*, Allen & Unwin, London.

Shackle, G. L. S. (1938) *Expectations, Investment and Income*, Clarendon Press, Oxford.

Shackle, G. L. S. (1967) *The Years of High Theory*, Cambridge University Press, Cambridge.

Shackle, G. L. S. (1983) 'The romantic mountain and the classic lake: Alan Coddington's Keynesian Economics', *Journal of Post Keynesian Economics*, 6, pp. 241–51.

Skidelsky, R. A. (ed.) (1977) *The End of the Keynesian Era*, Macmillan, London.

Skidelsky, R. A. (1983) *John Maynard Keynes: A Biography*, Macmillan, London.

Skinner, A. S. (1967) 'Say's Law: origins and content', *Economica*, n.s., 34, May, pp. 153–66.

Smith, A. (1958) *An Inquiry into the Nature and Causes of the Wealth of Nations*, Vol. I, Methuen, London.

Smith, P. (1979) 'Keynes' finance motive: some empirical evidence', *Journal of Post Keynesian Economics*, 1, pp. 55–68.

Snower, D. J. (1983) 'Imperfect competition, underemployment and crowding-out', *Oxford Economic Papers*, 35, pp. 245–70.

Solow, R. M. (1956) 'A contribution to the theory of economic growth', *Quarterly Journal of Economics*, 70, pp. 65–94.

Sraffa, P. (1932) 'Dr Hayek on money and capital', *Economic Journal*, 42, pp. 42–53.

Sraffa, P. (ed.) (1952) *The Works and Correspondence of David Ricardo*, Vol. 7, Cambridge University Press, Cambridge.

Sraffa, P. (1960) *The Production of Commodities by Means of Commodities*, Cambridge University Press, Cambridge.

Stamp, J. C. (1922) *Wealth and Taxable Capacity*, King, London.

Steedman, I. and Sweezy P. (eds) (1981) *The Value Controversy*, New Left Books, London.

Stewart, M. (1967) *Keynes and After*, Penguin, Harmondsworth.

Stigler, J. (1960) 'The influence of events and policies on economic theory', *American Economic Review*, 50, pp. 36–45.

Stone, R. (1945) 'The analysis of market demand', *Journal of the Royal Statistical Society*, 108, pp. 286–382.

Sweezy, P. (1946) 'John Maynard Keynes', *Science and Society*, 10, pp. 398–405.

Taussig, F. W. (1921) *Principles of Economics*, Macmillan, New York.

Taussig, F. W. (1927) *International Trade*, Macmillan, New York.

Tew, B. (1953) 'Keynesian Accounting', *Yorkshire Bulletin*, vol. 2, August, pp. 147–53.

Thirlwall, A. P. (ed.) (1976) *Keynes and International Monetary Relations*, Macmillan, London.

Thirlwall, A. P. (ed.) (1978) *Keynes and Laissez-Faire*, Macmillan, London.

Thomas, M. (1983) 'Rearmament and economic recovery in the late 1930s', *Economic History Review*, 2nd ser., 36, pp. 552–79.

Thomas, T. J. (1975) *Aspects of United Kingdom Macroeconomic Policy During the Interwar Period: A Study in Econometric History*, Cambridge PhD thesis.

Thurow, L. (1983) *Dangerous Currents: The State of Economics*, Oxford University Press, Oxford.

Tinbergen, J. (1933) 'The notions of horizons and expectancy in dynamic economics', *Econometrica*, 1, pp. 247–64.

Tinbergen, J. (1935) 'Annual survey: suggestions in quantitative business cycle theory,' *Econometrica*, 3, pp. 241–308.

Tobin, J. (1967) 'Unemployment and inflation: the cruel dilemma', in Phillips, A. and Williamson, O. E., *Prices: Issues in Theory and Public Policy*, University of Pennsylvania Press, Pennsylvania.

Tomlinson, J. (1981) 'Why was there never a "Keynesian Revolution" in economic policy?', *Economy and Society*, 10, pp. 72–87.

Tomlinson, J. (1984) 'A "Keynesian Revolution" in economic policy-making', *Economic History Review*, 2nd. ser., 37, pp. 258–62.

Trevithick, J. A. (1975) 'Keynes, inflation and money illusion', *Economic Journal*, 85, March, pp. 101–13.

Wallis, K. F. (ed.) (1984) *Models of the UK Economy*, Oxford University Press, Oxford.

Wattel, H. L. (ed.) (1986) *The Policy Consequences of J. M. Keynes*, Macmillan, London.

Watzlawick, P., Weabland, J. H. and Fisch, R. (1974) *Change*, Norton, New York.

Weeks, J. (1983) *Capital and Exploitation*, Princeton University Press, Princeton.

Weintraub, S. (ed.) (1973) *The Annals of the American Academy of Political and Social Science*, September.

Weitzman, M. L. (1982) 'Increasing returns and the foundations of unemployment theory', *Economic Journal*, 92, pp. 787–804.

Wicksell, J. G. K. (1934) *Lectures on Political Economy*, Routledge & Kegan Paul, London.

Wicksteed, P. H. (1910) *The Common Sense of Political Economy*, Macmillan, London.

Wiles, P. and Routh, G. (eds) (1984) *Economics in Disarray*, Basil Blackwell, Oxford.

Williamson, J. (1983) 'Keynes and the international economic order', in Worswick, D. and Trevithick, J. (eds) (1983).

Willoughby, J. A. (1982), 'A reconsideration of the protectionism debate. Keynes and import controls', *Journal of Economic Issues* XVI, 2, pp. 555–61.

Wilson, T. and Andrews P. W. S. (eds) (1951) *Oxford Studies in the Price Mechanism*, Oxford University Press, Oxford.

Winch, D. (1966) *James Mill: Selected Economic Writings*, University of Chicago Press, Chicago.

Winch, D. (1969) *Economics and Policy: A Historical Survey*, Hodder & Stoughton, London.

Worswick, G. D. N. and Trevithick, J. A. (eds) (1983) *Keynes and the Modern World*, Cambridge University Press, Cambridge.

Worswick, G. D. N. (1984) 'The sources of recovery in the UK in the 1930s', *National Insititute Economic Review*, 110, November, pp. 85–93.

Worswick, G. D. N. (1985) 'Jobs for all?', *Economic Journal*, 95, March, pp. 1–14.

Youngson, A. J. (1968) *Britain's Economic Growth, 1920–66*, 2nd edn, George Allen & Unwin, London.

Subject index

Name index

Allen, M. 21
Allen, R.G.D. 22
Ando, A. 131
Andrews, P.W.S. 40, 44n.
Arrow, K.J. 143

Balogh, T. 10, 39, 40, 171n.
Barrett, C.R. 87n
Barro, R.J. 63n., 137, 150
Baumol, W.J. 132
Beenstock, M. 84
Benham, F.C.G. 30
Benjamin, D.K. 84
Beveridge, W.H. 33, 74, 75, 85
Blair, W. 33, 34
Block, F.L. 171n.
Bohm-Bawerk, E. 23
Booth, A.E. 75–7, 80, 81
Bowley, A.L. 39
Bretherton, R.A. 21, 32, 33, 72
Broadberry, S.N. 86n.
Brothwell, J.F. 27, 186
Brown, A.J. vii
Bryce, R.B. 15
Burchardt, F.A. 32, 39, 40, 72

Capie, F.H. 84
Cassel, G. 22, 41
Chamberlin, E.H. 40
Chick, V. 63n, 191, 207n.
Clark, C. 42
Clay, H. 22
Clower, R.W. 55, 57, 62n., 136–8, 186, 187
Coddington, A. 149, 209
Cole, G.D.H. 20, 171n.
Crotty, J.R. 171n.

Dalton, H. 22, 29
Daniel, G. 33
Darby, M.R. 207n.
Davidson, P. 47, 48, 50, 57, 62n., 63n.

Drazen, A. 139

Eatwell, J. 16

Feinstein, C.H. 66
Fender, J. 62n.
Fisher, I. 23, 27
Flux, A.W. 42
Foley, D. 203
Ford, A. 83
Fraser, L. 21
Friedman, M. 46, 92, 131
Frisch, R. 37, 38, 43

Garegnani, P. 57, 58, 147
Garside, W.R. 78, 85n.
Glynn, S. 75, 77, 83
Goodwin, R. 33, 38
Graziani, A. 209n.
Griffiths, B. 84
Grossman, H.I. 137, 142, 150

Haavelmo, T. 36
Haberler, G. 25, 26, 37, 38
Hahn, F.H. 143
Hall, R. 21, 25, 28, 32, 40, 44n.
Hansen, B. 93
Hargreaves, E. 21, 29, 40
Harris, L. 207n.
Harrod, R.F. 4, 5, 16, 19, 21, 27, 28, 30, 35, 38, 40, 59, 132, 156, 171n.
Hart, O. 141
Hatton, T.J. 78
Hawtrey, R. 26, 37, 179
Hayek, F.A. von 7, 24, 26, 37, 39, 172–3, 179–84
Henderson, H.D. 20, 22, 29, 31, 40
Hession, C.H. 4
Hicks, J.R. 4, 21, 23, 28, 29, 35, 36, 37, 38, 50, 92, 126, 183
Hitch, C. 21, 23, 27, 32, 35, 40
Howells, P.G.A. 75, 85
Howitt, P. 144–5